Your Beagle's Life

Also Available from PRIMA PETS™

Your Beagle's Life by Kim Campbell Thornton

Your Boxer's Life by Kim D.R. Dearth

Your Cat's Life by Joanne Howl, D.V.M.

Your Chihuahua's Life by Kim Campbell Thornton

Your Dog's Life by Tracy Acosta, D.V.M.

Your German Shepherd's Life by Audrey Pavia

Your Golden Retriever's Life by Betsy Sikora Siino

Your Lab's Life by Virginia Parker Guidry

Your Rottweiler's Life by Kim D.R. Dearth

KIM CAMPBELL THORNTON
Joanne Howl, D.V.M., Series Editor

Your
BEAGLE'S
Life

Your Complete Guide to Raising
Your Pet from Puppy to Companion

PRIMA PETS

An Imprint of Prima Publishing

3000 Lava Ridge Court • Roseville, California 95661
(800) 632-8676 • www.primalifestyles.com

DISCLAIMER: While the Publisher and the author have designed this book to provide up-to-date information in regard to the subject matter covered, readers should be aware that medical information is constantly evolving. The information presented herein is of a general nature and is not intended as a substitute for professional medical advice. Readers should consult with a qualified veterinarian for specific instructions on the treatment and care of their pet. The author and Prima Publishing shall have neither liability nor responsibility to any person or entity with respect to any loss, damage, or injury caused or alleged to be caused directly or indirectly by the information contained in this book.

YOUR PET'S LIFE and PRIMA PETS are trademarks of Prima Communications, Inc. The Prima colophon is a trademark of Prima Communications, Inc., registered in the United States Patent and Trademark Office.

Interior photos by Kent Lacin Media Services
Color insert photos © Isabelle Français
Chapter 6 illustrations by Pam Tanzey © 2000 Prima Publishing
Beagles and their people: "Max," "Tess," "Crystal," "Norman," and "Blaze," and Timothy R. and Janet R. Aamodt of River Oaks Beagles; "Hogan," "Craig," "Penny," and Lynne Katusich; and "Nigel" and Rebecca Henshaw and Dan Martell.

Library of Congress Cataloging-in-Publication Data
Thornton, Kim Campbell.
    Your beagle's life : your complete guide to raising your pet from puppy to companion /
Kim Campbell Thornton.
       p.   cm. -- (Your pet's life)
   ISBN: 0-7615-2050-3
   1. Beagle (Dog breed) I. Title. II. Series.
  SF429.B3 T56 2000
636.753'7--dc21   00-022034

00 01 02 03 DD 10 9 8 7 6 5 4 3 2 1
Printed in the United States of America

How to Order

Single copies may be ordered from Prima Publishing, 3000 Lava Ridge Court, Roseville, CA 95661; telephone (800) 632-8676. Quantity discounts are also available. On your letterhead, include information concerning the intended use of the books and the number of books you wish to purchase.

Visit us online at www.primalifestyles.com

To Savanna and Bella,
my perfect dogs

Contents

Acknowledgments

The author's most grateful thanks go to the following people for their help, advice, and contributions: Janiece Harrison, Luisa Fallon, Judy Watts, Katie Williams, Janet Nieland, and everyone on the I-BARC list.

Introduction

Beagles are merry hounds. P. G. Wodehouse wrote: "It is fatal to let any dog know that he is funny, for he immediately loses his head and starts hamming it up." Surely he was writing about a Beagle. These comedians of the hound group keep their people constantly entertained with their humorous antics, which usually involve their much vaunted sniffing ability or their widely known love of food.

While the Beagle is always good for a laugh, he has many other great qualities as well. In the eyes of many dog lovers, the Beagle is a classic, with the good looks, working ability, and personality that make him a quintessential canine. His popularity as a pet is undeniable. The Beagle has long ranked among the American Kennel Club's (AKC's) top 10 most popular breeds, and it's estimated that 80 percent of all Beagles bred are sold as pets. It's easy to see why.

Lurking inside the Beagle's small body is the heart and personality of a large dog, one with admirable courage and stamina. Shining out of his soft brown or hazel eyes is a good-natured intelligence. With his boisterous nature and endless supply of energy, he's a willing playmate for rowdy kids of all ages and a ready companion for a hiker or rabbit hunter. With a weight range of 16 to 30 pounds, he's able to fit in any size home, although he prefers one with a yard where he can sniff to his heart's content. And who can resist a dog that always looks like a puppy, even at the advanced age of 14? Gentle and true, yet full of charm and *joie de vivre,* the Beagle is a fine friend for an active family who can give him the exercise and attention he loves.

If the Beagle sounds like it might be the breed for you, read on to learn more about whether it's suited to your personality and lifestyle.

An Overview of Beagle Ownership

The Beagle has many excellent qualities as a companion dog, including his small size, intelligence, ease of grooming, watchdog ability, and, last but not least, a lively and affectionate personality. The person who owns a Beagle can be assured of having a friend whose fun-loving disposition will bring many hours of laughter and joy. This breed thrives on affection and will return it many times over to the people he loves. To take a Beagle into your home requires an honest commitment of time, not simply to give the care that any dog needs but to give the attention and friendship that this social butterfly of a dog desires.

Dog Ownership:
The Many Sacrifices, the Many Joys

Owning a dog is much like having a child. It requires a serious commitment of time, money, and care. Among the potential expenses and responsibilities of dog ownership are license fees, food, grooming tools, training class, regular veterinary care (checkups, vaccinations, emergency treatment for accidents, or treatment for a serious disease), boarding kennel or pet-sitter costs, time or money spent grooming, and regular meals and exercise. The upside is that a dog won't demand an Ivy League education or designer clothing. The Beagle will be satisfied with a constant supply of dog biscuits and other taste treats.

For most people, the joys of owning a dog far outweigh the sacrifices. A dog is someone to cuddle with on a cold winter night, someone to tell secrets to who won't spill them to anyone else, someone who is always loving, never judgmental, no matter what. A dog is never demanding, except of two things that are free: love and attention. For the person who can provide these—and give them with a willing heart—a Beagle can be the companion of a lifetime.

What It Means to Have a Beagle in Your Life

Sharing a home with a Beagle brings many rewards besides companionship. The Beagle is a strong proponent of family togetherness. He is an active dog who enjoys being involved in all family activities, from supervising meal preparation to going camping.

He lives for the moment and is always on the lookout for a good time, especially if it involves following his nose—the one thing he's serious about besides food. This smallest of the hounds is ruled by his sense of smell, and he will take any opportunity to follow an interesting scent wherever it may lead him, even if it takes him miles from home. For this reason, Beagle owners must provide their pets with a securely fenced yard and walks on leash, because when the Beagle's nose takes over, all training goes by the wayside. As a prospective Beagle owner, you'll want to consider whether you're willing to exercise a dog on leash, because it takes a lot of training to teach a Beagle to come reliably in all situations. Beagles that are allowed to run free often end up dead under the wheels of cars because they become so distracted by the scent they're following that they have no idea what's going on around them.

The Beagle is not a breed to own if you want a highly attentive dog. There's no doubt that he's loving and affectionate, but he's also extremely distractible. He'll stick around as long as you show him a good time, but if something better wafts by on the breeze, he'll be off to check it out.

Beagles are bred to work independently of people, so they're not the easiest dogs to train. They can be stubborn or insistent on doing things their way. As a result, many people mistakenly label them stupid. The truth is that Beagles are a lot better at training us than we are at training them. It takes persistence and patience to train a Beagle effectively and, even then, you can never be sure of what he might do next. Beagles like to put their own spin on things, which is why they're not usually the top-scoring dogs at obedience trials.

Potential behavior problems include barking, howling, chewing, stealing food, house soiling, and roaming. Beagles can also become snappy and irritable if they're spoiled. These problem behaviors can usually be circumvented with early training and plenty of attention and playtime, but there's no guarantee.

When he's following a scent, the Beagle "gives tongue," or bays, a sound that is music to the ears of hound lovers. Most other times, he's quiet, unless he's distracted by a squirrel or announcing the arrival of a guest. Bored Beagles will howl to let you know of their displeasure, and it is this habit that most often causes neighbor complaints. Beagles also bark and howl when they're separated from their people. They are less likely to make noise when they sleep indoors at night and when they're kept inside at times when their people aren't home.

One family whose Beagle barked incessantly when they weren't home tried placing an antibark collar on the dog, which would squirt a mist of citronella scent into his face whenever he barked. They put the collar on the dog in the morning before they went to work, and came home to find that he had barked it empty (the collars contain enough scent for 20 corrections). He figured out that he could get the correction over with quickly and then be free to bark for the rest of the day.

Their habit of barking at whatever catches their attention gives Beagles the reputation of being good watchdogs, but watching is about all they do. A Beagle is more likely to lick an intruder to death than to scare him off. One Beagle owner says, "The only time I remember actually worrying that we had a burglar was when a large limb split from a tree in our backyard around 4 a.m. The noise was deafening, and it sounded as if someone was in the house knocking dishes off the counter. The Beagles just sat up in bed—dead silent—expecting us to look into the problem!"

Beagles have a highly endearing characteristic that makes up for their stubborn nature, loud vocalizations, and destructive habits. They have a wonderful way of finding the humor in any situation. Beagle owners, especially those who engage their dogs in obedience or agility competitions, often discover that their dogs' sense of humor comes at their expense, but the laughter they bring is always worth it. Even if he's not misbehaving, a Beagle is sure to do something funny that will make you grin. Peabody, owned by Anna Maria Caranci of St. Lazare, Quebec, Canada, buried a bone in one of the pigeonholes in her desk and covered it up with paper. "Now I've seen everything," says Anna Maria. "Beagles!"

How Much Thought Have You Given to Having a Beagle?

As you can see, deciding to bring a Beagle into your life requires a lot of thought. It's not a relationship that you should enter into lightly. Dogs, especially companionable breeds such as Beagles, become very attached to their people, so the acquisition of one should be made with the promise of a lifetime commitment, a time frame that can span 12 years or more. Do some serious research about the breed before committing yourself to it. Reading this book is an excellent start and will give you a foundation for talking to breeders and choosing the Beagle that will best suit your needs.

Look into your future. Are you currently single or childless? Consider whether your commitment to the dog will remain strong in the face of a fiancé or spouse who doesn't like dogs. A Beagle is a loving dog that will be unhappy if you stop paying attention to him because you've gotten married or had a baby. Will you still be willing to make time for a Beagle and protect him from tail-pulling and clumsy handling?

How's your sense of humor? Do you consider yourself a flexible person, able to go with the flow? Are you patient? All of these characteristics are typical of the successful dog owner. The ability to laugh instead of freeze in mortification when during a cocktail party your Beagle runs into the living room with your underwear in his mouth is essential, as is willingness to live with dog hairs here and there on furniture and carpets. You never know what a dog will do next, so don't expect to have a complete measure of control.

Talk to several people who own Beagles to find out what their experience has been like. Ask for an estimate of how much they spend annually on food and veterinary bills. The figure won't be comparable to what a Great Dane might run up, but you should still make sure it's within your budget. Assume that training classes will range from $50 to $100 for four to eight sessions. Private in-home training costs more, from $45 to $75 per hour. Boarding kennel stays range from $10 to $20 or more per day. A bath from a professional groomer will cost $15 to $20. And don't forget food. A high-quality diet costs about $1 per pound. Your Beagle will probably eat one to two cups of dry food daily, depending on his size.

Your veterinarian can comment on the health of the Beagles he or she sees in practice. That will give you an idea of how often your dog might be visiting the veterinarian, and why.

Finally, before you decide that a Beagle is the right dog for you, ask yourself the following questions: Do I have plenty of time to spend exercising, training, and playing with this dog? Will my income allow me to provide the dog with high-quality food and regular veterinary care? Am I willing to brush the dog once a week? Can I give a Beagle the emotional connection he desires? If you can answer yes to all of these questions, the Beagle may indeed be the ideal breed for you.

So, You Want a Beagle

In This Chapter

❍ What Makes a Beagle Special?
❍ Keys to Your Beagle's Happiness
❍ Where to Find the Perfect Beagle for You

I f you're reading this book before purchasing a Beagle, it's the best thing you can do. Starting with this chapter, you'll learn about the Beagle's history and appearance, what he's like to live with, and where to find one. Even if you already have your dog, the information you read here will be valuable in helping you get to know your new friend.

What Makes a Beagle Special?

All dogs are descended from wolves, which is more apparent in certain breeds, such as the Alaskan Malamute, than in others, such as the diminutive Chihuahua. Many years ago, man befriended the wolf and decided to harness this animal's considerable talents to suit his needs. Our ancestors then molded dogs into certain breeds to perform specific jobs, from hunting to herding, from guarding to companionship.

A Bit of History

Hounds have been around for centuries, prized for their ability to sight or track prey and bring it down. When the Beagle emerged as a distinct breed is not established, but there were little dogs called glove beagles—because they could fit on the palm of a glove—in the time of Henry VII of England. His granddaughter Queen Elizabeth I was known to hunt with dogs called pocket Beagles, so named because they could fit in the pocket of a huntsman's coat. By the mid-eighteenth century, English sportsmen had developed what was known as the North Country Beagle, a nimble, vigorous dog. His purpose was to accompany hunters on foot, who might spend all day hunting a single hare. This called for a dog with a good nose, persistence, and stamina, but not necessarily speed. Lesser landed gentry and well-to-do farmers who perhaps lacked the resources to keep packs of larger foxhounds kept packs of Beagles.

Eventually, farmers worried about crop damage began to breed for a speedier hound that could take a number of hares in a single day. These two styles of hunting, compounded by the rise of conformation showing in the late 1800s, led to differences within the breed besides its two size varieties (13-inch and 15-inch). So, while the Beagle might seem a perfectly straightforward hound, as with many breeds that come from a hunting heritage he has fallen victim to a split in

How the Beagle Got His Name

This dog is named for his size. The word "small" was similar whether it was spoken in a Celtic language (beag), French (begle), or Old English (beigh). This word became associated with the Beagle, the smallest of the hounds. References to the breed date to the work of Chaucer in the fourteenth century.

type, with field dogs, show dogs, and pets diverging in appearance and ability, although not in temperament.

At the turn of the twentieth century, all Beagles looked pretty much alike. Beagle lovers imported their dogs from England, using them for hunting and competing with them in field trials and conformation shows. Gradually, however, the people who showed their dogs in conformation lost interest in field trials and hunting, and vice versa. The Beagle soon began to look very different, depending on his purpose. People who used their Beagles for hunting or in field trials bred strictly for working ability and lost some of the look that made the Beagle unique. Beagles that were shown in conformation were evaluated strictly on appearance, without taking into consideration the qualities of a Beagle that can't be judged in a show ring: the real desire to hunt, a good nose, being able to tell when a rabbit has turned, and being able to follow the rabbit's trail accurately.

Besides the differences between field and show dogs, there are differences among the field dogs themselves, depending on whether their quarry is rabbit, which go to ground, or hare, which don't, as well as whether they compete in slow-moving brace trials or in large pack trials, which are best suited to sound dogs with plenty of stamina. Expect Beagles from field trial or hunting

What's the American Kennel Club?

Founded in 1884, the American Kennel Club (AKC) is a non-profit organization dedicated to the protection and advancement of purebred dogs. Composed of over 500 dog clubs from across the nation, the AKC's objectives include maintaining a registry of purebred dogs, promoting responsible dog ownership, and sponsoring events, such as breed shows and field trials, that promote interest in and appreciation of the purebred dog.

To be eligible for AKC registration, a puppy must be the offspring of individually registered AKC parents, and the breeder must obtain the proper paperwork before the puppy's sale. Once registered, a dog is eligible to compete in AKC-sanctioned events and, if bred with another AKC registered dog, to have his/her offspring registered.

The AKC approves an official breed standard for each of the 147 breeds currently eligible for registration. The standard is written and maintained by each individual breed club. An attempt to describe the "perfect" dog of each breed, the breed standard is the model responsible breeders use in their efforts to produce better dogs. Judges of AKC-sponsored events and competitions use the breed standards as the basis of their evaluations.

Because of the AKC's emphasis on excellence and high standards, it is a common misconception that "AKC registered" or "AKC registrable" is synonymous with quality. However, while a registration certificate identifies a dog and its progenitors as purebreds, it does not necessarily guarantee the health or quality of a dog. Some breeders breed for show quality, but others breed for profit, with little concern for breed standards. Thus, a potential buyer should not view AKC registration as an indication of a dog's quality.

lines to have higher energy levels than those from show lines—an important distinction if you're simply looking for a pet. Some Beagle breeders are working toward bringing back the all-around Beagle who is capable of going from the show ring to the field without missing a beat.

The Breed Standard

The official AKC breed standard calls for the Beagle to be a Foxhound in miniature, solid and big for his inches, with the wear-and-tear look of a hound that can last in the chase and follow the quarry to the death. You probably have the meaning of that wear-and-tear phrase demonstrated for you every time your Beagle goes haring off after something furry.

The Beagle is a nicely proportioned dog, more square than rectangular, with a pretty head and a pretty face. Dark brown or hazel eyes give him what may well be his greatest charm: a soft, pleading expression. If you draw his long ears forward, they reach almost to the end of his nose. (President Lyndon Johnson had two Beagles—Him and Her—and was heavily criticized after a photograph was released that showed him holding his dogs by their ears.)

> A proper Beagle has attitude and carries himself with confidence.

Unlike some scenthounds that are known for the amount of drool they produce, a Beagle has tight lips and doesn't salivate heavily—except maybe when he sees food. A proper Beagle has attitude and carries himself with confidence. One breeder says the dog's attitude should resemble that of a businessman with briefcase in hand, briskly marching off to matters of great importance.

What allows the Beagle to go all day in the field is his well-laid-back shoulders, strong, powerful rear, and a long rib cage that leaves plenty of room for heart and lung capacity. These components create smooth, alert movement without any wasted motion, such as weaving in and out. Whether he's in the field or the show ring, he should seem to almost float over the ground.

The tail, referred to as the stern, is set high and carried up in the air. A white tip helps make the dog visible in the field. A tail with a teapot curve, meaning that it is carried in an arch up and over the back, is not desirable for a show or field dog, because it's not as visible, but it doesn't detract from a Beagle's ability to be a good pet. Other faulty tails are those that are too long or that lack a brush, meaning that the tip is devoid of hair—known as a rat tail.

The Beagle's double coat is dense and waterproof. The fine undercoat keeps him warm and is covered by a coarse topcoat. Hard to the touch, the topcoat protects him as he scrambles through brambles and brush, and when it gets wet, all he needs to do is give himself a good shake to dry off. A soft, thin, or short coat just wouldn't provide the same protection. A good Beagle coat is medium-short in length, one-half inch to three-quarters of an inch long.

A Beagle may be any true hound color, which leaves plenty of room for variety. The classic Beagle is a tricolor, with a black saddle over his back, white legs, chest, and belly, and tan on his head. At birth, tricolor puppies are black and white, with the tan color developing as they mature. Some Beagles are red and white, with the red ranging from light tan to dark rust. Red-and-white Beagles are born with that coloration, or they may be born white, with the red shade appearing later. The same is true of lemon-and-white Beagles, whose off-white to dark yellow coloration emerges as they grow. More rarely seen are black and white Beagles, which sometimes have a gray saddle. It's possible for Beagles to be solid white or solid tan but, like the black-and-white Beagle, they're not commonly found. Other unusual colors are liver, chocolate, and blue. Beagles of these colorations tend to have light eyes, which may give a harsh expression, and light nose pigment, which is acceptable only on red-and-white and lemon-and-white Beagles. In the eyes of sportsmen, however, no good hound can be a bad color.

A Beagle of any color may have freckling, mottling, ticking, or grizzling. Freckles are just what they sound like: a sprinkling of pigmented spots on the coat, usually on the face. A mottled coat has a pattern of roundish dark blotches superimposed on a lighter background. Ticking occurs when there are small, isolated areas of black hairs on a white ground. Grizzling is described as a mixture of black or red hairs with white hairs.

Beagle Varieties   This breed is found in two sizes: 13-inch and 15-inch. As the names imply, 13-inch Beagles must not exceed 13 inches in height, and 15-inch Beagles stand more than 13 inches but not over 15 inches. Each has its advantages.

The 13-inch Beagles are a little slower than their big brothers, making them easier to keep up with if you're on foot, but they can get through a fence more easily and have no difficulty following a rabbit into heavy briars or brush piles. Maneuverability is their strength, and it serves them well in pursuit of cottontails.

The 15-inch Beagles have more speed, and they appeal to people who like a larger dog. Their purpose is to pursue the rabbit in the open field after it's been flushed by the 13-inch Beagle. They're also more suited to coursing snowshoe hares than cottontails. Other than in size, the two varieties should not differ in appearance, but each is judged separately in the show ring. The 13-inch Beagles usually weigh 16 to 20 pounds, the 15-inch Beagles 20 to 30 pounds.

Did You Know?

The first Beagle registered with the American Kennel Club (AKC) was Blunder, in 1885. No Beagle has ever won Best in Show at the Westminster Kennel Club.

The Song of the Beagle

In Thomas Bewick's General History of Quadrupeds, published in 1790, he wrote: "The Beagle's tones are soft and musical and add greatly to the pleasures of the chase." Beagles and other scenthounds howl to announce that they have detected their quarry. This baying, or "singing," of hounds, sometimes described in the American South as "mountain music," allows the hunter or handler to know where the dogs are. People have compared howls to music for centuries. In his book <u>Country Contentments</u>, published in 1615, Englishman Gervase Markham gave advice on how to combine hounds in a pack to create a symphony of sound.

People who hunt packs of Beagles usually prefer to have dogs that are similar in size. That similarity helps them run together so they can better function as a pack. The two sizes can be mixed, if they aren't too far apart in size, but the 15-inch Beagles will generally have an advantage as far as speed. A large 15-inch pack really moves and is a sight to see in action.

In the breed's homeland, only one size is recognized. Beagles in England have a desired minimum height of 13 inches and a maximum of 16 inches.

Personality and Temperament

Whether he's trailing a rabbit or hare, nosing his way around a show ring, or simply being a loveable family companion, the Beagle retains the cheerful yet workmanlike character that has made him popular for centuries.

"Beagles are the happiest dogs on earth," says Judy Watts of North Tustin, California, who shares her home with Virginia and

Hannah. "When we go for walks, they have to greet every person they encounter with tail wags and sniffs. They're the most positive, upbeat animals I've ever seen. Of course Beagles are appealing looking, but their personalities are even more appealing."

Personality and temperament are both generally defined as an individual dog's behavioral or emotional traits, or the characteristics that distinguish an individual dog or a breed. The two terms are usually used interchangeably, although some people differentiate them by saying that personality refers to the characteristics of individual dogs and temperament to the characteristics of a breed as a whole. Often the two definitions overlap, as in the following discussion.

The characteristics of a particular breed can be positive or negative, depending on what you're looking for in a dog. The temperament of most dogs is related to the purpose for which they were bred. A scenthound like the Beagle has a strong desire to follow prey by scent. To be successful at this job, he needs to be energetic, independent, outgoing, and tenacious. Both varieties of Beagle have this temperament.

> The typical Beagle is an extrovert, ideal for a home with kids or with people who like taking their dog with them wherever they go.

Other aspects of temperament include whether a dog is shy, passive, or aggressive. Beagles generally have a friendly temperament, and it's rare to find one that's snappish. Aggression is generally not a behavior problem for Beagles, although some can be shy. The typical Beagle is an extrovert, ideal for a home with kids or with people who like taking their dog with them wherever they go.

Before you begin your search for a Beagle, decide what type of personality best suits you and your family. Personality is an important consideration, not only for you but also for the dog. A

Beagle that tears through the house after imaginary rabbits won't be happy in a situation in which he's expected to be quiet and biddable (not really a reasonable expectation for any Beagle). The shy puppy who sits in the corner won't magically turn into a confident, outgoing dog once you take him home. A mismatch can mean unhappiness all the way around.

The first step in evaluating the temperament of a puppy you're considering buying is to look at the temperament of his parents. Are they outgoing or shy? Friendly or suspicious? Barky or quiet? Temperament is heritable, and in dogs, especially, there's a lot of truth in that old saying "Like mother, like daughter (or son)." Beagle puppies are with their mother constantly from birth until they go to their new homes at least eight weeks of age, so her influence on them is tremendous. Dad's temperament plays a role as well, but it's from Mom that puppies take their cues on how to react toward people, other animals, sounds, and other sensory events. Even pups that are carefully socialized by the breeder and the new owners can turn out to be timid or unfriendly because Mom's temperament genes were dominant over any environmental attempt to mold the puppies. Keep in mind that temperament doesn't fully emerge until a dog is 12 to 18 months old.

Ideally, you will be able to meet the mother as well as other dogs the breeder has produced. The more of them you can meet, the better you will be able to gauge a puppy's future temperament and select one that will grow to be confident and well adjusted.

In Beagles, there are all kinds of personalities. Some Beagles are lap dogs who will be happy to sit with you and watch television. Others are more independent and would rather explore the house and yard, checking in with you occasionally.

Dog Heaven

Among Beagle lovers, a favorite story says it all about their breed. At the gates of heaven, four friends approached and stood awaiting permission to enter. Saint Peter scowled and asked them to account for themselves.

The first of the four, a Poodle, proudly leaped forward and said, "I am the showman, winning many prizes for my beauty. See how fine I am? There was none better in my prime, and I was my master's pride and joy." He demonstrated his fine show stance.

Next was a Labrador, black and glossy. He said, "I am a field champion, keen for the gun and never missing a bird. I worked hard for my master."

Then the German Shepherd stepped forward, eager and alert. "I guarded my masters, keeping them safe. No strange foot trod the paths without my say. They feared not with me around."

Saint Peter turned to the last supplicant. "And you, sir," he inquired, "what of you?"

The dog replied, "I am a Beagle, maybe not so good, I confess. I chased the cat, fell to temptation, and stole food. I forgot to return at my master's call, leaving him to worry, then howled to show my disapproval at being left alone. Oh, and there was my chewing and other bad habits that drove my master crazy."

"But what did you give them?" asked St. Peter.

"I gave them light in their eyes and laughter in their voices," the Beagle replied.

With no further hesitation, Saint Peter swung the pearly gates wide open.

The lines from which a Beagle comes can also have a bearing on his personality. Beagles bred for the field tend to be a little more mouthy and pushy than Beagles bred by hobby breeders for the conformation ring. They are also more likely to be shy of strangers. Unlike someone who's breeding for a dog that might have potential in the show ring, breeders who are selecting primarily for field ability are usually less concerned with socialization, because they don't want their dogs to be willing to go off with any-one who finds them. The socialization a show breeder gives makes for a dog that's easier to handle as a pet.

Be sure you let the breeder know what you're looking for in a Beagle. That way, you can help him or her steer you to just the right pup. After all, the breeder has been watching these puppies for at least eight weeks and has a good idea of each one's person-ality. It's a much better bet to take the breeder's recommendation than it is to let the puppy choose you or to play eeny, meeny, miny, mo. When you take home just any old puppy, you run the risk of setting yourself and the dog up for failure, a situation that will result in stress and disappointment for both of you.

Intelligence

As in any breed, intelligence varies from dog to dog but, for the most part, Beagles are smart, with good memories. If they're properly motivated and kept entertained, they can be quick to learn. Reliability, however, comes only with frequent repetition over a long period. Expect Beagles to learn "bad" behaviors more quickly than good ones, and counter that tendency by giving them plenty of opportunities to do things the right way and few opportunities to get into trouble. Just because your Beagle is smart doesn't mean he's always going to be well behaved. You need to be a quick thinker to stay a step or two ahead of a Beagle.

Life Expectancy

One of the nice things about Beagles is that they have a relatively long life-span. With good care, Beagles can live 10 to 14 years. A few old-timers hang on for 17 or even 18 years.

The best way to ensure that a Beagle has a long and happy life is to provide him with plenty of exercise, a healthy, high-quality diet, regular veterinary care, and lots of love. Given these, a Beagle from good lines should rarely be ill.

> The best way to ensure that a Beagle has a long and happy life is to provide him with plenty of exercise, a healthy, high-quality diet, regular veterinary care, and lots of love.

Keys to Your Beagle's Happiness

Part of developing a great relationship with a Beagle is ensuring that you can provide an environment in which she will be happy. Things to consider before getting a Beagle include her needs for living space, exercise, training, grooming, and companionship, as well as her interactions with other pets.

How Much Space Does a Beagle Need?

Although the Beagle is a small breed, she does best in a home with a yard. Apartment or condo dwellers may not have a problem taking a Beagle out for regular walks, which are indeed important, but given that she's a scenthound it's nice for this breed to have a fenced yard. This gives her a place to cruise around with her nose on the ground and explore, something that you may not be willing to let her do if you only have a set amount of time for a walk or if you prefer to walk a particular route. Having access to a yard gives a Beagle her own private sniffing time and means that, when you do take her for a walk, you won't feel guilty for not permitting her to follow every interesting trail she comes across.

While having a yard is important for a Beagle, she's not a good "outside" dog. Being left alone outside with nothing to do only encourages her to bark, dig, and try to escape to some place more fun. To preclude the possibility of teasing by the neighbor kids, escape, or theft (Beagles are popular laboratory specimens because of their small size and sweet temperaments), consider keeping your Beagle indoors while you're gone or in a secure dog run with a top. You'll need a sturdy fence at least four feet high to keep your Beagle safely contained.

Can a City Beagle Be a Happy Beagle? In a word, yes. While a yard is ideal, plenty of satisfied Beagles and their people live in city apartments or condominiums. If their lives were documented on an HBO series, it might be called *Scent and the City*. "I think Beagles are rather good city dogs," says Jennifer Zickerman of Vancouver, British Columbia, Canada, who owns a Beagle named Oi. "Because of their overwhelming interest in scent and tracking, city streets are of great fascination to them—'Where's the hotdog? I know I smell hotdog around here somewhere.' They also tend to be friendly, which makes them tolerant of the variety of people they meet. I love it when the suit-and-briefcase dudes get all googly-eyed and baby-talking with the Oister. I also love it that the pimps and hookers and dealers want to make friends with her. It's good to know your neighbors—especially those neighbors. I think dogs make the city a more civilized and less sterile place for everyone."

To keep a city Beagle happy, provide her with a minimum of one daily hour-long (or longer) walk or two or three shorter walks, plus lots of playtime when you're home and a good variety of toys when you're not. Beagle owner Katie Williams, Lubbock,

Texas, recommends trying to find an older Beagle that is already house-trained. House-training a puppy is difficult if no one will be home during the day. If you can't get someone to come in and take the puppy out (such as a professional dog walker or pet sitter), set up a puppy pen in your kitchen, Williams says. "Put the crate inside the pen, with the door open and a snuggly blanket inside. An older Beagle is best, though. You'd be surprised at how small a Beagle puppy's bladder is, especially at eight weeks."

Another advantage of getting an older Beagle is that you'll know in advance whether she's a barker. Beagles can learn not to bark, but it's easier to get one who's already quiet. "A crate-trained Beagle who's given lots of attention can be fairly quiet. Teach him not to howl or bark when he's in the crate, and he'll be fine," says Williams, but she urges potential Beagle owners to think about the "what-ifs." If you get a Beagle that's noisy and you aren't able to retrain him, are you willing and able to move or would you just get rid of the dog? "Too often we expect dogs to adjust to us instead of being willing to work around their needs," she says.

Finally, always keep your city Beagle on lead. Even dogs with obedience titles have been hit by cars or attacked by other dogs because they didn't respond quickly enough to commands or because their owner's attention wandered. If you want to give your Beagle some time off lead, find a securely fenced dog park, baseball diamond, or tennis court, and don't neglect to pick up after her before you leave.

How Much Exercise?

One of the greatest things about Beagles is their adaptability. They can be content to spend much of their time asleep on

> **Did You Know?**
>
> The word for "dog" in the Australian aboriginal language Mbabaran happens to be "dog."

the couch while you're at work, but they enjoy several outings a week. Unlike some breeds, they don't need a brisk daily workout to burn up excess energy; a nice stroll through the neighborhood will suit them just fine, especially if they're allowed to follow their noses. That said, Beagles are athletic dogs and can stand up to a lot of exercise. Beagle owner Janiece Harrison of Nashville, Tennessee, says, "For the past four years, we've taken Annie and Bo hiking in Colorado and they do great on eight- to ten-mile hikes that include stream crossings and strenuous climbs."

How Much Training?

A good puppy kindergarten class, beginning when the dog is 10 to 12 weeks old, will help you lay the foundation for a mutually respectful relationship. Your Beagle will learn basic obedience commands, such as sit, down, stay, and come, and you will learn positive, nonforceful ways to provide guidance and discipline. These techniques are especially important with Beagles, who respond best to food, not force. Follow puppy kindergarten with an obedience class to reinforce the lessons your Beagle has already learned.

Beagles are good problem solvers and become bored easily. Avoid working them on the same trick or command over and over. Your Beagle will either start adding her own interpretation to what you're asking, or she'll simply quit, because it's not fun anymore. Keep her on her toes by introducing new commands, new rewards, new ways of doing things. The Beagle's attitude is often "What's in it for me?" so for everything you want her to do, you have to make it worth her while.

Since they are scenthounds, Beagles are highly motivated by food; used properly, it's the most effective training tool you can have. If you believe a

Trading Cookies for Contraband

Beagle owner Janiece Harrison tells a story that highlights the breed's cleverness and sense of humor. "I have been training Bo to retrieve for the obedience ring, so he's rewarded for bringing me things. It's also a great way to deal with his counter surfing since I can trade him a cookie for his stolen contraband. He now has a morning ritual. After we get up, he goes back to the bedroom and brings one item out after the next to trade. His usual morning booty includes his collar, shoes, the remote control, a necktie, and my husband's wallet. We can only get him to stop by closing the bedroom door. He's clearly quite pleased by his antics."

dog should possess an innate desire to please, the Beagle isn't the breed for you. On the other hand, if you're comfortable with the food-as-motivation approach, it can be great fun to train a Beagle, because he is so clever. Not all dog trainers approve of food rewards, so be sure to choose one who's experienced in working with Beagles or other scenthounds.

Beagles are intelligent, but don't expect yours to develop perfect behavior simply by attending six or eight weeks of puppy kindergarten or obedience class. This breed requires frequent practice to maintain his skills, and it may take many repetitions before the Beagle will do what you want on a consistent basis. If you want your Beagle to respond reliably to your requests—and she'll view them as requests, not commands—plan on working with her briefly a couple of times every day for the first two years she's with you. Once she's mature, regular refresher sessions are a good idea. A Beagle will never be a dog who is easily trained to be perfectly reliable, so make sure you're not expecting the impossible before you get one.

Will My Beagle Be Noisy?

One of the most common complaints expressed by the neighbors of Beagle owners is that the dogs bark. Beagles do have a reputation for barking constantly, but they normally don't bark unless they have a reason: someone is walking down the street, someone comes to the door, or it's feeding time. Beagles are especially likely to bark when they're separated from their people, either because they're left in the yard at night or because their people are at work during the day. For that reason, Beagles don't make good outdoor dogs.

"People always say that they used to live next door to a Beagle, and it barked all night. My response is that if the dog had been allowed to be indoors at night, he wouldn't have barked," says Janet Nieland of Stanton, California. "They're so people-oriented that they want to be around you, and they don't get it when you're inside and they're outside."

If your Beagle is barking excessively while you're at home, a spray of the hose or a squirt from a water bottle and saying "no" at the same time can silence him, if you're consistent about it, Nieland says. If you leave and the dog is allowed to bark all day without any kind of correction, he's on the path to becoming a habitual barker. To decrease the annoyance to neighbors, Nieland recommends keeping Beagles indoors when you're not at home. "When my guys go nuts, say if it's getting dark, I just bring them in and put them in their crates, and they're fine with that because they're with me," she says.

While some people are blessed with quiet Beagles, you should be prepared to deal with barking. Many Beagles are given up to animal shelters because their owners complain that they're too noisy. Beagles are scenthounds, and they respond to smells by letting you know that something is out there. Stay calm, and check it out so your Beagle will be satisfied that she's done her job and can stop barking.

Can My Beagle Stay Home All Day Without Me?

Beagles are definitely pack animals, originally bred to hunt together in groups. While they often do fine when left for an eight-hour workday, they don't adapt well to being alone for longer stretches, especially if they have nothing to keep them occupied. This is a busy breed, and if a Beagle doesn't have a good selection of toys or some other way to occupy herself while you're gone, she's perfectly capable of making her own loud, mischievous—and quite possibly destructive—fun. Beagles have been known to eat screens and chew holes through walls in their quests for entertainment.

Your Beagle can spend the day in your home or in a securely fenced yard or dog run (if barking isn't a problem) if you give her a good walk in the morning before you go to work and spend plenty of time with her when you get home. You may want to consider providing your Beagle with a friend or two—someone who can come in while you're gone and give her some play time, or another dog. Some Beagle owners crate their dogs all day, but that should be done only if the dog receives a lengthy walk before and after crating. Be sure she has a safe chew toy to keep her occupied. One Beagle owner leaves the television on for her pet— *Animal Planet*, natch.

Double the Beagles, Double the Fun

Beagles are like potato chips: it's hard to have just one. Having a second Beagle gives your dog a like-minded playmate with a similar energy level. Beagle fan Teresa Bridgman of Centreville, Virginia, who's involved in Beagle rescue, suggests having at least two Beagles if the breed is going to be part of your household. If you're adding a second Beagle as a playmate for your puppy, she recommends getting a one- to three-year-old. "That dog will be young enough to play with your pup, but old enough to house-train if necessary, and will be a little more independent," she says. Just be sure you're ready to be a two-Beagle household, and take your time in choosing one so that he will be the right "fit" for the entire family.

Katie Williams advises selecting an older Beagle (18 months or more) who loves to play but is calm enough to be gentle with a puppy. Two puppies can be trouble, making house-training more difficult, she says, and a four-month-old puppy can play too roughly with one that's only eight weeks old.

"The best decision I ever made was to get two Beagles," says Liz Highleyman of San Francisco, California. "They keep each other company, whether playing or napping, when we are away at work. They are generally quiet except when other dogs are outside our apartment. Rasken and Tekla are inseparable, and watching them interact is great fun. I imagine a single dog would be very lonely, which could lead to boredom and frustration-related barking and destruction."

Beagles and Other Pets

Since they're pack animals, Beagles generally get along well with other dogs and are always happier with another dog around. Unlike some breeds, they don't necessarily prefer the company of other Beagles but do tend to be dominant over other breeds. Beagle breeder Janet Nieland tells the story of Dolly, a 13-inch Beagle who had finished her championship and gone to Idaho to live with a family that wanted a small dog for their daughter to handle in junior showmanship. The family's other dogs were Newfoundlands, and Dolly's new owners said she walked into the kennel of 15 Newfoundlands and, in effect, told them, "Okay, guys, I'm in charge now." And she was, from that day forward.

In most instances, Beagles get along well with larger dogs but may take a dislike to smaller dogs. Nieland used to show a Beagle that paid no attention to larger dogs at shows but went ballistic at the sight of little dogs with a lot of hair. Cats, too, can be iffy. Some Beagles will chase them, while others ignore them. Expect the cat to determine what the relationship will be. A cat who stands her ground will most likely be left alone, but one that turns tail and runs has just set a lifetime pattern of encouraging the Beagle to chase her. Like any dog, a Beagle's personality depends in large part on what she's exposed to and how well she's socialized to new situations as a puppy, but in general the Beagle is adaptable when it comes to accepting other animals.

Katie Williams says having a second dog made her Beagle, Sally, much easier to handle. "When we brought Andy the Pug home, Sally was a four-month-old energizer bunny," she says. "Sally was so full of energy that she could easily wear my husband and me out. Andy made it easier for us. Sally was still energetic, but had a buddy to steal chewies from and run wildly around the house with. She really loved the company. At first, we put up baby gates to keep the two separated because we were afraid Sally would be too rough, but she scaled the gates to lie next to her friend. So being good Beagle people, and since Andy was faring well with Sally, we admitted defeat and removed the barriers. Dog company isn't a substitute for human companionship, but I believe Sally would miss it if she went back to being the only canine."

Surefire Ways to Make Your Beagle's Life Unpleasant

An unhappy Beagle is likely to develop behavior problems or even physical illness. No dog deserves to live in conditions for which he's unsuited, so consider carefully whether your home and family life will meet this dog's basic needs.

Things a Beagle Simply Cannot Live With

○ Lack of protection from children too young to treat him with care and respect. Beagles love kids and make great playmates for them, but that doesn't mean they should have to tolerate children who pull their ears and tails. Teach your child how to pet the dog nicely, and supervise all interaction between young children and Beagles to prevent them from hurting one another. Another consideration to keep in mind before getting a Beagle is that it's a mouthy breed. Beagles use their mouths to explore everything around them; chewing can be part of their exploration. That exploration may include grabbing onto your child's (or your) hand or arm, not in an attempt to bite but as a form of play. You can teach a Beagle not to do this, but it's something you should be aware of when he's around children.

> Teach your child how to pet the dog nicely, and supervise all interaction between young children and Beagles to prevent them from hurting one another.

○ Lack of companionship. For centuries, Beagles were bred to run in packs. They are highly sociable dogs that will become lonely without the company of another dog or of their people.

○ Lack of exercise. A Beagle's exercise needs are moderate. He is a moseyer, not a maniac, but he will become destructive without an outlet for his energy.

Maybe a Beagle Isn't the Dog for Me

If you are reading this book after already acquiring a Beagle, you may be learning some things about the breed that you didn't know and perhaps getting a better understanding of the new dog who is sharing your life. All is not lost if you are discovering that there are certain things you should have taken into consideration before getting a Beagle.

If your allergies are acting up because of the dog's presence, or you have decided that you can't give a Beagle the life he needs, there are several steps you can take to help resolve the situation. If you bought the dog from a breeder, give her a call. Responsible breeders are concerned for the well-being of every dog they've bred and will either be willing to take the dog back, no matter how long you've had him or why you're giving him up, or to help you place him in a good foster or adoptive home. Of course, you shouldn't expect to receive your money back, unless you've had the dog for only a week or two; then the breeder may be willing to give you a full or partial refund.

If you've lost touch with the breeder, contact a Beagle rescue group in your area. The people with the rescue group can help you better adjust to living with your Beagle, or they can try to place him in a more appropriate home. Rescue organizations may or may not charge for taking and placing your dog, but their costs in time, boarding, and veterinary expenses are high, so it would be a gracious gesture to give them a substantial donation for their efforts. (See the appendix for information on where to find a rescue group.)

Where to Find the Perfect Beagle for You

The Beagle is a relatively popular breed, so the dogs tend to be widely available without a long wait. They can be found through breeders and are sometimes available from animal shelters or Beagle rescue organizations. The avenue you choose may depend on whether you have your heart set on a puppy or a dog of show quality or if you like the idea of skipping the hassles of puppy-hood or giving a home to a dog that really needs one.

Puppies Versus Older Dogs

There's nothing more fun than watching a puppy grow up, but there can also be nothing more frustrating. Puppies chew on expensive shoes, pee or poop on expensive rugs, and must be kept under constant surveillance to make sure they don't hurt themselves or destroy something you value. Be sure you can afford to replace anything the puppy might destroy, or place it out of reach.

Puppies require a strict feeding and elimination schedule so they can be house-trained. Someone who's not home during the day will face difficulty in arranging for the number of meals and outings a puppy needs.

On the other hand, puppy antics are pretty entertaining, and there's a lot of pleasure to be gained from bonding with a puppy who is a member of a one-person breed. If you wouldn't miss that experience for the world—messes and all—then a puppy is the right choice for you.

Adolescent or adult dogs have advantages that puppies don't. They may already be house-trained or have some obedience training. They've already been through the destructive chewing stage, so you are less likely to have to fear for your possessions. Sometimes, they're already spayed or neutered, which is a savings. Older dogs need only one or two feedings daily, so it's easier to fit mealtimes into a busy work schedule.

An adult Beagle is more likely to be reliable in the house without the minute-by-minute supervision a puppy demands.

An adult dog requires fewer initial veterinary visits and vaccinations than a puppy does. Usually, by the time a dog reaches maturity, any health problems he may have are evident. Adopting an older dog allows you to select one that you know is healthy, or at least to go into Beagle ownership knowing what health problems your dog faces rather than being surprised by them down the road. You also don't have to guess about what size he's going to be.

It's not true that an older dog won't be able to bond to new people. All you need to win a Beagle's heart is a good supply of treats. He'll quickly become your best friend. If you can set aside the fleeting joys of puppyhood for the greater pleasure of teasing out a relationship with a Beagle who has retired from breeding or the show ring, or whose first home didn't work out, then an adult dog is for you.

Buying from a Breeder: What Is a Good Breeder?

A good breeder can be the source for a fine puppy or a well-adjusted older dog who has retired from breeding or the show ring. But what defines a good breeder? Anyone can hang out a shingle and call himself a breeder. A breeder could be your Aunt Sarah, who bred her dog because she thought it would be fun to have puppies and earn a little extra money, the commercial breeding operation just outside the town limits, or your neighbor down the street, who shows her dogs and produces a litter only once every couple of years. Which one of these qualifies as a "good" breeder?

> **Did You Know?**
>
> The Saluki, a hunting dog raised by ancient Egyptians, is the oldest known breed.

A good breeder is someone who has an interest in Beagles and has educated herself about them by studying their history, health, and the pedigrees of well-known dogs in the breed. She's knowledgeable about Beagle genetics and breed type, as well as the ins and outs of line breeding, inbreeding, and outcrossing. She doesn't breed her dogs until they're physically and emotionally mature, and she doesn't breed dogs whose ancestors have a history of genetic disease. She shows her dogs in conformation classes so that other Beagle breeders and judges can see and evaluate the results of her breeding program. When the puppies are born, a good breeder handles them frequently and makes sure they are accustomed to the sights and sounds of a typical household. That way, they'll adjust well when they go to their new homes at eight weeks of age. The money a breeder makes from her puppies typically helps cover the veterinary expenses of breeding and whelping a litter, but doesn't leave much of a profit.

> A good breeder is someone who has an interest in Beagles and has educated herself about them by studying their history, health, and the pedigrees of well-known dogs in the breed.

In contrast to the good breeder, while she may have the best intentions in the world, a backyard breeder like your Aunt Sarah typically doesn't have much of a plan before she breeds her Beagle. She simply makes an appointment with an acquaintance who has a male Beagle, and they put the dogs together and hope for the best. She isn't aware that Beagles have genetic diseases, so she doesn't do any testing beforehand. She isn't really sure when the pups are due or what to do when her dog goes into labor. She just figures the dog can handle things on her own. When the puppies are born, she sticks them and their mother in a box in the garage so they won't get in the way. She starts trying to sell them

The Ins and Outs of Breeding

When we hear the term inbreeding, we automatically think of dogs born with physical or mental defects, but inbreeding, along with linebreeding and out-crossing, is a valid technique in breeding, as long as it's done properly.

Inbreeding is the mating of dogs that are closely related, such as father to daughter or brother to sister. Inbreeding is a way to set type, or good characteristics. When the dogs used for inbreeding are free of hereditary disease and have excellent conformation and temperament, the result can be a litter of beautiful, healthy puppies. While inbreeding works well when the dogs involved have superior attributes and few or no defects, it can lead to serious problems if the opposite is true. Inbreeding intensifies good qualities, but it also magnifies flaws. Inbreeding requires in-depth knowledge of the pedigrees of both dogs so that the breeder is knowledgeable about and prepared for any diseases or defects that could occur from the breeding.

Like inbreeding, linebreeding is the mating of related dogs, but the degree of relationship is not so close. Examples of linebreeding would be a bitch to her grandsire (grandfather) or a dog to his granddam (grandmother). It's another way to enhance good characteristics and express defects that need to be eliminated from the breeder's line. Again, dogs being linebred should be of the highest quality in health, conformation, and temperament.

An outcross is the breeding of two unrelated dogs. It's used when a breeder wants to introduce a desirable attribute into her line.

to people when they are only six weeks old, because she is tired of the hassle.

Also in contrast to the good breeder, the commercial breeder, known as a puppy mill, runs a large-scale operation and supplies pet stores all over the country. His Beagles spend most of their time in cages, with little human contact. The puppies go to pet stores at six to eight weeks of age, while they're still at the cute stage but before they have completed the all-important socialization lessons they need to learn from their mother and siblings as well as from regular handling by people.

While it can certainly be easier to acquire your Beagle from breeder number one—Aunt Sarah—or more convenient to stop in at the pet store and pick one up on impulse, buying a Beagle should be entered into with more thought. If you are expecting to pay several hundred dollars for a purebred dog, you should get the best puppy for your money. You may think that your Beagle is simply going to be a pet, not a show dog, but that's even more reason for him to come from a breeder who is concerned about healthy bloodlines and good socialization. A Beagle who is going to be a family companion should come from the very healthiest, most temperamentally sound stock available.

Get to know several breeders and their dogs before making your decision. It's tempting to take home the first big-eyed puppy that snuggles into your neck, but if you wait and compare you'll be a more informed consumer, better able to choose the Beagle that's right for you.

Prices for Beagles vary according to location and the sex and quality of the puppy you're getting. A reputable breeder on the West Coast might price puppies between $600 and $800. In the South, Midwest, and on the East Coast, all places where Beagles are as thick as flies on honey, they generally go for somewhat less. Females tend to go for more than males.

A backyard breeder like Aunt Sarah might price her puppies as low as $50 or as high as $200, depending on how sick she is of having them underfoot and how much she thinks she can get for them.

Some breeders charge less for pet-quality puppies than for puppies with potential as show dogs. Reasons a puppy might be sold as pet quality include being oversize, or having such cosmetic defects as a straight shoulder, asymmetrical markings, blue eyes, short, stiff ears, ears that are set too low, an undershot or overshot bite, or missing teeth. Other reasons are gun shyness or a lack of hunting ability. If the dog is healthy, none of these flaws will detract from his ability to be a fine pet, although a Beagle that's gun shy may panic at thunderstorms or other loud noises.

Pet-quality puppies to avoid are those with excessively shy or aggressive temperaments, flat feet, lameness, or an unhealthy or scrawny-looking appearance. Beware, too, of a puppy that's unusually large for his age. Check the "growth knobs" at his wrist and ankles. If they are very large, tender, or hot to the touch, the dog is likely to be prone to joint problems later in life.

As the Beagle is such a popular breed, finding a good breeder is paramount. You'll want to deal with someone whose primary concern is the best interest of the breed, not a person who's simply capitalizing on the Beagle's popularity to make a quick buck.

How to Find a Breeder

Word of mouth is a good way to start your search for a breeder. Ask a satisfied Beagle-owning friend for a recommendation. Your veterinarian may have a Beagle breeder as a client, and the vet can advise you on the health of that person's dogs and confirm whether he or she had proper preliminary health certifications performed.

Visit a dog show and talk to the Beagle breeders there. They won't have puppies for sale at the show, but it's a good place to get to know a breeder informally. If you like what you hear, you can ask to set up an appointment to visit the breeder's home and meet his other dogs and puppies.

The National Beagle Club (NBC) is a good source of information (see the appendix). The club's secretary or breed information

Overbreeding and
Overpopulation—The Facts

Every year, an estimated 10 million to 20 million animals are turned in to animal shelters by owners who no longer want them. The majority of them are euthanized. That's not an exaggeration. And the problem of pet overpopulation is not limited to mixed breeds.

The number of Beagles surrendered to animal shelters is high because they are such a popular breed. Beagles end up in animal shelters for a variety of reasons: their owners didn't take the time to learn about their characteristics before acquiring them; their owners didn't spend the time and patience required for successful house-training; their people moved to a place that didn't allow pets; they developed behavioral problems through neglect or lack of training; or a new baby came along and suddenly there was no more time for the Beagle. In most cases these dogs are not bad; they are simply either the victims of circumstance or ill-equipped for change.

Responsible breeders know all too well the reasons why dogs suddenly find themselves homeless, and that's why they inquire so carefully into the backgrounds and motives of people who want to buy their puppies. They want to make sure that their Beagles are going to lifelong homes. That's also why they are concerned when new Beagle owners express an interest in breeding. Beagles are a popular breed. It is all too easy for a popular breed to slide into the gaping maw of public demand, there to be overbred by the uninformed and the puppy millers until the breed is but a shadow of its former self. Then, no one can remember why anyone would want a dog with so many health, temperament, and conformation problems—all brought about by excessive popularity. Many breeds have gone through this cycle—German Shepherds, Doberman Pinschers, Collies, Cocker Spaniels, Dalmatians, Saint Bernards. While each eventually recovered, it often took many years and many sad, short dog lives before these breeds regained their proper temperament and appearance. Concerned Beagle breeders fear that the same thing could happen to their dogs.

Heavy demand for a particular breed can be troubling for breeders, who voice concern about health problems exacerbated by overbreeding and about the dogs ending up in families that aren't suited to them. Responsible retailers have similar concerns. They must balance a customer's desire for a certain animal not only with supply but also with their own concerns about placing pets appropriately. Fortunately, there are a number of ways that the worries on each side can be handled.

Bob Vella, owner of Pet Stop in Bakersfield, California, says he advises people to research breeds carefully before buying. "What amazes me is that when you buy a computer, you don't just sit down in front of it and you're a computer expert," he says. "Everyone always reads the manual or something to become literate on the subject. When they buy a puppy, why doesn't the same thing apply?" He recommends that potential pet owners buy a book about the breed first or go to the library to learn more about it. Vella, who also hosts a weekly radio show about pets, doesn't stop there. Noting that the number one reason that dogs are turned in to animal shelters is behavioral problems, he says: "We do the best we can to ensure that the puppy's going to go through the proper steps of becoming a good member of the family. We talk to buyers about obedience training, about vaccinations and other medical situations, so they get off on the right foot."

At Tail Waggers Pet Shop in Holyoke, Colorado, same-day sales are discouraged. Owner Vicki Ocken also takes the time to screen prospective buyers to make sure a particular breed is right for them, and she says customers respond well to her advice. "There are always going to be some people who are determined they're going to have certain breeds, but with most of them, once they're educated, they're much better about choosing a breed," she says. Like Vella, Ocken suggests that people read books about their chosen breed before buying, and she refers them to the store's veterinarian who can discuss any medical drawbacks to the breed. "We also give them names of people who actually own the animals and have them talk to them," she says.

Spaying and neutering pets can also help reduce the problem of surplus Beagles, but it goes hand in hand with educated buyers. If you or someone you know is considering buying a Beagle, take the time to learn about the breed and find a good breeder. Your effort and concern will help keep the breed in good shape.

representative can refer you to reputable breeders in your area. If you write to the club or to a breeder, be sure to send a self-addressed stamped envelope for the reply.

Once you have some names, you can start interviewing breeders. Good questions to ask include how long the breeder has been in Beagles, whether he shows his dogs, what breed clubs he belongs to, what health problems he has seen in his line, how often he produces a litter, and whether he can provide you with references from other buyers. Ask about the show or performance records of the sire and dam (male and female parent). Are they really worthy of being bred? You'll also want to know if the puppies you're looking at come from show or field lines. The two types can have vastly different personalities and appearances. Find out what vaccinations and deworming medications the puppies have received, and whether the breeder guarantees the health of his puppies.

These are all good things to know, because they will give you an idea of how committed the breeder is to Beagles and how long he has been in the breed. Someone who exhibits his dogs is proud of what he has produced and is willing for them to be judged by other Beagle fanciers. Club membership indicates a desire to keep up with what's happening in the breed, especially in the area of health-related issues.

A breeder who admits to problems in the breed, or even his own line, is simply being honest. There is no breed that's free of hereditary problems, and anyone who makes that claim is not someone from whom you want to buy a dog. Ask the breeder what he's doing to eliminate health problems.

Beagles are susceptible to several hereditary diseases: hypothyroidism, epilepsy, epiphyseal dysplasia, and cherry eye. Even though the Beagle is a small breed, the dogs can suffer from hip dysplasia, also a hereditary condition. Hypothyroidism is a deficiency of thyroid hormones. Epilepsy is a seizure disorder. Epiphyseal dysplasia, also known as chondrodysplasia, is an abnormality of the growth plates of the long bones (legs). Cherry eye is a swelling of the gland of the third eyelid. Hip dysplasia is a deformity of the hip joint and causes mild to severe lameness.

Many of these conditions can't be tested for or don't show up until later in life, but the breeder should be using dogs that are currently free of disease and have a family history that's relatively free of these diseases. They should also test dog and bitch for brucellosis (a sexually transmitted disease) and thyroid function before breeding. A Beagle breeder who x-rays the hips of breeding stock and has the radiographs evaluated by the Orthopedic Foundation for Animals is to be highly commended.

Ask the breeder to go over the pedigree with you and tell you about the medical history of her pups' ancestors. Unfortunately, problems such as epilepsy and hypothyroidism usually don't show up until a dog is middle-aged or older, after it has already passed on its genes. If a dog or bitch develops hypothyroidism or begins to have seizures late in life, all of that dog's descendants must be considered carriers. There's currently no way to do DNA testing to determine which dogs are definitely carriers, so all breeders can do is to eliminate those dogs from their breeding program.

Did You Know?

The United States and France have the highest rates of dog ownership in the world (for countries in which such statistics are available), with almost one dog for every three families. Germany and Switzerland have the lowest rates, with just one dog for every ten families.

Some breeders offer health guarantees, with a promise of a replacement puppy or a refund if the dog develops a hereditary problem. A guarantee is usually good for a limited time: two weeks, one year, or even two years. It doesn't ensure that a pup will be free of problems, but it does mean the breeder has confidence in his dogs' good health.

The Breeder's Concerns

Expect the breeder to interview you thoroughly as well. He wants to make sure his puppies go only to the very best homes, where they'll be loved and appreciated. Rather than taking his questions personally or being insulted if he is concerned about some aspect of your lifestyle, such as the age of your children, remember that he is only concerned for the welfare of his pups. You would ask lots of questions too if your children were going to a new home. Your brain should send up a warning flag if the breeder doesn't seem interested in knowing about you.

> Expect the breeder to interview you thoroughly as well. He wants to make sure his puppies go only to the very best homes, where they'll be loved and appreciated.

Questions the breeder may ask include whether someone will be home during the day, who will be responsible for the dog's care, whether everyone in the family wants a Beagle, whether you have a fenced yard, where you expect the Beagle to sleep, whether you plan to spay or neuter your pet, what your plans are for training the dog, whether anyone in the family suffers from allergies, and what happened to previous pets—for instance, did they die of old age or get hit by cars after only a couple of years? He should require that the dog be returned to him if there's ever any reason you can't keep it—no matter how many years later it is.

Talk to a number of breeders and look at lots of puppies so you can get a good overview of the breed. Once you've found a breeder you're happy with—and who approves of you—the fun part begins: checking out the puppies.

How Do I Choose the Pick of the Litter?

You will probably first see the puppies when they are six or seven weeks old. The breeder won't want to risk infection from outside sources before then. At that age, puppies are still in need of time with their mother and littermates so they won't miss out on any important social development, but you can still get a good idea of each one's personality.

Based on what you've told the breeder about the kind of dog you want, she can point you in the direction of the pup that meets your needs. In fact, some breeders don't even let prospective buyers see all the puppies. They only show the ones that are available for sale. That way, people don't fall in love with a pup the breeder is planning to keep or has already promised to someone else.

Temperament Tests

Predicting a puppy's adult personality and temperament isn't an exact science, but there are some clues you can look for that will help you make an appropriate choice. Activity level, interaction with siblings, and reaction to people can all be evaluated and, to some extent, are indicators of what a pup will be like when she grows up.

Find out how the puppies have been socialized. Have they been exposed to a variety of people or only to the breeder and his family? It's important for young dogs to encounter as many people as possible in their first four months of life so they don't bond only with the breeder's family. Beagle puppies should view all people as a source of pleasure and entertainment.

When you first encounter the puppies, simply stand still and wait to see how they respond to you. Look at the puppies' general demeanor. While some may be more cautious than others, expect to see signs of curiosity, friendliness, and trust in people. Some puppies come readily, while their littermates take a little more time to evaluate the situation. Caution is not a bad thing, and it shouldn't be confused with shyness.

Shyness and suspicion are traits you want to avoid in the puppy you take home. You may feel sorry for the puppy who is hiding in a corner, but shyness is extremely difficult to overcome. It's no fun having a dog that runs away from everyone who approaches it or startles at any unusual sound.

Although it might seem likely that the suspicious pup would make a good watchdog, this is not a characteristic that should be evident in such a young dog. An overly suspicious puppy may well develop into a fearful adult.

Test the pups' response to sound by clapping your hands. Do they look around or run away? If they run away, do they come back quickly to investigate? The pup who looks around to see what the noise is or who comes back quickly after running off is curious, or maybe just a little cautious. There's nothing wrong with that, but avoid the pup that takes off for the hills and never comes back.

How do the puppies behave with each other? Is one more dominant than the rest, jumping on her littermates and taking toys from them? Or is there one that all the other pups pick on? For most people, a Beagle that falls between these two extremes is a good choice. Dominant dogs want to run the show and can be difficult to train, while picked-on pups may have low self-esteem, which can lead to problem behaviors.

After you've looked over the puppies for a few minutes, see how each one feels about being picked up. Does she squirm and struggle or happily relax into your arms? Does she squirm a little and then relax? This is a stressful situation for a puppy, and you want

> Dominant dogs want to run the show and can be difficult to train, while picked-on pups may have low self-esteem, which can lead to problem behaviors.

to choose one that is able to calm down in a reasonable amount of time. The pup who's unable to control her fear or her desire to be in charge is likely headed for future behavior problems.

Then walk away with the pup. See if she shows alarm at being separated from her mother and littermates. Some unease is natural, of course, but if the puppy trusts people, it should eventually relax and enjoy the ride. A pup's demeanor may change as well, with a quiet puppy becoming more inquisitive and active or a bold one becoming a little insecure. A puppy that becomes extremely fearful probably isn't a good choice.

Sit down and see if a particular puppy will come to you. Your Beagle should be people oriented. Note whether she's excited to see you or somewhat submissive. Tail wagging and ears up are the signs of a confident pup. Offer a treat. If the puppy trusts you enough to come forward and take it, you're looking at a Beagle with good training potential. Avoid the puppy that backs away with an anxious bark. Speak softly to the puppy. Is she interested in listening to you? In most cases, you'll want a puppy that sticks around to be with you, but if you plan to hunt your Beagle or teach her to track, you may prefer the pup who's intent on following a scent and leaves you to follow her nose.

Gently roll the puppy on her back and gauge her reaction. Does she squeal with indignation and struggle to get up or is she happy to relax as you scratch her tummy? The squealer is likely to be a domineering Beagle and will need plenty of consistent training so she won't take over the household. Be sure you differentiate between the puppy who is merely high-spirited or assertive and one who is aggressive, fearful, or suspicious. The latter puppy may try to bite, which is not a good sign.

Another good test is of the puppy's willingness to follow. Walk away; then encourage the puppy to come to you. A nice Beagle with a moderate temperament will comply without a lot of antic behavior, such as running in circles, barking, or dashing away.

Test a puppy's sensitivity to touch and sound as well. While you're holding her, squeeze the webbing between her paws, letting up as soon as you get a response. Look for a puppy that pulls her paw away, but doesn't yelp or try to bite. The latter reactions indicate a puppy who probably won't respond well to handling by young children or handling required for grooming.

To see if a puppy is noise shy, wait until she's not looking and then clap your hands or drop something that will make a noise. Puppy reactions will range from ignoring the noise altogether to investigating the sound to running away. A confident puppy will respond by ignoring the sound or checking it out. That's the one you want. (Deafness isn't a common problem in Beagles, but if the puppy totally ignores the noise, you'll want to have her checked by a veterinarian to make sure she doesn't have a hearing disorder.)

Just as humans have work styles—for instance, the go-getter versus the laid-back employee—dogs have play styles. Toss a toy and see how the puppy reacts. Does she run helter-skelter after it or proceed in a more deliberate fashion? Her actions will give you a clue as to her future personality. When you take the toy away, does the puppy give it up politely or hang on for dear life, growling through her teeth? Prefer the polite puppy to the growler.

Finally, the puppy should be used to having all parts of her body handled. The breeder should be able to show you how willing the puppy is to have her teeth or ears looked at and her nails trimmed.

By this time, you and the breeder should have a good idea of which puppy suits you best. Now you just need to make sure she's in sparkling good health.

Signs of Good Health

As you were evaluating the puppies, you were probably taking note of their surroundings as well. Breeders are normal people who sometimes have messy houses, but there's a difference between messy and filthy. A healthy puppy is rarely going to emerge from highly unsanitary conditions. Keep an eye out for such things as whether fly-ridden piles of feces are lying around the yard or dog dishes are encrusted with old food.

Then there's the puppy herself. Active and alert, she should have bright eyes, clean ears, pink gums, white teeth, and a shiny coat without sores. Nose and eyes should be free of discharge, not runny or red.

Even though you can't see inside a puppy, his outward appearance can suggest internal problems such as worms. A dull coat and a distended stomach— giving the puppy the appearance of having a beer belly—can be signs of internal parasites such as roundworms. Say no thanks if you encounter a puppy that

Did You Know?

Barry Manilow is the proud pop of two Beagles—Bagel and Biscuit.

looks like this. Sure, internal parasites are easily treated, but the puppy's condition doesn't say much for the breeder's husbandry or care for the dogs.

It's kind of gross, but take a look at the feces if the puppy eliminates while you're there. Are they small and firm, or does the pup show signs of diarrhea? Blood or worms in the stool are also caution signals.

If everything checks out, though, it's time to talk to the breeder about purchasing one of her pups. They likely will be ready to go to their new homes at seven or eight weeks of age.

Buying Long Distance

It's not always possible to find the perfect breeder living right next door, or even in your hometown. Sometimes you will have to look farther afield for the puppy of your dreams. Buying a Beagle sight unseen may seem like the stuff of nightmares, but it can be done successfully.

Expect to spend lots of time on the phone with the breeder so the two of you can get to know each other. It's not unusual for a phone interview to go on for a couple of hours, or for briefer periods over several days or weeks. It's very important for both you and the breeder to be comfortable with each other.

Check out each other's references. The breeder may be able to steer you to someone in your area who has bought one of her puppies. She may have a friend in your city who can visit your home and report back to her. And you may have a relative in her city who can give a thumbs-up to the breeder's home. Ask your veterinarian or dog trainer if they'd be willing to provide written testimonials about your experience as a pet owner.

The postal service and the Internet are your friends as well. The breeder can mail photos or videos of her dogs, or direct you to her Web site. Ask for copies of health certifications, just as you would if you were meeting the breeder in person.

Most breeders are familiar with shipping dogs and will choose the flight that will be fastest and safest for the puppy, usually priority parcel or counter-to-counter. A puppy being shipped by air must be at least eight weeks old and accompanied by a health certificate. If the breeder knows someone who's heading in your direction, he may even be able to have the puppy hand-delivered to you at the airport. Be sure you bring a collar and leash with you to the airport so you can take the pup out for a potty break before heading home.

The agreement with the breeder should include a 48-hour, no-questions-asked return policy, so make the veterinarian's office your first stop after the airport pickup, to make sure the puppy's health checks out. You don't want to get attached to her and then find out she has a serious health problem. Avoid breeders who sell only on a "no returns allowed" basis.

If all is well, it's time to take the puppy home, let the breeder know she arrived safely, and start enjoying life with your Beagle.

Adopting from an Animal Shelter

Amazing as it may sound, purebred dogs, especially popular breeds such as Beagles, are often available at animal shelters. Many of them land there through no fault of their own, because their people died, moved to places where pets weren't allowed, didn't have time for them, or decided they were too much work. If you like the idea of owning a Beagle, but want to give a chance to a dog who needs a good home, start your search at local public and private animal shelters.

You may not find a Beagle your first time through, but explain to the shelter staff what you're looking for and ask to be placed on a waiting list. If a Beagle comes in, they'll know to give you a call. It might help to leave a photo of a Beagle to serve as a visual reminder.

If you do find a Beagle in a shelter, ask if you can take her out on a leash. Some shelters have playrooms, where people can get to know pets in a friendlier environment than a cage. If the Beagle is a puppy or adolescent, perform the same temperament tests you would if you were at a breeder's home (see pages 35–39). People who work at the shelter see the dogs on a daily basis, and it is helpful to get their opinion on the dog's temperament as well.

Shelter personnel may be able to tell you something about the Beagle's background, such as how old she is, whether she came from a home with children or other pets, and why she was given up. Questions to ask include whether the dog has a good appetite and whether she came with any health records or other paperwork.

Remember that a dog in a shelter is probably frightened, and that may color her attitude. This may be her first time away from her canine or human family; that's upsetting for anyone, let alone a dog that lands in a noisy, unfamiliar place like a public shelter. A Beagle separated from her previous owner may go through a period of mourning, so she may seem depressed or withdrawn. Once she's in a less stressful environment, such as a visitation room or an outdoor exercise area, she may perk up a little. Evaluate the dog's physical condition as well, checking for the same things noted in the earlier section, "Signs of Good Health."

You may go into a shelter hoping to find a puppy, but don't pass up a grown Beagle or even one of advanced age. Giving a home to an older dog can be a wonderful experience. Although she may not be with you for as many years as a puppy, the rewards of taking her into your home can far outweigh the eventual loss.

Hunter's Story—An Adoption Success

Our adoption of a Beagle came from a purely selfish need and a wonderful stroke of luck. About two years ago, we adopted a Jack Russell Terrier from our neighbors, who could no longer handle the needs of this very active breed once their first child was born. The JRT became a "daddy's girl" and was often in my husband's lap, leaving my lap cold. We started looking for a second dog, and thus began the weekly trips to the pound.

It took two to three months of looking before I found the dog I was waiting for. He was a poor skinny Beagle, just wagging his tail and looking at me with those big brown eyes. I immediately went to the office and asked to see the file on the dog, whose name was Hunter. He had been dropped off by a family because he wouldn't stop running away. I had had a Spaniel when I was growing up who ran away often, and this wasn't fun, but as long as it wasn't a biting problem I thought we'd be okay. When we saw that Hunter and our other dog got along, we decided to give him a try. It was the week before Christmas.

After a bath and lots of cookies, Hunter joined our family. For the next few weeks, we spoiled him with hamburgers from the drive-through, leftovers, and lots of love. Eventually his ribs disappeared, he let us touch his head, and the pads on his feet toughened up (after many walks). We had to teach him what "love" was, what a "sidewalk" was (no, you can't run down the middle of the street), where "home" was and who his new "pack" was. Now, nine months later, Hunter has gone from running away every week (the little squirmer always managed to find some way to escape—jumping on rock, going over the fence, sneaking through a door slightly ajar) to a great big snuggle bunny who is more concerned about keeping his yard free of kitties than about escaping to another place.

Seeing his progress has been a great experience. I would encourage everyone looking for a dog to check the local pound on a regular basis. You can find some wonderful dogs there. Most important, research the breed you are interested in. We have three rescue dogs that were dropped at the pound or given up because the owner could not handle behaviors that were common to their breeds. Our dogs' behaviors and the reasons why they were given up are exactly what you would find described if you picked up a book about Jack Russells or Beagles. Jack Russells are big dogs in little bodies and Beagles follow their noses. Educate yourself so you can learn to love their faults.

—Kristen Gose

Adopting from a Rescue Group

A Beagle rescue group is another excellent place to look for a dog. A dog may be placed with a rescue group for the same reasons he lands in a shelter. The National Beagle Club does not sponsor a rescue group, but several clubs and individuals across the country are making a good effort to place homeless Beagles (see the appendix). Each rescue group might place up to 130 or more Beagles annually.

There are several reasons why people give Beagles up to rescue organizations. If the Beagle is less than a year old, the owners probably bought the dog from a source that didn't educate them about his need for a yard and exercise and his desire to roam. Things were okay while the puppy was young, but as he moved into adolescence, his energy level became too high for them to deal with in an apartment or condo. Many Beagles that are given up are two or three years old. The owners are moving or decide that they're just not Beagle people; they're tired of dealing with the breed's stubbornness. Common complaints Beagle rescuers hear are "He won't come when I call" or "He won't stay in the backyard."

Questions to ask yourself before adopting a Beagle are those you should consider before getting any dog: What is the dog's activity level? How much exercise will he need? Does the breed or individual dog have any severe health problems? Does the dog get along with children and other animals? Does someone need to be home with the dog all day? Are two better than one?

A Beagle has many advantages in that he's usually great with kids, easy to groom, and generally gets along well with other animals, but the disadvantages—the instinct to roam and the difficulty of training—should not be overlooked. Also keep in mind that Beagles placed with rescue groups often have health or behavioral problems with which you are going to have to deal. You'll need to give him extra patience, care, and understanding for the adoption to be successful. On the plus side, you'll know exactly what size the dog is going to be and what his habits are.

Evaluate a Beagle from a rescue group the same way you would a dog from a breeder or shelter. If you're considering an adolescent or mature dog, ask ahead of time if you can take the dog for a walk through the neighborhood or at a nearby park. Note the dog's reaction to the approach of bikes, cars, or strollers, and to sudden sounds or movements. Ideally, he will be confident and relaxed, recovering quickly from a startling situation and proceeding with tail up.

> A Beagle has many advantages in that he's usually great with kids, easy to groom, and generally gets along well with other animals, but the disadvantages—the instinct to roam and the difficulty of training—should not be overlooked.

As you approach people, pay attention to the dog's response. Be wary of taking home a Beagle who shrinks away from people, tail between his legs, or tries frantically to climb up into your arms. This dog will require lots of socialization. Acceptable reactions range from indifference to caution to friendliness and curiosity.

Be sure to ask from what type of situation the dog came. If he was given up because he didn't get along with a family's children or other pets, you don't want to take him home to your children or pets. Some Beagles simply want to be the center of attention, and they do best with childless or older couples who can give them the time they need. On the other hand, if the dog was given up for behavior problems caused by lack of attention, that's something you can remedy with training and time.

A Boy or a Girl?

Unlike many breeds, there's little difference in size or temperament between the Beagle sexes. Both generally tend to be sweet and loving. "Bo was our first male," says Janiece Harrison. "I hadn't planned on ever having a boy because I thought a boy wouldn't be as sweet as our girls had been. But he was in a situation where he needed a new home, so we gave it a try. He has turned out to be my soul mate. He's loving and devoted, and he and I have really connected."

In terms of how males and females relate to other dogs in the family, it's not uncommon for a female Beagle to end up as top dog. If you have more than one dog, it's usually recommended that they be of the opposite sex, but if they're introduced on neutral territory, some Beagles are mellow enough that two of the same sex can live together without problems. It's likely that you'll be happy with a male or a female Beagle, but each has aspects you may want to consider before making a final decision.

Unless a female is spayed, she will go into season for about three weeks twice a year, usually every five to seven months. A bitch in season has swollen genitals, which she licks frequently, and a bloody discharge that can be light or heavy. During this hormone-driven period, your Beagle may enthusiastically hump anything or anyone she can find. Without careful supervision, she'll become an escape artist in search of any male to satisfy her urges.

Elimination habits also differ between males and females. Males will lift their legs on just about anything, from your freshly painted fence to a wall or sofa indoors. Females squat neatly.

In both sexes, spaying or neutering can reduce or eliminate these unpleasant behaviors. Spay/neuter surgery also has health advantages. Spaying prevents serious uterine infections and, if done before the dog's first heat, can significantly decrease the chance that she will develop mammary cancer later in life. Spayed females are also spared the hormonal disruption of a false pregnancy, in which the uterus swells and the nipples engorge with milk. This can be disturbing to the dog both emotionally and physically.

Neutered males are protected from testicular cancer, prostate disease, and perianal adenomas, growths around the anus which are testosterone-dependent. They are also less likely to lick their genitals, lift their legs, or hump guests. Nor do they have any reason to roam in search of a willing female. As neutered animals of both sexes have no desire to procreate, they are happy to devote all their love and attention to their people.

The Sniffer

Beagles belong to a group of dogs known as scenthounds, which were originally bred for their ability to track prey by scent. Few of us need to hunt for our meals anymore, but our dogs still retain their ancestral fervor for following a trail. Bloodhounds are the most famous of the scenthounds, but Beagles aren't slackers when it comes to using their noses.

How does a Beagle follow a scent trail? Our bodies constantly give off scent. Scent is made up of flakes of dead skin that carry our unique odor, which is determined by such factors as the type of soap, shampoo, and perfume we use, how often we bathe, what we eat, and even our genetic heritage. The scent trail stays near the ground when weather conditions are cool or damp and rises into the air when the weather heats up.

A Beagle is able to follow this trail because of the high number of receptor cells located inside his nasal cavity. The receptor cells continuously feed sensory information about odors to the olfactory nerve, which runs directly to the area of the brain where scent information is processed. The larger and longer a dog's nose is, the better his sense of smell. Whereas people have only about five million receptor cells, a Beagle has 125 million or more.

Even more amazing is a dog's ability to discriminate among different odors, even when they're heavily masked. Dogs have been trained to sniff out the scent of currency paper and ink, explosives and weapons, accelerants used by arsonists, and illegal drugs such as cocaine, heroin, methamphetamines, and marijuana.

Due to their affable nature, size, and scenting ability, Beagles are used by the United States Department of Agriculture's Animal and Plant Health Inspection Services to detect prohibited fruit and meat in the baggage of passengers arriving from overseas. They're called the Beagle Brigade; you may have seen them in their bright green jackets patrolling luggage areas. Some of them can identify up to 50 different odors. Their job is to help prevent the importation of foreign animal and plant pests and diseases that could affect or even wipe out American crops.

Snoopy

The world's most famous Beagle may well be the comic strip character Snoopy, who debuted in print on October 4, 1950, a birth date that also makes him the world's longest lived Beagle. Born at the Daisy Hill Puppy Farm, he's one of the rarely seen black-and-white Beagles, and an extrovert with a Walter Mitty complex. Perched atop his doghouse, he lets loose with his vivid imagination, which takes him through space and time to become a World War I flying ace in a dogfight with his archenemy the Red Baron; a put-upon writer whose every literary attempt meets with failure; a vulture surveying the landscape for carrion; a member of the French Foreign Legion; and campus hero Joe Cool. But like every other Beagle in the world, he's always back in time for supper.

Adopting from an animal shelter or breed rescue group is not as simple as going in and saying "I'll take that one." Requirements for adopting a Beagle may include having a fenced yard and letting the dog sleep indoors at night. Expect to be required to spay or neuter the dog and to return him if he doesn't fit into your home. Adoption fees range from $85 to $110 or more and usually include spaying/neutering and microchipping for identification purposes. You may be asked to fill out an extensive application form and go through an interview just as grueling as that given by the most careful of breeders, and for the same good reason: shelter personnel and rescue groups want to make absolutely certain that the animals they place are going to appropriate homes where they'll be loved and cherished.

Other Sources

A number of pet food companies use Beagles to test new food formulations. It's hard to imagine a better taste-tester. Often,

A Model Dog: The Beagle in Art

Before the advent of photography, people had portraits painted of their loved ones or their prized possessions. Animal portraiture reached its zenith during the Victorian era, thanks to the sportsmen who wanted visual records of their sporting dogs, hounds, and horses. Naturally, Beagles were among those favored animals. Among the depictions of Beagles are a work by well-known artist Maud Earl entitled <u>A Check</u> (oil on canvas) and <u>The Beagles Gudger, Betsey and Tuner</u> (oil on panel), by W. Murray. A more modern work, entitled <u>Beagle in a Basket</u>, by Duane Hanson, portrays a member of the breed in a rare state—repose.

these dogs are used for only a limited period and are then made available for adoption. It's in the companies' best interests to give the dogs the best of health care, and they receive regular handling from kennel attendants. If you live near the headquarters of Iams, Purina, Science Diet, or another major pet food manufacturer, it's worth checking with them to see if they have a Beagle adoption program.

Sometimes the United States Department of Agriculture has Beagles available for adoption from the National Detector Dog Training Center in Orlando, Florida. These dogs are either retired from service with the Beagle Brigade (see "The Sniffer, page 47) or didn't make it through evaluations and training. For more information on adopting a Beagle from the National Detector Dog Training Center, call (407) 816-1192.

2

Welcome Home!

In This Chapter

- ○ Preparing for Your Beagle's Arrival
- ○ Beagle-Proofing Your House
- ○ Which Supplies Do You Really Need?
- ○ The First Night with Your Beagle Puppy

There are few events in life more memorable than the first day with a new puppy or dog. What follows is a guide to the necessary preparation and get-acquainted period with your pet. Prepare now, and you'll have more time to enjoy the special moments that will become treasured "remember-whens" years down the road.

Preparing for Your Beagle's Arrival

The big day is almost here. In just a week or two, your new Beagle will be arriving to spend the next 10 or so years with you. Starting off on the right paw will help ensure that the coming years are happy ones. Before the pup arrives, the family needs to sit down and discuss how the new dog will fit into the household, and who will be responsible for such things as meals, grooming, playtime, and poop patrol. You also need to prepare a puppy layette so your Beagle will feel right at home, and Beagle-proof your house and yard.

Setting Boundaries: Decisions You Need to Make before You Bring Your Beagle Home

Dogs are conservatives at heart. They like to know where they stand, and they're not big on change. Beagles are no exception. They respond best to consistency, so you should begin as you mean to go on. If you let the puppy get away with things that are cute at the puppy stage but not so cute as the months and years go by, your dog will be confused when you start correcting her for behavior you used to laugh at. So before you bring your Beagle home, go down the following list and decide what's okay and what's not.

○ Where will the dog sleep? If you have kids, they're sure to clamor for allowing the dog to sleep with them. Whether you approve or disapprove of letting dogs sleep on the bed, keep in mind that puppies aren't physiologically able to control their elimination habits reliably at this early age. You'll want to house-train your Beagle and wait several months to a year to make sure she's capable of avoiding accidents without being confined to a crate. Offer a compromise by allowing the dog to sleep in a crate in the child's room—on the condition that the child be responsible for taking the dog to eliminate first thing every morning when she wakes, even if that means getting up at 6 a.m. instead of 6:30 or 7. You should only offer this compromise to a child who is old enough to carry it out without being constantly reminded. If you have multiple kids, puppy and crate can rotate to a different room each week. You can determine which kid gets him first by age, alphabetical order, or drawing names out of a hat.

○ If you don't have children or if they're too young for such an arrangement, consider letting the puppy or dog sleep in a crate in your room. She'll feel less lonely there, and you'll be able to hear her in the morning when she wakes and needs to go out. It's also easier to correct her immediately if she barks, whines, or howls during the night. Sleeping in your room allows the Beagle to become accustomed to your scent and is a good bonding experience.

> If you let the puppy get away with things that are cute at the puppy stage but not so cute as the months and years go by, your dog will be confused when you start correcting her for behavior you used to laugh at.

○ Is the dog allowed on the furniture? Most Beagle owners enjoy sharing a sofa or chair with their pets, but if you prefer that the dog stay on the floor, on her own bed, or on a particularly ratty piece of furniture designated just for her, then eliminate the word "sometimes" from your vocabulary. If you let the dog up on the "good" sofa occasionally, she will soon want to be up there all the time and won't understand when you don't let her stay.

○ Who is responsible for training the dog? At least one family member should regularly attend training class, but it's best if everyone goes. That way, you'll all understand the training techniques and commands and how to implement them. Take turns training the dog during the week. That way, everyone will get some practice, and the dog will learn that she should respond to commands given by any family member.

"What Do You Mean It's My Turn?"

Use this checklist to make a Beagle care schedule. Post it in a prominent spot, such as on the refrigerator or by the front door, so no one can make the claim "I forgot" or "I didn't know it was my turn."

○ **Mealtime.** Schedule three to four meals daily for puppies, one or two meals daily for adults.

○ **Elimination.** Puppies need to go out immediately upon waking, after every meal, and just before bedtime. If they get plenty of opportunities to go outside, they shouldn't make any messes in the house. In case of accident, make sure everyone knows where the stain and odor remover is kept and how to use it.

○ **Exercise.** Beagle puppies are very active. They come in two speeds: full throttle and crash (naptime). Channel their energy with several daily 15-minute walks or playtimes.

○ **Grooming.** Weekly, take about 15 minutes to brush coat and teeth, clean ears, and trim nails as needed. Daily, check eyes for discharge and wipe away the "sleepies" in the corners.

○ **Training.** Classes usually take place weekly, for five to eight weeks. Schedule at least two brief daily training sessions at home as well.

○ **Health.** Note any upcoming veterinary visits for booster shots and who's responsible for taking the dog to the vet.

○ Who is responsible for feeding and watering the dog? This can be delegated to one person, or you can design a schedule delegating the chore to various family members. If children are involved, a parent must be responsible for making sure the Beagle gets meals on time. The dog shouldn't suffer because of a child's forgetfulness or activity schedule.

○ Who is responsible for grooming the dog? The 15 minutes that it takes each week to groom a Beagle shouldn't be a problem for any family member to handle. Make sure everyone knows how to properly use each grooming tool.

Cleaning Up Pet Accidents

A puppy accident in the house doesn't have to be a disaster. If you clean it up properly, you won't even know it was there. For urination, use a towel (fabric, not paper) to blot up as much of the liquid as possible. Then, following the directions on the container, apply stain and odor remover. (Two products that I have found to work extremely well are Resolve carpet cleaner, available at grocery stores, and Odor Mute, found at pet supply stores.) Then put a dry towel on the area and top it with some heavy books. This helps remove moisture from the carpet. For solid messes, use a towel or plastic bag to lift up as much of the stool as possible and dispose of it in the toilet or garbage can. Apply stain and odor remover as directed on the bottle.

Beagle-Proofing Your House

Dogs are curious by nature, and Beagles more so than most, thanks to their sensitive sniffers. Puppies, especially, are natural-born explorers, programmed to learn about the world by testing everything with their mouths and paws. Because paws aren't very good for picking up and holding things, puppies bite or chew on items to find out how they taste, what they feel like, and whether they might be good to eat. Your Beagle, puppy or adult, has the potential to cause a great deal of damage, so be extra-careful about what you leave within his reach.

How Your Beagle Sees Your House

For this nosey breed, the whole world is a giant pantry. Beagles will sniff out anything that has the potential of being food, and everything has possibilities. Since these natural-born explorers don't have hands with opposable thumbs, they stand ready to test anything and everything with their mouths, biting or chewing on items to find out their taste and texture and whether they might be good to eat or fun to gnaw on. Beagle puppies are inveterate chewers. Judy Watts' puppy Hannah chewed a four-inch hole in the wall when she was teething. Your Beagle puppy might be small, but he's capable of a good deal of destruction, so make sure you're prepared before you bring him home.

> Puppies, especially, are natural-born explorers, programmed to learn about the world by testing everything with their mouths and paws.

Adult Beagles require the same amount of dog-proofing. While some may have polite manners, you're more likely to end up with a dog that's capable of opening cabinets and refrigerator doors. One seven-year-old Beagle, a former show dog, was discovered going through his owners' closet, pulling down clothes and checking the pockets for liver bait. He also grabbed a steak out of the refrigerator, ate a couple of screens, and got on the dining room table and tore up some paperwork. All of this occurred at night or during the one or two hours each day that no one was home with him. The people who adopted him returned him because they couldn't bring themselves to use a crate for even a brief period to keep him out of trouble.

To make sure your home is safe for exploration, go through it room by room, looking at everything from a Beagle's point of view. That means getting down on your hands and knees so you can spot hazards that a puppy might think will be fun to investigate. If nothing else, getting a Beagle will result in your house becoming very neat and organized, with a place for everything and everything in its place. Expandable child or dog gates are a good way to keep a puppy out of rooms where he shouldn't be or off the expensive Oriental carpets. Make sure the gate you use offers no way for the puppy to stick his head through and get caught.

"It's best not to give a puppy the run of the house," says breeder Janet Nieland. "Block off your kitchen or some other area, and let the puppy explore that, under your supervision. Beagles have a huge age range as far as when they can become dependable in the house. Some are fine within six or seven months, and others are two years old before it's safe to give them the run of the house. Some of them are never able to handle that much responsibility. I have a Beagle that's going to be 14 next month, and I still don't think I could trust her cruising around the house without us here."

House Hazards

Each and every part of your house contains certain dangers for your Beagle. Let's take a look at each room (and the garage) to help you eliminate as many potential hazards as possible.

Bathrooms Put cleansers, makeup, medications, and trash away from prying puppy paws. Child locks on cabinet doors keep even the most determined pup out. Put dangling cords from blow dryers and curling irons out of reach, so your Beagle doesn't pull them down on his head or electrocute himself by chewing them. Keep toilet lids down, toilet bowls free of chemicals and cleansers, and make sure toilet paper isn't dangling, enticing your puppy to run with it through the house.

Bedroom Shoes and dirty clothes on the floor are an open invitation for a puppy to chew on them or drag them into the living room while the boss is visiting (and swallowed socks could mean an intestinal obstruction and emergency surgery). Keep laundry and shoes behind closed doors or otherwise out of reach. If they're within puppy's reach, put away breakables, such as glass picture frames or other knick-knacks, and chewables, such as prized photo albums or books. Save your Beagle from a shocking experience: use tough plastic cable ties, available at electronics stores, to wrap up the cords of clock radios, phones, and televisions so they're not accessible, or coat them with a nasty-tasting substance such as Bitter Apple or hot sauce (for example, Tabasco). Wrapping cords in aluminum foil is a good deterrent as well. Biting down on it isn't a pleasant experience. Don't wrap frayed cords with aluminum foil, however, as it could serve as a conductor for electricity. If cords are frayed, it's best simply to replace them. They aren't safe, even without a puppy around.

Kitchen Keep cleansers and medications up high or behind cabinets with child-proof locks. Candy, especially chocolate, should be out of reach as well. The trashcan is full of things that smell wonderful to the sensitive nose of a Beagle. Make sure it's securely covered or located in an area where it can't be tipped over or climbed into. You don't want your puppy swallowing such items as twist ties, rubber bands, cellophane wrappers, poultry skin, fat trimmings from meat, or bones of any kind.

Store dog food in a Beagle-proof container. "I put a 40-pound bag of dog food on the table, thinking it was safe," says Katie Williams. "Distracted for just a few seconds, I came back to find my adventurous Beagle puppy's rear end sticking out of the bag. She had jumped on top of her crate, then to the top of the grooming table, then to the kitchen table. And they say dogs have no problem-solving abilities! Marcy was only nine or ten weeks old at the time."

Antifreeze

Antifreeze has a sweet taste that's appealing to children and dogs. Lapping up less than a tablespoon of antifreeze can kill a Beagle if he's not treated in time. Keep it well out of reach, and wipe up spills right away. To be on the safer side, buy antifreeze that contains propylene glycol, which is still toxic but less so than that containing ethylene glycol. If you suspect that your puppy has ingested antifreeze, rush him to the veterinarian.

Den/Office/Living Room Again, put breakables, prized items, and remote controls out of reach, and wrap the cords of computers, televisions, cable service, VCRs, and stereo equipment. Be sure houseplants are safe for nibbling (see list of toxic plants on page 63). Don't leave anything down low that you don't want puppy tooth marks on or that you don't want to disappear down the puppy's gullet.

Garage This area is full of dangers to dogs: chemical hazards such as antifreeze, cleansers, fertilizers, pesticides, paint, strippers, and glue; sharp-edged tools; and boxes storing who knows what. Store chemicals up high or behind closed doors, and clean up any oil spots or antifreeze drips. Put tools away, and make sure boxes are tightly closed so they can't be climbed into.

Beagle-Proofing Your Yard

For a Beagle, your yard is a jungle, ripe for exploration yet full of hidden dangers. Before you let your pup out on safari, give the

Top 10 Common Household Hazards

- ○ Aspirin, acetaminophen, ibuprofen, and other medications
- ○ Ceramic or glass knickknacks; other breakables
- ○ Chocolate
- ○ Electrical cords
- ○ Garbage: wrappers, meat trimmings, bones, cans with sharp edges

- ○ Household cleansers
- ○ Rubber bands and twist ties
- ○ Toxic houseplants
- ○ Toys, especially items small enough to be swallowed, like Lego pieces
- ○ Unsecured heavy items that a puppy can pull over on himself

yard a thorough going-over for poisonous plants, holes in fences, sharp or pointed edges along fencing, poisonous bait laid out for snails or other pests, tools lying around, and other hazards.

Repair any spots in the fence where a dog might be able to wiggle through, and sand down sharp edges. Loose wire could entangle a pup or poke him in the eye. Gates should latch securely. Take up bait and put away fertilizers and pesticides. Hoses, tools, and any toys the kids have left lying around should be returned to their proper spots as well.

What about your pool or spa? A Beagle could drown quickly if he fell in when no one was looking. Keep a pool or spa securely covered if you're not there to supervise. If the pool or spa is surrounded by a fence, again, make sure the gate latches securely.

If you don't want your Beagle nibbling on your strawberries or tomatoes, fence them off as well. A white picket fence will look nice and help keep your Beagle out of tasting range.

Placing barriers around your yard isn't always practical; you may want to consider putting a wire exercise pen in a safe area where your Beagle can play, or even building a dog run. You can make a good-sized yard pen for a Beagle—to play under supervision—from four-foot-high chain link with a strip of 18-inch chicken wire around the outside bottom to prevent him from digging his way out. A run where the dog can play without supervision should be long enough to give him plenty of sniffing area and at least six feet high or covered to keep him from escaping to follow his nose. Beagles are escape artists, given the opportunity. They will figure a way to get out of just about anyplace, if it is at all possible. Remember, they're smart!

> Beagles are escape artists, given the opportunity. They will figure a way to get out of just about anyplace, if it is at all possible.

Which Supplies Do You Really Need?

You spent months researching, planning, interviewing. First, you learned all about the Beagle and decided it was the breed for you. Then, you had to find just the right breeder. Your preparation paid off, and she added you to her list of potential buyers for her next litter. When the pups were born, one of them turned out to be exactly what you were looking for. Now the day has finally come for you to take home the Beagle puppy of your dreams.

But are you ready to bring a puppy home? Just like a baby, a puppy needs all kinds of equipment for his new life as your companion. Before you pick up your puppy from the breeder, be sure you have the following supplies on hand.

Forms of ID

When you get your new Beagle, it's for keeps. The two of you will share a lifetime of play, cuddling, and just vegging out together,

Prevent Digging Out

To Beagle-proof a chain link fence so your dog can't dig out, follow this advice from Beagle owner Diane Wiest of Halifax, Pennsylvania. Buy a roll of chicken wire or wire garden fencing with square holes. Cut it into long strips about two inches wide, then use wire to fasten it to the bottom of the chain link, as if you're sewing the two pieces of fence together. (Aluminum wire meant for an electric fence is relatively inexpensive and won't rust.) Be sure to clip any rough ends of the wire so your Beagle doesn't cut himself. The piece of fence that lies on the ground can be covered with several inches of dirt or stone for a border. If you use dirt, you can plant grass over it so the area will look nice.

forging a bond of companionship like no other. To ensure that this special bond isn't broken by loss, your Beagle needs identification that is safe, permanent, easily recognized, and widely available.

There are three types of identification available to dog owners: tags, tattoos, and microchips. Used separately, each has advantages and disadvantages, but no one method offers complete protection. Used together, however, they meet the above criteria and can give your Beagle his best chance of getting home if lost.

Tags The traditional collar and tag is the most common form of pet identification. A tag is small but identifiable, and everyone understands the concept of checking a tag for an owner's name and phone number. However, the collar/tag combination has some drawbacks. A collar and tag are easily removed, either by the dog himself or by unscrupulous people who want the dog for their own ends. Tags must be updated when addresses or phone numbers change, something that often gets relegated to "later"

Poisonous Plants in Home and Yard

Commonly found plants, trees, and shrubs can cause symptoms ranging from rashes or dermatitis to vomiting and diarrhea to abdominal pain and convulsions. Some are toxic enough to cause death if the dog isn't treated quickly. Listed below are some of the most common plants whose leaves, seeds, bulbs, or other parts are toxic to dogs. The National Animal Poison Control Center also has a good book available for $15. See the appendix for contact information.

House

Amaryllis

Asparagus fern

Boston ivy

Caladium

Creeping fig

Dieffenbachia

Elephant ears

Heart ivy

Jerusalem cherry

Philodendron

Pot chrysanthemum

Spider chrysanthemum

Umbrella plant

Weeping fig

Yard

Apricot, cherry, or peach pits

Azalea

Bird of paradise

Buttercup

Chinaberry

Chrysanthemum

Daffodil

Delphinium

English holly

Foxglove

Horse chestnut

Jasmine

Mayapple

Monkey pod

Morning glory

Nightshade

Oleander

Privet

Rain tree

Water hemlock

Wisteria

Yew—American, English, and Western

during the hustle and bustle of a move. If a dog wearing outdated tags is lost in an unfamiliar area, the information on the tag may be useless to whoever finds the dog. And tags can be annoyingly noisy, especially when there is more than one on a collar.

Nevertheless, a collar and tag are the first line of defense against loss. An engraved tag should include your name and two phone numbers at which you can be reached. Don't put your dog's name on the tag. This gives leverage to any person who wants to lure your dog—"Come on, Joker, follow me"—or claim ownership.

Tags come in a variety of shapes, sizes, and colors. Choose something distinctive, so if your dog gets lost, his tag will stand out to people looking for him. There are a lot of Beagles in the world, but not all of them wear neon-green, bone-shaped tags.

Plastic and metal tags each have advantages and disadvantages. Plastic is quieter than metal, but it can fade and become brittle with age. Metal is durable, but it can rust. Instead of a tag, a tiny metal or plastic barrel can be attached to the collar. These barrels unscrew to reveal a slip of paper on which you can write important information about your dog such as a phone number, your veterinarian's name, or any medications the dog needs. Engraved metal plates can be attached to collars to reduce not only jingling but also the possibility that the tag could get caught on something. Some nylon collars can be woven or imprinted with a phone number.

Tattoos A tattoo is also a visible form of identification but, unlike a tag, it is permanent. Employees at research laboratories and animal shelters know to look for tattoos, and federal law does not permit laboratories to use tattooed dogs. A sticker or sign on your car, fence, or your dog's kennel noting that your pet is tattooed can ward off dog thieves.

Most tattoos are placed on a dog's belly or thigh, and it's best to tattoo a dog after he has reached his full growth, so the lettering remains legible. Avoid tattooing the inside of a dog's ear (as is done with racing Greyhounds); thieves have been known to cut off tattooed ears to prevent identification.

Tattooing can be done at a veterinary office, with the dog under anesthesia, or by a qualified individual at a dog club or other organization. The procedure is not painful, but it is noisy and time consuming, so a squirmy Beagle may require anesthesia.

Although a tattoo is permanent, it must be registered to be of any use. Otherwise, the finder has no way of contacting the owner of a lost dog. It's best to tattoo your Beagle with a number that can't be duplicated, such as your Social Security number, the dog's AKC number, or a computer-assigned number from the registry. Some registries assign specific codes for breeders, shelters, or communities. Phone numbers and birth dates are poor choices because the former change frequently and the latter can be shared by a large number of people.

The disadvantage of a tattoo is that not everyone knows how to contact a registry. Tags and tattoos can be used in combination, however, with the dog wearing a tag that bears a registry phone number. Thus, it's important to keep registries informed of any change in address or phone number.

Microchips Microchips are a way of permanently identifying dogs six months or older; ideally, a dog can get a microchip when he gets his vaccinations. Implantation is painless, with no sedation or anesthesia required. A microchip lasts for the dog's entire life, without fading or getting lost. Available only through veterinarians, microchips are tiny, about the size of a grain of rice. The battery-free devices are programmed with a unique, unalterable code number, and include electronic circuitry to send out the code number, a small copper coil that serves as an antenna, and a capacitor for tuning. Before the microchip is injected beneath the skin in the scruff of the neck, the veterinarian scans it to confirm the code. Once the microchip is implanted, it is scanned again to verify the code and ensure that the microchip is working properly.

A microchip sends a signal only when a scanning device activates it. The scanner decodes the signal and displays the identification code on a liquid-crystal display window. Veterinary and humane organizations as well as dog registries recommend microchipping as a safe and effective way of identifying lost pets and ensuring their return. This method of identification has the potential to save the lives of thousands of dogs that would otherwise die in shelters, unrecognized and unclaimed.

> Veterinary and humane organizations as well as dog registries recommend microchipping as a safe and effective way of identifying lost pets and ensuring their return.

Yet despite their high-tech advantages, even microchips have drawbacks. For one thing, they are invisible. People unfamiliar with microchip technology may be unaware that a dog is chipped. Not all shelters and laboratories have scanning devices, although pet product manufacturers and registries such as the American Kennel Club and the United Kennel Club are working with microchip/scanner companies and animal welfare organizations to ensure that animal shelters nationwide are properly equipped.

Why Register? There are advantages to enrolling a tattooed or microchipped dog with a national registry. A registry usually provides 24-hour notification and a tag with the registry's phone number along with a statement that the dog is tattooed or microchipped. Often, registries are affiliated with shelters across the

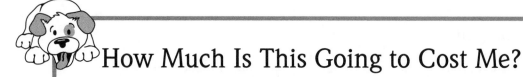

How Much Is This Going to Cost Me?

The basic supplies for your new dog can come with a hefty price tag depending on size and quality, and often it's a price you'll be paying more than once. Remember to factor in these costs when making the decision to get a dog. Prices likely will vary depending on where you live, but the following should give you a good idea of what to expect.

Item	Low Price	High Price
Crate	$20.00	$200.00
Food and Water Bowls	3.00	60.00
Collar	4.00	40.00
Leash	4.00	50.00
ID Tag	3.00	15.00
Pet Stain/Odor Remover	4.00	10.00
Brush	4.00	20.00
Toys	1.00	40.00
Food (8 lb. bag)	4.00	9.00
Bed	10.00	200.00
TOTAL	$57.00	$644.00

country. Even if you choose not to register your dog with one of these organizations, a shelter or laboratory can still locate and notify the veterinarian who implanted the chip.

If he isn't already, your Beagle will soon be a beloved member of your family. Protect him from permanent loss by ensuring that he is well identified. Should he ever escape from your watchful eye, as Beagles are prone to do, you'll be glad you did.

Collar or Halter

For everyday wear, your Beagle needs a flat, buckle-style leather or nylon collar. Both materials are long lasting. Look for a collar that's well made, with fine stitching and a sturdy buckle. Leather has a classic look while nylon comes in a range of colors and designs. The disadvantage of leather is that its scent and texture is attractive to puppies, who quickly discover that it makes a fine chew toy. If you prefer the look and feel of leather, wait to buy this type of collar until your Beagle's chewing is no longer destructive.

Check the collar regularly as your puppy grows to make sure it hasn't tightened. A rule of thumb is that two fingers should comfortably fit between the collar and the puppy's neck.

There's no need to purchase a nylon or chain "choke" collar yet. It won't be necessary for puppy kindergarten, and many trainers are moving away from using choke collars altogether, even in basic obedience classes. This is especially true with dogs, such as Beagles, that respond better to rewards than correction.

Leash

Beagles are controlled by their noses. A leash is a must to keep them in sight and safe from harm. "Although I work my two Beagles off-lead in obedience and agility," says Janiece Harrison, "I would never feel comfortable hiking with them off lead. I've watched them pick up a scent too many times and just tune me out. I was thankful they were on lead when these incidents happened."

Buy a lightweight leash that is well constructed. Leashes are typically made of leather, nylon, or chain. Leather leashes have the same advantages and disadvantages as leather collars, and skin oils can stain them. Nylon leashes are colorful and sturdy. They usually can be purchased in matching pairs with nylon collars. Chain leashes are heavy and noisy. Who wants to listen to a leash clink all the way around the block? A retractable leash lets your puppy move out at his own pace while giving you the security of being able to reel him in as needed.

Crate

A crate is one of the most useful and versatile items a dog owner can buy. It serves as a house-training tool, a safe mode of transportation, a bed, and a place of refuge for a Beagle who's pooped from chasing squirrels. Wherever the crate is—car, hotel, showgrounds—that is home for the dog who has been properly introduced to this portable den.

With the growing number of uses for the crate have come innovations in crate design. Recent models include collapsible plastic crates, soft-sided carriers, and domed designs with a space-age look; there are crates that fit under airline seats, fold flat for storage, or roll on wheels through airports and showgrounds. Accessories such as designer covers, cushions, and mats turn them into cozy beds.

But with greater choice come tougher decisions. "Which crate should I get?" you may wonder, as you eye stacks of wire and plastic crates. Not to worry. Selection is easily determined by considering your Beagle's lifestyle. By taking a few minutes to think about how the crate will be used, you can come to the best decision for your circumstances.

People have different experiences with different types of crates. "When we

Did You Know?

The average cost per year for owning and maintaining a dog in the United States is $1220.

brought Cricket home, we had purchased a wire crate," says one Beagle owner. "She was able to climb the wires and squeeze out of them. It was cute, but it also scared us, as we didn't want her doing that when we weren't there. We were afraid she'd get caught between the wires. We switched to a plastic Varikennel, and she loved it. Now that she's older, she has one of my old comforters in there and hangs out in the crate for hours."

On the other hand, Luisa Fallo, of Falkirk, Scotland, is very happy with the wire crates she uses. "They're easy to fold flat and put in the car. I also think my dogs would feel too enclosed in a plastic crate. At night or when it's cold, I put a light blanket over their crate to make a cozy den, and they seem to like that."

Both types have advantages, says Janiece Harrison. "We have always used wire crates, but I think if I were starting out with a new puppy today and needed to crate him at night and during the day, I would use a plastic crate since they seem to provide a more den-like atmosphere. However, I like the wire crates because I can easily see inside them and tell whether the dogs look restless or are sacked out. I also think they allow for better airflow if you're in a situation other than home where you're worried it might be warm. The most critical thing is to make sure your Beagle likes the crate. Feed him in the crate, and give him a toy stuffed with treats when he's in the crate. Dr. Ian Dunbar, Ph.D., B.Vet.Med., M.R.C.V.S. [a well-known British veterinary behaviorist] suggests putting the dog's dinner in the crate a few minutes before mealtime and shutting the door so the dog can't get inside. That way the dog is absolutely dying to get into the crate."

As for size, your Beagle should be able to stand up and turn around inside his crate. There shouldn't be so much room inside it that he can eliminate in one corner and then move to another area to get away from the mess. "We normally recommend the Varikennel 200 size," Nieland says. "People often get talked into a bigger size at the pet store, but it doesn't work for house-training. Usually when we sell a puppy, the purchase price includes a 200 crate, and we lend them one of our 100s until the puppy gets big enough for the 200."

To learn more about types of crates and the best uses for each, see the sections on house-training (in chapter 6, pages 210–212) and travel (in chapter 8, pages 266–269). Ideally, your Beagle's crate should give him a good view of everything that's going on; place it in an area of the home where everyone spends a lot of time, such as the den or kitchen. Move it to your bedroom at night.

Food

To fuel his growth, a puppy needs food containing high-quality protein. Ask your veterinarian for a recommendation, or look for a food that is specially formulated for puppies. Good sources of protein that you should see on dog food labels include chicken, eggs, and cheese. Be sure that the food you choose is labeled "complete and balanced." The label should state that feeding trials confirmed the nutritional value of the food.

Before taking your puppy home, ask when the puppy last ate, how often he eats, and what brand of food he usually gets. If you will be feeding a different brand, introduce it a little bit at a time, over a two- to three-week period. You don't want to bring on diarrhea or vomiting caused by a rapid change in diet. Plan on feeding a food formulated for puppies until your Beagle is six to twelve months old, when you can switch to a maintenance food (check with your vet to see when he or she recommends changing).

Feeding Dishes

Food and water dishes can be utilitarian or decorative, depending on which material you choose. If you're the practical type, go for metal dishes. They last forever, and they're easy to throw in the dishwasher. One drawback is that they can't be used to warm food in the microwave, which some people like to do because it intensifies the aroma and increases palatability, especially with canned food that's been sitting in the refrigerator. Another is that they're lightweight, making it easy for excitable puppies to bat them around the floor, spilling water and food.

Ceramic dishes come in many colors and designs and can be personalized with your Beagle's name. They're heavier than metal dishes, making them more stable, but if dropped they can shatter. If you like ceramic dishes, make sure they're dishwasher and microwave safe. Avoid foreign-made ceramic dishes, which may contain high amounts of lead.

For low cost and ease of cleaning, plastic dishes can't be beat, but your breeder or veterinarian may recommend against them because many dogs develop allergies to plastic. Plastic is also known for retaining food odors, which can be unpleasant for you and the dog.

"I use stainless steel bowls for their food," says Luisa Fallon. "They're easy to clean, and Beagles don't like metal in their mouths, so they don't try to chew it. I have a plastic bowl for traveling, and it's a little chewed around the edges. I use a heavy earthenware [ceramic] bowl for their water because it doesn't tip as easily as stainless steel bowls."

The size of the bowl often depends on the type of food you're giving. A bowl with a small diameter is good for canned food because the dog's ears will hang outside it and won't get messy. That's not so much of a problem if you're feeding dry food. Since her Beagles inhale their food so quickly, Janiece Harrison prefers fairly large bowls. "It seems to slow the dogs down a little to have the food spread out on a larger surface rather than mounded in a small bowl," she says.

Heather Trinque highly recommends a water dish that has a "guard" around it. "Cricket slurps her water, and if we didn't have this kind of dish, there would be puddles all over the floor," she says. "We use one that was originally meant for traveling and prevents spilling during movement."

Grooming Tools

For a Beagle, all you need are a metal flea comb, a natural bristle brush or a hound glove, a nail trimmer made for use with dogs, and a toothbrush and toothpaste formulated for dogs. (For more information about grooming tools, see chapter 7, page 231.)

First-Aid Kit

Pet first-aid kits are available at pet supply stores, or you can assemble one yourself. Include antibiotic ointment, bandaging tape, cotton swabs and cotton balls, gauze bandages, an eyedropper, a rectal thermometer, petroleum jelly or K-Y jelly to lubricate the thermometer, scissors, a needleless syringe for dispensing liquid medication, and tweezers. In a pinch, sanitary napkins can be used as bandages. Hydrogen peroxide is useful for cleaning wounds, and activated charcoal tablets are used to absorb poisons. In the case of poisoning, you may need to use activated charcoal if for some reason you aren't able to get your Beagle to the veterinarian right away. (Call the veterinarian or the ASPCA's National Animal Poison Control Center, (800) 548-2423, for advice.)

Also good to have on hand are a blanket or towel, a cold pack, and rubber gloves. Be sure the kit is within easy reach and contains your veterinarian's phone number, the phone number of and directions to the nearest animal emergency hospital, and a first-aid handbook. Some ready-made kits come with first-aid booklets as well as stickers or pet health records on which you can record phone numbers and other important information.

Toys

The energy expended by a puppy could light up Paris. To channel that energy, offer a variety of toys that will keep your Beagle interested and active. A hard rubber chew toy is durable and will help soothe the ache caused by teething. Stuff a hollow chew toy such as a Kong with peanut butter or fill it with smelly dog treats to make it even more enticing. The noise emitted by a squeaky toy will quickly attract a puppy's attention. Be sure sharp puppy teeth can't detach the noisemaker inside—it could choke him. Many Beagles love cuddling up to a soft stuffed toy, while others will aggressively shake it or toss it in the air. Either way, the dog is having fun. Make sure soft toys are well made, with no bells, button eyes, or ribbons to be chewed off and swallowed.

Bedding

The only bed your Beagle will need at first is his crate, lined with a pad, towel, or blanket, or bare if he insists on chewing and eating his bedding. The crate will keep him from roaming the house at night and having accidents in the house. When he's older, if he hasn't wormed his way into your bed, your Beagle will appreciate a comfy bed where he can relax after a long day of sniffing. From four-posters to futons, hunt prints to tapestries, there are beds to suit any Beagle and any decor. Look for a bed that's well built and machine washable. Sweet dreams! Both of you will need to rest after your first exciting day together!

The First Night with Your Beagle Puppy

Things will go more smoothly if you've bought all your supplies beforehand. That way, you don't have to run out at the last minute to get food or some other necessary item.

The most important thing you can do to help your puppy feel at home is to spend plenty of time with her. She may be shy at first, even if she was outgoing at the breeder's home. She was comfortable there, and it may take a few days for her to adjust to you and your home. She will be missing her mother and litter-mates, so the more you can distract her with play and attention, the less time she will have to think about being lonely. She'll also be more tired and more willing to sleep through the night.

At bedtime, take the puppy out for one last potty trip, then put her in her crate. You should already have decided where the dog would sleep so there won't be any arguments about it at bed-time. A bedroom is ideal. If the puppy is next to your bed, your presence will help her feel less alone in this big new world that she's discovering. Consider putting a blanket or other bedding inside her crate that's the same size or color as the one she was used to at the breeder's home.

It's especially important not to give in to puppy cries at night, notes Heather Trinque. "I felt horrible hearing Cricket cry and would go in and comfort her. After a few nights of this, I was exhausted. Because I did this, it made the transition time a little longer."

Naming Your Beagle

Classic Beagle names are usually short and easy to yell out. That's important for a dog who is likely to wander off somewhere. Old-time beaglers used to give their dogs "people" names that were easy to say: Molly, Betty, Jack, Bill, Tom, Clyde, Susy, Janie, and Pete, for instance. Ace, Buddy, Buster, Rebel, and Slick are traditional dog names that suit the Beagle.

Riffing off a registered name or names in the dog's pedigree is another way to go. "Annie is our first and only Beagle from a conformation kennel, and her full name is Whiskey Creek's Annie Oakley," Janiece Harrison says. "As we always say, 'She's a pistol'. Our other Beagle was a rescue, and his previous name was Beau. At the time we got him, Bo Jackson the football/baseball player was popular, so we changed the spelling from Beau to Bo. There was a Nike commercial at the time that featured Bo Jackson, and the tag line was 'Bo knows football' or 'Bo knows baseball'. We were always saying 'Bo knows walking' or 'Bo knows eating'. It was a silly ritual, but for me that simple spelling change really meant a lot psychologically for Bo's personality."

Circumstances can dictate a dog's name as well. "Cricket was nameless for a few days because we couldn't decide, but wanted a name that fit her," says Heather Trinque. "One day, while my husband and I were playing with her, she started hopping around and squeaking from excitement. My husband said she was like a little cricket, and the name stuck."

Plenty of Beagles are named after media figures. There are Beagles named Snoopy, of course, and Peabody, after the character on the Rocky and Bullwinkle Show. Luisa Fallon's Beagle Floyd was named after a television cook. "We liked the show and wanted a name that wasn't typically 'doggy'," she says. "Floyd seemed like a good hound name. Rigsby came already named, also from a TV personality. There was a television show years ago called Rising Damp, whose main character was a landlord called Mr. Rigsby. Rigsby's previous owner named him this because she liked the show. His kennel name is Caurniehill Rigs O'Barley."

The Beagle's British heritage and historical associations as well as his popularity in the American South also offer fertile territory for names. The names below will help get you started. Remember to choose a name that's only one or two syllables, or that can easily be shortened. Unless you plan to use a different word for correction, try not to pick a name that could be confused with the word "No" (for instance, Bo or Moe).

Males

Arthur—in Welsh mythology, the spirit of King Arthur leads "the Wild Hunt," a ghostly pack of hounds.

Bayou (pronounced byoo)—a good name for a Louisiana Beagle, especially one that likes to bay.

Beachcomber—for a coastal Beagle who's always finding things. Beach for short.

Belvedere—a handsome Beagle with the charming personality of a playboy.

Chaucer—after the writer who first put Beagles in print.

Clootie—Scottish nickname for the devil. For a mischievous Beagle.

Cody—in honor of frontiersman Buffalo Bill.

Darwin—the naturalist who spent three years exploring the world on the HMS <u>Beagle</u>.

Drake—after the famous explorer.

Huckleberry—after the cartoon hound. Huck for short.

Females

Abby—short for Abigail, a name meaning "source of joy."

Bliss—a Beagle that's happy all the time.

Blithe—for a carefree Beagle.

Daisy—for a pretty, sweet Beagle.

Dixie—for a Southern Beagle.

Lucy—for a comedic Beagle.

Mandy—short for Amanda, meaning "worthy of love." A common Southern girl's name.

Sibyl—after the ancient Greek prophetess. For a Beagle that likes to "talk" and tell you what's going on.

Sally—a nickname for Sarah, which means "princess."

Sister—a common Southern name or nickname.

Remember that each Beagle is different, and what works for one may not work for another. Some are inconsolable, while others settle in just fine. "We got Floyd as a nine-week-old puppy," says Luisa Fallon. "We played with him all day so he was very tired on his first night. We put him in his crate in the kitchen, with a big fluffy blanket and his toys, and left the radio on in the background, turned down low. He fell asleep and didn't wake up until 6 a.m. I have to admit that we slept in the living room that night just to make sure he'd be okay."

Be prepared for the first couple of nights to be tough. It's difficult to hear a lonely puppy whine without going to comfort her, but your puppy will soon adjust. Your best bet is to keep things fairly low key, and offer lots of treats and companionship during the day. Beagles thrive on both.

Making an Older Beagle Feel Welcome

The move to a new home is stressful for a dog of any age, but most adjust well given a little time. Treat an older Beagle the way you would a puppy. Give her attention and playtime, but if she prefers to just sit back and observe for a while, respect her decision. Don't overwhelm her with a lot of new people all at once, but give her plenty of opportunities to do things she enjoys, such as going for walks. This will help her relax.

She may feel a little confused at first in her new home. If you know what her previous routine and environment were like, it may help to make things as similar as possible. This means using the same food, the same type of food dishes, and the same type of bedding. Whenever you can, make changes slowly.

Give the dog a place she can call her own, such as a crate or a bed, where she can go to think things over. Again, the dog should sleep in a crate in your bedroom. Even though you're asleep, the time together will help begin the bonding process.

With a puppy or an older dog, get her used to short periods of your absence right away. Start by leaving her on her own in a room for a few minutes, and build on this until she learns that there are times when she's alone or that you aren't going to give her attention. One thing you can do is to give some kind of signal to indicate to the dog that this isn't "her" time, says Luisa Fallon. She'll begin to recognize and associate the signal with being left to her own devices. "Some people I know bring out a small radio when they're about to go out, and their dog knows to go to her bed. Other people hang a towel up on a door or even put a sign up. It sounds silly, but the key is to do this every time, even for the shortest periods, and make sure the dog sees you doing it," Fallon says. One dog knows that when she sees her people closing off the kitchen with a gate (so she can't get to the cat food), it's time to jump up on the sofa and await a treat and the command "Guard the sofa until we get back."

Another way to decrease anxiety is to reduce the amount of attention you give just before you leave the dog. When you return, don't make a big fuss over her; just greet her calmly. It's hard to do, but it's for the best.

> Give the dog a place she can call her own, such as a crate or a bed, where she can go to think things over.

Food for Thought

We all learned in grade school that we are what we eat. The same is true for our dogs. But what exactly does that mean?

Why Does Good Nutrition Matter?

Good nutrition is the foundation of a long and healthy life. Food contains nutrients that are the building blocks of the dog's body, which it uses to form strong bones and muscles, supple skin, and a full coat, as well as a powerful immune system to fight off disease. These nutrients—

protein, carbohydrates, fats, vitamins, and minerals, along with water—work in combination to keep the body functioning at peak levels. When the level of nutrients is low—due to a poor diet, for instance—the body functions less efficiently. Hair becomes dull or falls out, teeth loosen, eyes lose their shine, and the skin loses its elasticity. It's easy to tell at a glance when a dog is or isn't eating correctly.

Each nutrient plays a specific role in the body's maintenance and function. Protein contains amino acids, which the body needs for tissue growth and repair. The body itself produces some amino acids, but others—the 10 "essential" amino acids—must be obtained from food. Meat, eggs, and dairy products are high in protein and contain all the essential amino acids. Grains and vegetables also contain protein, but are lacking in some of the amino acids. They are known as incomplete proteins. Both animal and non-animal sources of protein are important to a dog's well-being.

Carbohydrates provide the energy a Beagle uses to follow a scent for hours on end, run barking to the door when a guest arrives, and jump on a table to steal food. Quick energy comes from simple sugars such as glucose, while starches and complex sugars give more long-lasting energy. Corn, rice, wheat, and oats are common sources of carbohydrates; they add fiber to the diet, too, which is helpful for smooth functioning of the intestines.

Fat is also a source of energy, but it has other purposes as well. Fat cushions the internal organs and helps the body conserve heat, transport nutrients, and send nerve impulses. Oleic, linoleic, and linolenic acids—known as the fatty acids—contain vitamins A, D, E, and K and are necessary for such bodily functions as gastric acid secretion, inflammation control, and muscle contraction. Fat has a bad reputation, but in the right amounts it's a must for every dog's diet.

The Importance of Water

Water makes up about 65 percent of your Beagle's body, so it's a very important substance indeed. Lack of water can of course lead to dehydration, but water is also a vital element of cell and organ function. Without it, the body couldn't maintain proper temperature, transport nutrients, circulate blood, digest food, or eliminate waste products. Fresh water daily is a must for your Beagle. Recent news reports have cast doubt on the quality and safety of municipal drinking water nationwide, so consider giving your Beagle the same bottled or filtered water you drink yourself.

Dogs need only minute amounts of various vitamins and minerals, but without them they would suffer serious health problems. Vitamins and minerals are involved in almost every aspect of the body's operation, from tissue formation to cell maintenance and growth to the transformation of proteins, carbohydrates, and fats into energy. Veterinary nutritionists agree that a high-quality balanced diet contains all the vitamins and minerals your Beagle needs.

Whether he's a pet, a show dog, or a hunting dog, good nutrition is important for the energetic Beagle. He's meant to be solid and big for his inches, with plenty of stamina. He needs an owner who will provide him with a high-quality diet, give him plenty of exercise, and prevent him from overeating. Read on to find out more about choosing a food, good feeding practices, and giving treats and supplements.

What's the Best Food for My Beagle?

There is no generic version of a dog. Each is an individual, with unique needs. Just as not every food is tasty or agreeable to us, not every formulated diet is best for all dogs. Choosing the right food is a matter of experimenting to find a high-quality diet that suits your Beagle's nutritional needs.

When evaluating a dog food, you need to consider the quality of ingredients, their digestibility, the amount of energy the food provides, and the food's taste, or palatability—that is, does your Beagle like it? Price and availability are important as well, but they shouldn't be the primary factors in your decision.

> Choosing the right food is a matter of experimenting to find a high-quality diet that suits your Beagle's nutritional needs.

Any food you are considering should be labeled "complete and balanced." Such a food is formulated to contain the correct levels of all the nutrients a dog needs. The Association of American Feed Control Officials regulates these nutrient levels and requires pet food manufacturers to prove their claims through feeding trials or chemical analysis before they can use the AAFCO name on their labels.

Feeding trials are preferable to chemical analysis because they provide physical evidence of a food's nutritional value. If a food hasn't been tested on dogs, there's no way to know whether dogs are able to digest and absorb the nutrients. For instance, the label on a food might state that it contains 25 percent protein, but if the dog can use only 10 percent of that, the other 15 percent isn't doing the dog any good. Look for foods that carry the phrase "feeding tests," "AAFCO feeding test protocols" or "AAFCO feeding studies."

The amount of usable nutrients a food contains determines its digestibility. Nutrients that aren't absorbed by the body are eliminated as waste. A food's digestibility is not something you can find on the label—the proof is in your dog. A highly digestible food is evident in a healthy dog who produces small, firm stools. Food that isn't being well digested often results in flatulence (gas), loose, large stools, or even diarrhea.

Choosing a food involves being aware of your Beagle's energy needs. Beagles are small dogs and, pound for pound, small dogs in general have greater energy requirements than large-breed dogs. Like many sporting and hound breeds, however, Beagles vary greatly in lifestyle, which influences their nutritional needs. Beagles that are actively hunting or performing other sports or activities need more calories from their food. These Beagles need a dense, nutrient-rich food that's high in protein and fat, especially if they're doing a lot of running during the season or traveling to shows. The more typical pet Beagles whose activity is minimal likely have lower energy needs than other dogs their size. Beagle puppies need more energy—to fuel their growth—than adult Beagles do.

> Beagles are small dogs and, pound for pound, small dogs in general have greater energy requirements than large-breed dogs.

Like nutritional quality and digestibility, the amount of energy a food provides—its metabolizable energy—is determined through feeding trials. Labels must include a nutritional adequacy statement advising consumers what life stage a food is appropriate for, such as puppy, adult, active dog, or senior.

Palatability is another factor that can be tested only by your Beagle. No matter how great a food's ingredients are, if your Beagle won't eat it, then it won't do the dog any good. Of course, just because your Beagle scarfs up a particular food doesn't mean the food is good for her. Beagles will eat anything, after all. That's where reading labels comes in handy. Your Beagle can't do it, so you need to do it for her.

After making sure the label states that a food is complete and balanced, take a look at the ingredient list. The label must list

What Are Dry-Matter Percentages?

When a guaranteed analysis panel reports nutrient levels, the content doesn't take into account the amount of water in the food. The moisture levels in canned foods are much higher than those in dry foods, and even the moisture levels in different brands of dry foods can vary, so before you can truly compare them, you need to figure out what's called the dry-matter percentage.

To calculate dry-matter percentage, divide the percentage of the given nutrient you'd like to compare (protein, for instance) by the proportion of dry matter in the diet. Here's how to do it. First, subtract the percentage of moisture shown on the label (the guaranteed analysis panel). For instance, suppose a food has 11 percent moisture. That leaves 89 percent dry matter. To find the percentage of protein in that food, look at the label for the protein percentage and divide this number by the dry-matter percentage. So, in this case, if the label lists 34 percent protein, you would divide 34 percent by the dry-matter percentage, 89 percent, and multiply by 100 to arrive at 38, the percentage of protein in the food. The same formula works for all foods—dry, canned, and semi-moist.

ingredients by weight in decreasing order. That is, the ingredient listed first—usually some form of animal protein—is not exceeded in weight by any of the following ingredients. That seems straightforward enough, but manufacturers can get around this requirement by a practice called split-ingredient labeling, in which ingredients of the same type are spread out so they will appear farther down on the label. For instance, a grain such as corn, wheat, or rice might appear on the label in several different forms, such as flour, flakes, middlings, or bran. A food labeled in this way might actually contain more protein from grain sources than from animal sources.

Quality ingredients, which should appear first or second on the ingredient list, include animal protein, eggs, or cheese. All the added vitamins in the world can't turn a food with poor-quality ingredients into a product that's nutritionally sound.

Labels also include a guaranteed analysis of the percentages of crude protein, crude fat, crude fiber, and moisture the food contains. This information has only superficial value, however. The guaranteed analysis doesn't list exact amounts of nutrients, only minimum and maximum percentages. If you want to figure out dry-matter percentages of nutrients so you can compare one brand of food to another, call the manufacturer's toll-free number, which is usually listed on the bag. The customer service department can give you the information you need.

It's not enough to simply read the label the first time you buy a food. Check it regularly to see if the formulation has changed. Ideally, the manufacturer is using a fixed formula, meaning that the ingredients remain the same from batch to batch, rather than fluctuating based on availability of ingredients and market prices. A change in formula could cause stomach upset in a Beagle with a sensitive digestive system.

As a rule, Beagles are easy keepers, meaning that they're generally healthy and seem to do quite well on almost any good diet, says Dorothy Laflamme, D.V.M., Ph.D., a veterinary nutritionist with Purina Pet foods in St. Louis, Missouri. "This does create one problem in that they are predisposed to obesity," she says. "The same amount of food that would keep another dog in good shape may contain too many calories for the laid-back Beagle. In my experience, Beagles do not tend to become overweight until they are mature, but then, watch out!"

Each dog is an individual, so you may need to experiment until you find a diet that suits your Beagle perfectly, with just the right mix of protein, carbohydrates, fats, vitamins, and minerals. Experienced

Beagle owners such as Katie Williams recommend starting your search with a premium dry kibble. "Canned food makes it harder to keep teeth clean," she says. Canned food is also more palatable because it's higher in fat, so dogs will eat (and want) more of it, not a good thing for an obesity-prone breed. Williams also recommends staying away from foods that contain rice or lamb. "These should be reserved for dogs with allergies," she says. "If you have fed a diet that contains lamb and rice and your dog develops food allergies, it's going to be difficult to find economical alternatives."

The true test of a food's quality is how well your dog does on it. Once you've made your decision, stick with the food you've chosen for as long as your Beagle has good health, plenty of energy, a shiny coat, and easily maintains her weight.

Premium Foods and Grocery Store Foods— Is There a Difference?

We always hear that we should give our dogs a high-quality food, but what does that mean? Should you buy a high-priced premium brand from a pet store, or can a dog's nutritional needs be met just as well by a name-brand food from the grocery store? Veterinarians and breeders differ in their answers; in the end, what really matters is your dog's individual needs. Each dog is different, and no one food can meet the needs of every dog.

The difference between premium and nonpremium foods is density per volume. In other words, a tablespoon of a premium food is likely to have more nutrients that are digested and absorbed than a tablespoon of nonpremium food. What that means is that the higher cost of a premium food is made up in savings of amount served and then later eliminated by the dog. It can actually cost less to feed a high-quality food, because your Beagle is eating less of it but getting a higher percentage of nutrients. In the average healthy dog, stool volume is the most obvious difference between premium and nonpremium foods.

If your Beagle could stand to put on a little weight (not usually a problem in this breed), premium foods pack more nutrients into a smaller amount. But can a premium food actually make a difference in a dog's health? Many veterinarians, breeders, and pet owners believe it can, citing examples of improved health, coat quality, and digestibility. "Our first Beagles, Daisy and Sadie, were from a backyard breeder and grew up on grocery store dog food," says Janiece Harrison. "They had about every health problem typical of Beagles. Daisy had epilepsy and a cherry eye. Sadie developed back problems as she grew older and grew lots of fatty growths called lipomas. Both often had ear infections and skin problems. Bo is a rescue Beagle, also from a backyard breeder, and Annie is from a well-bred line of conformation dogs. Both are much healthier than Daisy and Sadie, and I think a lot of it—no epilepsy, healthier coat and ears—is due to the better diet they receive."

> Each dog is different, and no one food can meet the needs of every dog.

Cost Differences—Why They Exist, What They Mean Name-brand grocery store foods also have a loyal following of veterinarians, breeders, and pet owners, who say that these foods are just as high in nutrition as pricier premium brands. The corporations that make pet food—whether it's premium or a grocery store brand—all spend big bucks on nutritional studies, feeding trials, and consumer hotlines. The price differences in their products generally are based on types and amounts of ingredients. For instance, a premium food might contain turkey or venison rather than the more common beef or chicken, or grain that's grown organically instead of being treated with pesticides. It may contain more animal protein than grain protein, or be free of dyes or synthetic preservatives.

Whether you choose a premium diet or a grocery store name brand, you can be sure of its nutritional quality, but couldn't you save a little money by buying one of those generic foods that come in a plain white bag or can? You might, in the short term, but your pocketbook would eventually groan under the weight of the excessive amount of food your Beagle would need to eat to get the same nutritional benefits he would from a better food. Dogs that eat generic foods often experience slow or retarded growth and skeletal abnormalities, and suffer from poor skin condition and coat quality. Even though a generic food might be labeled "complete and balanced," its nutritional benefits were probably obtained through chemical analysis or calculation rather than feeding trials. Essentially, your Beagle would be serving as a guinea pig for the generic food manufacturer. The potential health problems your dog would face—not to mention the resulting veterinary bills—aren't worth the savings.

To determine a food's cost per day, mark the price on the calendar on the day you start feeding it. Then track how many days the food lasts and divide that number by the price. For instance, if a bag of premium food contains 67 cups and costs $32.97, it will last for 67 days—or a little more than two months—if you are feeding one cup per day. The cost per day is approximately 49 cents.

Average Portions for Different Weights/Ages

Just as with palatability or sensitivity to a particular ingredient, dogs are individuals when it comes to serving size. The serving portions listed on food labels are merely guides, which you can use in conjunction with advice from the breeder or your veterinarian. Your Beagle may do better with more or less than the recommended daily amount.

Don't be afraid to experiment. If your puppy is getting too fat on her puppy food, try a brand with a lower fat and protein content. If she's not putting on weight but is otherwise healthy, keep her on puppy formula a little longer than you might normally. Most Beagles make the switch from puppy to maintenance food at one year of age.

When it comes to nutrition for Beagles, it's important to remember that the breed comes in two sizes. Each has its own unique nutritional needs. A 13-inch Beagle doesn't need the same amount of food as a 15-inch Beagle.

"Generally, mature 13-inch Beagles eat a cup to a cup and a half of a good-quality dry food daily, depending on their weight," says breeder Janet Nieland. The 15-inch Beagles generally eat about two cups daily.

An aging Beagle usually has a lower activity level and metabolic rate than a younger dog, so she may eat less food and still maintain a good body weight. She still needs the same amount of nutrients, though, so it's especially important that the senior Beagle gets a high-quality, nutrient-rich food. "The food manufacturers recommend switching them to a senior diet at seven years, but we find that they're still too active at that age and we have trouble maintaining their weight on a senior diet," says Nieland. "We wait until they're nine or ten years old, or seem to be putting on weight with the same amount of food. I had one old guy who was still eating a mixture of half senior/half maintenance when he was 14 years old."

The Big Question: Dry or Canned?

We all want to choose the best for our dogs, especially when it comes to food. That's why the choice between dry and canned food can be a difficult decision. Each has advantages and disadvantages, and you'll want to weigh your needs against those of your dog when making the final choice.

If dogs had their druthers, they'd probably choose canned. Dogs seem hard-wired to come running at the sound of a can opener, the modern equivalent of Pavlov's bell. They love the taste and smell of meaty wet food.

On the down side, canned food is expensive, especially for a product that contains as much as 70 percent water by weight. Once it has been opened, it doesn't keep well. You can't just plop it into a bowl and leave it out all day unless you're using a dish that comes with an icepack to keep the food cold. Many pet owners are also concerned about the quality of the meat used in canned products.

> She still needs the same amount of nutrients, though, so it's especially important that the senior Beagle gets a high-quality, nutrient-rich food.

If you choose to feed canned food, be sure to buy a high-quality brand, based on the factors discussed above. Many pet food manufacturers produce small cans of dog food, just the right size for a meal or two. To keep leftover food fresh, take it out of the can, wrap it tightly in plastic, and refrigerate it. The food lasts longer and tastes better when stored in this way.

Dogs also appreciate semi-moist or soft-moist food. It resembles canned food in texture and taste, but it lasts longer and isn't as messy to serve. The odor is still tantalizing to dogs but more acceptable to people than the often unpleasant smell of canned food. The single-serving packets are convenient as well.

However, semi-moist foods are made with lots of sugar and preservatives, which give them that long shelf life. They're not a good choice for Beagles with diabetes or those who have a propensity to overeat (that means most of them). And, like most convenience foods, they are expensive.

Although their dogs might disagree, many pet owners favor dry food for its nutritive value, convenience, and low cost. Nutritionally, dry food is equivalent to canned food and superior to soft-moist food, since it doesn't contain as much sugar. As dry food contains less fat than canned food, it's often the best choice for a tubby Beagle. It can be left out all day for dogs to snack on, and it goes down with a satisfying crunch. The lower cost of dry food is also an advantage, especially if you have multiple Beagles or are living on a fixed income.

Another benefit of dry food is that it helps prevent the buildup of plaque and tartar on teeth. Animals that eat a hard, abrasive diet have been shown to form plaque at a slower rate than animals fed a soft diet. Since Beagles are predisposed to dental problems, a dry food is usually the best choice for them. If you're dealing with a Beagle who already has dental problems and has a difficult time eating dry food, you may need to moisten the dry food or give canned food.

For owners of that rare specimen, the finicky Beagle, mixing a little wet food in with dry kibble can make the meal more aromatic, and therefore more appealing to the dog. It's not often, though, that such an enticement is necessary. Whatever you choose to feed, it's a good bet that your Beagle will scarf it down in about 30 seconds. If she doesn't, there's

Beagle Food Episodes

A British Beagle owner was looking forward to going home and eating the trifle (pudding) that was awaiting him in the refrigerator. When he arrived, he noticed that his Beagle was looking a little subdued but thought he must just be tired. Then he opened the refrigerator. The trifle was gone, and the interior of the refrigerator looked as if a bomb had gone off inside it. The Beagle had opened the refrigerator door, helped himself to the trifle, and then closed the door behind him.

Another Beagle lived with an owner who ran a boarding kennel. She noticed one day that she hadn't seen the Beagle in a while and after searching found him in the storage room where she kept the dog food. He was almost unable to move because he was stuffed so full of food, but he was still sticking out his tongue, trying to reach a dog biscuit that lay just out of reach.

Luisa Fallon reports that her Beagle Floyd once got into his bag of dry dog food when the cupboard door wasn't properly shut. He was so stuffed that he couldn't get up the stairs. "The extent to which he 'stretched' outwardly was quite worrying," Fallon says. Her advice? "Never leave any food accessible, even if you think it's safe on a countertop or tabletop. Beagles will go to any length to eat."

probably something wrong. Most Beagles are voracious eaters who stick their faces in the bowl and eat whatever's put before them. Beagles have no sense when it comes to food.

All-Natural Foods

With the increased interest in the link between healthful eating and a longer life, it's not surprising that pet owners are demanding higher quality meals for their dogs as well. Certain types of foods and supplements are gaining a "magic bullet" reputation for their ability to improve health and, in the past decade, manufacturers have increasingly begun providing diets touted as "all-natural."

When it comes to pet foods, there's not really a good definition for what makes a food "natural." Generally, a natural food is defined as a commercial diet made without preservatives or with natural preservatives such as vitamin E or ascorbic acid. Some foods calling themselves natural contain organic meats and grains or human-grade ingredients.

Most pet foods falling under these definitions are premium products that are available only in pet supply stores, natural-food grocery stores such as Wild Oats or Mother's Market, at dog shows, or even on the Internet. They include brands such as Flint River Ranch, Innova, Balance Diet, and Solid Gold. Many Beagle owners turn to natural diets when they're not satisfied with the performance or ingredients of premium or grocery store brands but are unwilling or unable to feed a homemade or raw diet. As long as such food has been proven in feeding trials, it can be an excellent choice for your Beagle.

Preparing Your Beagle's Meals Yourself

Along with the interest in commercial natural diets has come a rise in the desire to provide dogs with meals that are more like human foods: homemade or fresh foods, and even raw diets. According to a survey conducted by the American Animal Hospital Association, 49 percent of dogs eat food specially prepared by their owners. Europeans frequently buy fresh pet food from the butcher, and it's not out of the question that in the coming decade, fresh pet food counters will appear in American grocery stores. Already, bakeries, delicatessens, and drive-through

Did You Know?

Veterinarians estimate that between 30 percent and 50 percent of today's dog population is overweight.

Diet for a Natural Beagle

"Our dogs eat an all-natural, preservative-free food," Janiece Harrison says. "It's a little lower in fat than some foods, and it definitely helps with weight control. We feed about half a cup morning and evening and supplement it with cottage cheese, brown rice, vegetables, and/or all-natural baby foods. As they get older, we'll keep them on this food but probably up the protein further by adding beans, eggs, or tuna fish. Beagles are prone to epilepsy, and there's some anecdotal evidence that preservatives in dog foods can be a culprit in triggering it."

restaurants in several cities cater to pets only. More and more pet owners—and some veterinarians—are beginning to believe that homemade or raw foods are fresher, better, and healthier for their animals.

The advantage of making your own dog food is that you know exactly what's in it. A homemade diet can also be beneficial if your Beagle has food allergies, is sensitive to artificial dyes or preservatives, or has a particular health problem such as kidney or heart disease or a skin condition. Advocates of raw food say it is beneficial because it retains the enzymes and other healthful substances that cooking destroys, and they cite such benefits as better health, a beautiful coat, few or no skin problems, and improved dental health.

Whether you decide to feed your Beagle a homemade cooked or raw diet, make sure the recipe is nutritionally balanced to meet your dog's needs. Just as with any other food, you should be able to tell by looking at your Beagle whether the meals you're preparing agree with her.

There are many good sources for homemade recipes and raw diets. The best sources include *Dr. Pitcairn's Natural Health for Dogs and Cats,* by Richard H. Pitcairn, D.V.M., and *Home-Prepared Dog and Cat Diets* by Donald R. Strombeck, D.V.M., Ph.D.

Elsewhere in this chapter is a warning against feeding raw meat, but if it comes from an organic butcher and has been frozen first, risks are minimized, though not completely eliminated. Flash-freezing in sub-zero refrigeration units can reduce risks even further. Organic foods are highly nutritious because of their low chemical residue, so if you plan to prepare homemade meals for your Beagle, buy her only the best and freshest foods, just as you would for yourself. Look for organic foods at natural or health food stores, or buy them from farm co-ops or individuals who raise organic meat, grains, and vegetables. A copy of the National Organic Directory is available from the nonprofit Community Alliance with Family Farmers; (800) 852-3832.

> More and more pet owners— and some veterinarians— are beginning to believe that homemade or raw foods are fresher, better, and healthier for their animals.

Use your common sense if you decide to go the home-prepared route. Read several books on the subject, or let a holistic veterinarian, or better yet, a board certified veterinary nutritionist, be your guide. Use the freshest ingredients, not old foods or your leftovers. Freeze portions you don't use so the food will retain its peak level of nutrition. Supplement as directed so your Beagle doesn't develop any deficiencies. Introduce any new food gradually, over a period of at least a week. And be willing to experiment to find the foods and combinations that work best for and are most pleasing to your Beagle.

Can My Beagle Go Vegetarian?

The health benefits of vegetarian diets for people have spurred greater interest in vegetarian foods for dogs. Technically, dogs are omnivores, meaning they can extract nutrition from a variety of foods, so they can exist on a vegetarian diet. Meat contains nutrients that dogs need, though, so deficiencies can develop if a vegetarian diet isn't properly formulated with supplements to make up the difference. Commercial vegetarian diets are available at pet supply stores.

Again, dogs are individuals. Some do quite well on a vegetarian diet, while others demonstrate through their coat or stool quality that, for them, a meat-based diet is the better choice.

How Often and How Much Do I Feed My Beagle?

The breeder and your veterinarian can advise you on how often your Beagle needs to eat. A puppy's body spends calories with abandon on growth, play, and exploration, so the pup needs to eat frequently. Feed your Beagle puppy at least three meals a day—one every four hours or so during normal waking hours.

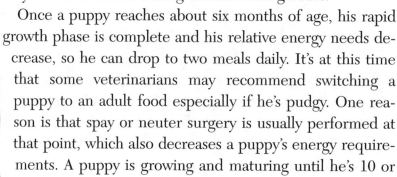

Once a puppy reaches about six months of age, his rapid growth phase is complete and his relative energy needs decrease, so he can drop to two meals daily. It's at this time that some veterinarians may recommend switching a puppy to an adult food especially if he's pudgy. One reason is that spay or neuter surgery is usually performed at that point, which also decreases a puppy's energy requirements. A puppy is growing and maturing until he's 10 or

12 months old, though, so he still has increased nutrient requirements during that period.

Rather than making the change to an adult food, Dr. Laflamme recommends a transitional diet of a food suited for all life stages. "They do need to be on a calorie-controlled regimen at that age so they don't become overweight," she says, "but some adult foods are minimalistic in terms of their nutrient content because they're designed for the inactive adult dog who has reduced energy and nutrient needs. Puppies should be on a food that is specifically formulated for puppy growth up until they're at least a year old."

Controlling a Beagle puppy's growth rate is important. A puppy needs lots of calories to fuel his rapid development, but too many calories simply make him fat. That excess weight is often the determining factor in the development of orthopedic problems.

The Importance of a Feeding Routine

When it comes to change, dogs are conservatives. They like to know that things are going to stay pretty much the same from day to day—including mealtimes. In today's busy world, few things are set in stone, but if your Beagle knows that he can expect to eat at approximately the same time each day, you'll probably both be happier. Pick a time that

> If your Beagle knows that he can expect to eat at approximately the same time each day, you'll probably both be happier.

will allow you a little leeway in case you get stuck in traffic or have to work late, or use a timed feeder that will pop open at a given hour whether you're home or not.

Be aware of how much your Beagle eats. The best way to do this is to feed a certain amount at each meal rather than leaving food out all the time. The recommended amount on the pet food label is simply a starting point; your dog may require more or less.

Put the food down for 10 or 15 minutes. If your dog doesn't eat it (highly unlikely with this breed), take it up until the next mealtime. Don't ever leave a Beagle with as much food as he wants, whenever he wants. If those sad hound eyes are pleading with you for more food, mix in vegetables such as green beans or carrots. They're low in calories, but they give the dog something to eat so he feels full.

Puppy Feeding Schedules and Amounts

A feeding routine is especially useful during puppyhood. House-training goes more smoothly when you take a puppy outside immediately after eating or drinking. Schedule three to four meals daily for a puppy, depending on how old he is (see page 98 for guidelines). Space them three or four hours apart.

Feeding Your Adult Beagle

Most Beagle owners find that feeding their adult dogs twice a day works well. Your dog will probably adapt nicely to whatever schedule works well for you.

Whether he's a pet or a show dog, a Beagle's nutritional needs change with age. Due to lifestyle differences and the onset of health problems, an older dog may show more individual variability in his nutritional needs than a younger dog or even a puppy. And while his energy requirements decrease, his need for protein, vitamins, minerals, and other nutrients remains the same. In fact, Dr. Laflamme says, evidence shows that older dogs need more protein than younger dogs.

Rather than cutting back on the amount of food an older Beagle eats, Dr. Laflamme recommends switching him to a diet that's lower in calories. "When you reduce the amount of food the dog eats, you're not only cutting back on calories, you're cutting back on protein and other nutrients," she says. With a lower calorie food, you're simply reducing the calories, not the other nutrients.

If your older Beagle's sense of smell has begun to deteriorate, consider warming his food in the microwave. This enhances the food's aroma and makes it more enticing. Some people warm their dog's food simply because they don't like the idea of the dog eating cold food. Before you feed the dog, test the food with your finger to make sure it's not too hot, and stir it well to eliminate tongue-scorching hot spots that microwaves often produce.

Is It Okay to Share My Food?

Feeding table scraps is rarely a good idea. People food is usually high in fat and too rich for a dog's sensitive digestive system. And what might seem like a small amount to you is probably a lot for a small dog such as a Beagle. "Giving an animal a few bites from the table is okay," says Kathy Gaughan, D.V.M., a veterinarian at the Kansas State University Veterinary Medical Teaching Hospital, "but it's not a good idea to feed them the fat off meat or scraps like that. I tell people that if it's not good enough for them to eat, do not feed it to a pet."

On the other hand, some people foods are perfectly fine to give—on special occasions and in reasonable amounts. Read the following section on treats to

Did You Know?

Dogs and cats in the United States consume almost $7 billion worth of pet food a year.

find out the kinds of foods your Beagle will enjoy. Limit her daily intake of these snacks to a tablespoon or two.

Healthy Treats

It doesn't take a rocket scientist to figure out why people enjoy giving dogs treats. The look of anticipation on a dog's face, and her pure enjoyment of a special food, make giving more than worthwhile. Treats are also invaluable during the training process. The trick is in giving dogs treats that are both healthy and tasty.

Fruits and vegetables fill the bill nicely. Many Beagles love bits of baby carrot, chopped apple, or banana. Some will even eat broccoli florets and frozen mixed vegetables. Fruits and veggies are low in calories, so you can give them without a guilty conscience. Don't give too much, though. An excess of fruit—especially fruits that are high in water, such as grapes—can cause diarrhea. Also, fruits are high in sugar and can be dangerous snacks for diabetic dogs.

Carrots broken in half and placed in the freezer until they're chilled are a good treat for teething puppies. They're fun to gnaw on, and they help numb sore gums.

Hard biscuits are also canine favorites. Besides being fun to crunch on, they're great for helping to keep your Beagle's teeth tartar-free. Break a single biscuit into two or more pieces. Your Beagle is more interested in getting something—anything—than in how much she gets. Giving several pieces of a single biscuit is more calorie-effective than giving several biscuits. Some dog biscuits are high in fat and calories, so give them in moderation.

Treats are ideal training incentives for Beagles. The best treats for this purpose are small and easy for the dog to eat quickly so you can move on with the lesson. Good training rewards include bits of kibble, small chunks of cheese or hot dogs, or bite-size pieces of soft commercial treats.

Homemade treats are popular as well. These can include freshly baked dog biscuits or "cookies," meatball snacks, jerky, scrambled eggs (about half an egg per Beagle), and other yummy delights. Topping a regular meal with a little yogurt, cottage cheese, or grated hard cheese is also a special but healthy treat. An easy homemade treat is "cookies" made from canned dog food. Form the food into balls and bake in the oven at 350 degrees until they reach a cookie-like texture—about 10 to 15 minutes. Don't forget the old standby—air-popped popcorn. Your Beagle will have a blast trying to catch the pieces you throw.

> A good rule to remember is that treats and table scraps should never make up more than five to ten percent of your Beagle's daily caloric intake.

Beagle owners often recommend against feeding pig ears and rawhides because of the possibility of choking. Let your own Beagle be your guide. If she doesn't gobble them, but rather chews on them slowly without trying to eat them, they are probably safe to give under supervision. Take them away if you can't be there to watch. Rawhide can become lodged in the esophagus if your dog swallows a big piece. And dogs that eat rawhide often suffer diarrhea the next day. Be sure you buy high-quality American rawhide; foreign-made rawhide may be treated with harmful chemicals.

What about natural bones? They seem to be the quintessential dog treat, but are they really good for dogs? As a rule, no, says Dr. Gaughan. "Bird bones splinter very easily and can cause intestinal tract problems, creating an obstruction, or blockage," she says. "Or the bone can actually go through the intestinal wall and create an infection in the abdomen, which can end up being very

An Unpleasant Habit

A Beagle's favorite treat can also be the most repulsive, says Katie Williams. Coprophagy—or eating feces—is a common problem in the breed. Beagle owners have tried all sorts of remedies, including sprinkling the feces with meat tenderizer or topping them with Bitter Apple to mixing food with expensive prescription powders, pumpkin, and alfalfa pellets to make the feces taste unpleasant to the dog. For some dogs, these measures just add to the flavor. The best thing to do, Williams advises, is to remove feces promptly and limit access to the cat's litter box. Other options include supplying the dog with plenty of toys and exercise so he won't be bored, changing his diet to a food that's higher in fiber, fat, or protein, and teaching a "don't touch" command. Schedule a veterinary exam as well, to make sure he hasn't acquired internal parasites from his nasty habit.

serious and costly to treat." Beef bones splinter the least, she says, but even if they don't cause internal damage, your dog can break a tooth on them.

When you give any kind of treat, reduce by a little bit the amount of regular dog food you give. That way, you don't have to worry about your Beagle gradually packing on the pounds. A good rule to remember is that treats and table scraps should never make up more than five to ten percent of your Beagle's daily caloric intake.

Preventing Obesity

Pets that are too fat are one of the most common concerns of veterinarians. About 25 percent of the animals seen by veterinarians are overweight, meaning that their body weight is 15 percent or more above the normal weight for their breed or species. When dogs get fat, their medical problems begin to increase. They are more prone to diet-linked diseases such as diabetes as well as orthopedic problems caused by carrying too much weight on their frame.

Beagles are prone to obesity and can quickly balloon up to outlandish proportions. A fat Beagle is neither a pretty sight nor a healthy one. He waddles when he walks and has difficulty going very far or jumping up into a lap. Musculoskeletal problems can develop as well. Obese Beagles tend to develop knee problems and are predisposed to vertebral disk problems, which are often aggravated by excess body weight.

Among the reasons for the canine predisposition to obesity are the appetizing flavors of commercial pet foods, owners who leave food out all the time, and a sedentary lifestyle. All of these factors, plus the scenthound tendency to sniff out food wherever it can be found, are applicable to Beagles. If you own a Beagle, you'll know what the phrase "to hound someone" means. Beagles are very persistent when it comes to getting what they want, which is usually food. "The minute the refrigerator door opens, ours are right there with their heads inside," says Janiece Harrison. "We can't leave our plates unattended. Bo recently managed to get an egg out of the carton on the kitchen counter."

Beagles must be prevented from gaining weight, and that comes down to feeding the dog, not the food bowl. It's very easy to overfeed this breed, especially when he's looking longingly at you with those big pleading eyes.

Eye your dog objectively and give him the hands-on test: Can you feel his ribs (but not see them) or are they well padded with fat? From above, your Beagle should have a visible waist behind his ribs. A rounded or bulging abdomen and no waist are signs that your dog has been eating a little too much and not exercising enough. Perform a monthly rib check to gauge your Beagle's condition.

If your Beagle is a chowhound, and most of them are, you need to take steps to keep his weight at an appropriate level. Long before little rolls of fat start appearing around your Beagle's middle, you should have an obesity prevention plan in place. Puppyhood is not too soon to begin. Dogs are very much like people. If they're allowed to become fat when they're growing, they're going to be more predisposed to obesity later in life. If you think weight may be an issue later in your pup's life, but he is svelte now, work with your vet to establish an obesity prevention plan.

If, however, your pooch is beginning to get pudgy, the following tips will help you get him back in shape. Be sure to check with your veterinarian first to make sure there are no health factors that would preclude a dietary change or increased exercise.

○ Reduce the amount of food you give. Something as simple as giving a level cup instead of a heaping one can reduce the amount of calories your dog gets.

○ If reducing the amount of food isn't practical, switch to a brand with fewer calories. There are many reduced-calorie dog foods on the market.

○ Introduce the new food gradually, over a seven- to ten-day period.

○ If you change foods, don't suddenly switch to a type that your Beagle isn't used to. For example, if he's used to eating canned food, switch to a diet canned food, not a dry one. Or take several weeks of mixing the two to allow him to adjust.

○ Increase the amount of fiber your dog gets in his diet. Adding frozen (warmed) or canned green beans, carrots, or pumpkin to his food will help him feel full without adding a lot of extra calories. (Rinse canned vegetables before serving to reduce the amount of sodium in them.)

○ Offer several small meals daily. More frequent meals will help satisfy your Beagle's desire to eat and help prevent him from realizing that he's getting less food.

○ Besides controlling the amount of food your Beagle eats, add more activity to his routine. This is a hardy, vigorous dog that's born to be active. Exercise, from throwing a ball to increasing the length of his daily walks, is the best way to keep obesity at bay. If he's really over-weight, start slowly and keep exercise sessions brief. As he loses weight, you can increase the length and intensity of exercise.

It takes a lot of willpower to keep a Beagle trim. These dogs will eat until they pop and have pleading expressions that are difficult to resist. And as dogs are so individual, there's no simple rule you can follow that will guarantee your Beagle a sleek physique if you just feed a given amount of food. Within a single breed, gender and age group, energy requirements can vary by about 30 percent, so it's easy to overfeed one dog while under-feeding another, even if they're getting the same amount of food. So cast an unsparing eye on your Beagle's body: If he's starting to get fat, cut back on the food; if he's starting to get too skinny, feed a little more. A Beagle's ideal weight depends on his size and frame. For a 13-inch Beagle, the weight range is 16 to 20 pounds. For 15-inch Beagles, expect a range of 20 to 30 pounds.

Many of us equate giving food with an expression of love, but too much of anything can be detrimental. If you're concerned that by putting your Beagle on a diet or cutting down the treats you're reducing your ex-pression of love, consider the situation from a differ-ent point of view. What you're really doing is showing even more love by ensuring that your Beagle lives a long and healthy life.

Beagle Eating Habits

"My experience has been that if you don't want a Beagle to eat something, don't leave it anywhere near him," says Janiece Harrison. "Ours have managed to open the refrigerator door a couple of times when we didn't close it carefully. We can't store potatoes in low cabinets because they will open those and eat raw potatoes. I've found the only way to manage their weight is by using a measuring cup and being ruthless. While the tendency to anything and everything does have some drawbacks, it's actually one of my favorite Beagle traits. The fact that they'll eat anything makes them a real joy to train. Also, it's a wonderful indicator of health. If my guys wouldn't eat, I'd know something was wrong and we'd be off to the vet right away."

What's All the Fuss about Supplements?

One of the hot topics in human and veterinary medicine is the use of antioxidant vitamins (such as vitamins A, C, and E) to reduce the rate at which cells degrade, thus decreasing the incidence of age-related diseases such as cancer, heart disease, reduced immune response, cataracts, and arthritis. Seminars at recent veterinary conferences have covered this subject as well as other pet nutritional topics. The veterinary nutrition specialty is a relatively recent one, and nutrition will take on much greater importance as more veterinarians become more educated about it.

Nutritionists know that vitamins and minerals are necessary to maintain good health, but there's not a lot of evidence yet about the optimal amounts of vitamins and minerals the human body needs, let alone the canine body. They do know, however, that an imbalance of vitamins and minerals—whether too many or too few—can cause serious health problems. As commercial dog foods already contain what is believed to be an appropriate level of vita-

Toxic Treats:
Dangerous Foods for Dogs

Chocolate and Beagles don't go together. Dogs are sensitive to a chemical in chocolate called theobromine. Too much chocolate can lead to vomiting, diarrhea, panting, restlessness, and muscle tremors. Dogs have even been known to die from an overdose of the sweet treat. Unsweetened baking chocolate and dark chocolate contain more theobromine than candy, which is adulterated with sugars and other ingredients, but all types should be kept well out of your Beagle's reach.

Other foods that can be harmful to dogs include raw or cooked onions, raw eggs, and raw poultry or meat. A chemical in onions can destroy a dog's red blood cells, causing a serious or even fatal case of anemia. Raw animal products may be infected with salmonella, E. coli, or other bacteria. A case of food poisoning can cause diarrhea and vomiting, and some bacterial infections, such as salmonella, can be passed between dogs and people.

mins and minerals, most veterinarians and veterinary nutritionists recommend against giving supplements to a dog that's eating this type of food. Exceptions include dogs who have been ill or are suffering from malnutrition, in which case, your veterinarian may recommend a supplement to help build the dog back up.

Some pet owners and holistic veterinarians believe that enzyme supplements are useful for dogs on commercial diets. These supplements replace the enzymes in food that are destroyed in the cooking process.

Dogs who eat homemade or raw diets generally do require supplements. The appropriate amounts should be included in any recipe used. If they're not, don't guess. Enlist the help of a qualified holistic veterinary nutritionist. "Dogs have a lot of special nutritional requirements, and making a meal that contains all the necessary vitamins and minerals in the right proportions is difficult," says Katie Williams, who has a bachelor's degree in animal science. "There's a reason they taught us to balance rations using a computer program in my animal feeds and feeding class."

Does My Puppy Need Supplements?

A puppy that's eating a well-balanced diet shouldn't need supplements of any kind. Calcium supplements, especially, can cause skeletal abnormalities in a growing puppy. Check with your veterinarian before giving your Beagle puppy any kind of supplement.

What about My Older Dog?

In most cases, a healthy older dog doesn't need a supplement. Your veterinarian may recommend one, however, if your dog starts to show signs of age-related problems. B-vitamin supplements are important for dogs with reduced kidney function. Fatty acids, vitamin E and zinc may be useful to improve dry, itchy skin and bring a gloss to the coat. Your veterinarian can recommend an appropriate supplement for your older Beagle's needs.

No matter how old your Beagle is, there's one sure way to know whether he's getting the right nutrition: trust your eyes. A look at your Beagle should show you a trim, confident dog wearing a shiny coat, eyes sparkling with intelligence and good health, ready for whatever comes her way.

Medical Care
Every Beagle Needs

In This Chapter

○ Going to the Veterinarian
○ Preventive Medicine
○ Sick Calls and Emergencies

The veterinarian is your partner in your Beagle's health care. Through regular exams, inoculations, and expeditious treatment during the—hopefully—rare emergency, your veterinarian provides the foundation for your Beagle's physical well-being. You can build on that foundation through observation of your dog's normal behavior—and quick response when something isn't right. Together, you and the vet can work toward ensuring your dog a long and happy life.

Going to the Veterinarian

Since each breed is prone to different health problems, it's a good idea to choose a veterinarian who is familiar with the breed. Veterinarians who see a lot of Beagles in their practices frequently deal with ear infections, cherry eye, and hypothyroidism, to name a few of the conditions that often affect Beagles.

Finding the right veterinarian is much like searching for any other professional. The first step is to seek the opinions of people you trust. According to a survey done by the American Animal Hospital Association, 34 percent of the respondents found their veterinarian through a recommendation from a friend. Ask your Beagle's breeder (if she lives in your area) or your friends, neighbors, coworkers, and nearby relatives where they take their dogs for veterinary care and why they chose that particular veterinarian or clinic. Your local Beagle club may keep a list of veterinarians who know the quirks of the breed. You may want to contact your local or state veterinary association for a referral to a veterinarian in your area. The American Animal Hospital Association provides references to veterinary hospitals that meet its standards in areas such as surgery, medical records, anesthesia, and dentistry (see the appendix for contact information).

This word-of-mouth campaign is sure to net you the names of several veterinarians that practice near your home. Now comes the information-gathering phase. Call their offices and ask if the office manager has time to answer some questions for you. You'll want to know such things as the office hours, fees for routine procedures such as annual exams, vaccinations, and spay/neuter surgery, and how payments can be made—cash, check, or credit card. (See also

Ten Questions to Ask before Making a Veterinary Appointment

❍ How do you handle after-hours emergencies? Are you affiliated with a nearby animal emergency center?

❍ Do you provide 24-hour coverage for hospitalized animals? If not, how often are overnight patients checked?

❍ Approximately what percentage of your clinic's patients are dogs? Of those, how many are Beagles?

❍ Does the veterinarian specialize in any areas, such as allergies, dentistry, ophthalmology, orthopedics, or surgery?

❍ Does the veterinarian make house calls? Under what circumstances?

❍ Who provides care when the veterinarian is not available?

"Ten Questions to Ask before Making a Veterinary Appointment" above.)

Expect your questions to be answered in a pleasant and help-ful tone. A bored or rushed delivery may suggest that you'll be treated the same way in person. If you're satisfied with the office manager's replies and the office is conveniently located, make an appointment for a personal interview. You'll want to assure your-self that the clinic is clean and odor-free and that pet patients are housed appropriately if they need to be kept overnight.

This personal visit is an opportunity for you to talk to the vet-erinarian about his or her educational background, continuing education, and practice philosophy. Naturally, you want a veteri-narian who's up to date on the latest advances in veterinary medi-cine. And if you're interested in alternative therapies, you need to know if the veterinarian supports this type of treatment or pooh-poohs it. Ask if the veterinarian is familiar with the conditions common to Beagles and how he or she treats them.

One of the most important aspects of good health care is communication. You should be able to understand what the veterinarian tells you without having to slog through a lot of jargon or big medical terms, and you should feel comfortable asking questions about your Beagle's care. Cross off your list any veterinarian who makes you feel ignorant or demanding.

> You should be able to understand what the veterinarian tells you without having to slog through a lot of jargon or big medical terms.

When you find a veterinarian who meets your standards, it's time to schedule a visit with your Beagle so he can check out the vet's petside manner. A routine physical—without vaccinations—makes a good test visit. If the three of you are happy with each other, your search is over.

Your Beagle's First Visit

If you've bought a Beagle puppy, she's likely to have already experienced a couple of veterinary visits for vaccinations. Your veterinarian's office will probably be new to her, though, so you'll want to make sure that the experience is a pleasant one.

What to Expect

A veterinary exam usually begins with an assessment of your Beagle's health. You may be asked to fill out a questionnaire describing your Beagle's age, sex, condition, activity level, eating and elimination habits, and so on. This information will become the foundation of your Beagle's medical history and can be used as a baseline for future checkups. As the medical history grows over the years, the information in it gives your veterinarian a record of the types of problems your Beagle has had as well as what has and hasn't worked in the past, which is important for any recurring problems.

Other information that will help the veterinarian evaluate your dog includes where you acquired her (from a breeder, pet store, or shelter), what kind of care she received before coming to live with you, and previous vaccination records. Knowing the dog's original environment can help the veterinarian determine what types of things to look for. For instance, a Beagle acquired from an animal shelter or pet store may have been exposed to canine cough or other diseases that thrive in crowded conditions.

Be prepared to describe your Beagle's home environment, too. What other pets does she live with? How often does she go for walks? What kind of food does she eat, and how often? If you slip your Beagle table scraps now and then, don't hide it. The more your veterinarian knows about your Beagle's lifestyle, the better able he will be to make an accurate diagnosis when something's wrong.

The veterinarian may ask for a stool sample to check for the presence of parasites. These nasty little critters can cause serious problems if undetected and untreated, so the veterinarian will want to make sure your Beagle is starting off with a parasite-free belly.

If your Beagle is not already spayed or neutered, your veterinarian will probably discuss these options with you. Spaying and neutering provide health and

Did You Know?

Shelters in the United States take in nearly 11 million cats and dogs each year. Nearly 75 percent percent of those animals have to be euthanized.

behavior benefits, prevent unwanted pregnancies in your dog, and help control the burgeoning population of homeless animals.

Preventive Medicine

For both people and animals, medicine has evolved from a reactive state—when we only saw the doctor or veterinarian because of illness—to a proactive state, in which doctor and client work together to ensure good health. This new approach is called preventive medicine and, in the case of pets, it can be visualized as a triangle. Annual exams and vaccinations are two sides of the triangle, and spay/neuter surgery forms the third.

> Spaying and neutering provide health and behavior benefits, prevent unwanted pregnancies in your dog, and help control the burgeoning population of homeless animals.

Annual Visits

An annual exam is more than just an opportunity for the veterinarian to give your Beagle his vaccinations. Even though your Beagle may appear to be in perfect health, an annual exam gives the veterinarian a chance to go over him with the metaphorical fine-tooth comb to make sure no problems are lurking unseen. Veterinarians are trained observers, and they often spot things overlooked by even the most conscientious of owners. When health problems are detected early, they are often less expensive to treat and do less damage. Besides regular exams, the most common reasons Beagles are taken to the veterinarian are related to their eating habits, says Luisa Fallon, who works as a veterinary assistant. These include obesity, dental problems, getting

A Few Questions to Ask at the First Vet Visit

○ How much does my Beagle need to eat?

○ How do I know if he's putting on too much weight?

○ Do those floppy ears need special care?

○ What emergency situations do I need to be concerned about?

○ What preventive medicine routine do you recommend?

into the trash, and eating inappropriate objects, from address books to entire rabbits.

A thorough veterinary exam begins with a check of temperature, pulse, respiration rate, and body weight, followed by a hands-on, head-to-tail body check. Careful scrutiny of the head area can reveal myriad conditions. Eye appearance can indicate such problems as anemia, infections, and jaundice, as well as glaucoma, corneal abrasions, and other eye diseases and injuries. If your Beagle has been shaking his head, scratching his ears, or giving off an unpleasant odor, he may have an ear infection.

Among the things a veterinarian looks for at an annual visit are: any inflammation or unusual discharge from the eyes, ears, and nose; changes in color, texture, moisture, or shape of the nose; nasal obstructions or foreign objects in the mouth; and dental disease, bad breath, or abnormal growths in or around the mouth.

Moving on to the rest of the body, the veterinarian listens to the heart and lungs with a stethoscope. Early heart disease is often discovered during an annual health exam. Then the veterinarian palpates the entire body, feeling for organ position and size, abnormal lumps or bumps, and any areas that seem painful.

Palpation also indicates the condition of the joints, muscles, skin, lymph nodes, and hair. He also checks the genital area for discharges and growths.

At the same time, the veterinarian is giving your Beagle a visual going-over, seeing how he moves, looking at the condition of the skin and coat, and checking for fleas, ticks, and other external parasites. He may discuss how much your dog weighs and whether he needs less food and more exercise. The annual exam is also your opportunity to ask questions or express concerns.

If all is well, your Beagle will get a clean bill of health, and you can take him home knowing that you've been doing a great job of caring for him. But sometimes even the best-cared-for dogs get sick or injured. Unless the problem is external—an abscess, for instance—some form of diagnostic test will probably be required. Based on the findings of the exam, your veterinarian may suggest performing a complete blood count, a chemistry profile, a urinalysis, a fecal exam, a chest x ray, ultrasonography, endoscopy, or an electrocardiogram. These diagnostic aids can help the veterinarian identify what's troubling your Beagle.

Vaccinations

Infectious disease was once one of the greatest killers of dogs, but immunizations can prevent most of those fatal or debilitating canine diseases. A series of vaccinations, along with occasional booster shots, is one of the best tools of preventive medicine.

For some time after birth, puppies are protected from disease by the antibodies they receive in their mother's milk. This passive immunity decreases as the pup grows, and gradually disappears between 6 and 16 weeks of age. Your puppy receives a series of vaccinations during this

Keeping a Pet Diary

Writing down observations of your dog's daily eating and elimination habits, behavior, and activities is a great way to keep track of what's normal for him. This is important because it will help you see patterns develop. By recording even minor changes in activity, such as choosing an unusual place to sleep, you will be better able to notice when something's wrong. And if your Beagle becomes ill, your diary will be invaluable to the veterinarian, serving as a quick, easy reference about his behavior and the length of time since the symptoms started. A simple spiral-bound notebook is all you need to get started. Write a paragraph each night, and you'll soon have not only a great veterinary resource but also a record of your Beagle's days.

time, when he's most susceptible to infection. Maternal antibodies don't disappear all at once. They slowly decrease, and it's possible for a puppy to have maternal antibodies that aren't numerous enough to fight off disease but are still able to interfere with the antibodies produced by immunization. It's during this window of opportunity that your pup is most vulnerable to disease.

Vaccines work by stimulating the immune system to produce antibodies to disease. A vaccine contains antigens, or pieces of infectious agents, for a particular disease, and when these antigens enter the body, the immune system springs into action, manufacturing antibodies to repel the foreign invader. After the antigen is defeated, the antibodies remain on guard, ready to respond the next time that particular antigen appears. A series of puppy shots given over a period of several weeks phases in immunity as the maternal antibodies disappear.

Of course, nothing in life is fail-safe and, occasionally, even vaccines don't do their job. A vaccine can fail if maternal antibodies are still in force, if the dog has already been exposed to the disease against which he's being vaccinated, if the dog is sick (stress or illness can depress immune response), or if he's taking certain medications such as steroids, which can interfere with the vaccine's potency. Vaccines that have been stored or administered incorrectly are another source of failure. Fortunately, vaccine failure is rare, and it shouldn't be used as an excuse not to vaccinate your Beagle.

When to Vaccinate For years, veterinarians and pharmaceutical companies have recommended that pets receive annual vaccinations, but that is beginning to change. According to veterinarians at Colorado State University, there is little scientific evidence to support the need for annual vaccination. They are also concerned by increasing documentation that overvaccination has been associated with harmful side effects, such as autoimmune hemolytic anemia in dogs and vaccine-associated sarcomas in cats.

> A series of vaccinations, along with occasional booster shots, is one of the best tools of preventive medicine.

CSU, Texas A&M, the University of Wisconsin, and other veterinary schools are now recommending that after the initial series of vaccines and a booster at one year, immunizations for many diseases need to be given only once every three years. Some veterinarians believe vaccinations aren't necessary for older animals that rarely leave home. It's not likely that the practice of giving annual vaccinations will disappear overnight, but over the years, as newly trained veterinarians enter practice, triennial vaccinations will probably become standard procedure.

The CSU program recommends a standard three-shot series of four vaccines for puppies—parvovirus, adenovirus 2, parainfluenza and distemper followed by a rabies vaccination after 16

What about Homeopathic Vaccines?

A nosode is a homeopathic remedy produced by a technique that involves diluting the original substance so completely that nothing is left of it. The theory in homeopathy is that the smaller the dose, the greater the effect. Unfortunately, there is no substantial evidence that nosodes are effective in preventing disease, writes homeopathic veterinarian Susan G. Wynn, a contributor to the American Holistic Veterinary Medical Association Web site. According to the results of one well-controlled study, she notes, parvovirus nosodes were completely ineffective in preventing parvoviral disease. Dr. Wynn, who has completed postdoctoral research in viral and vaccine immunology, recommends that puppies receive an initial vaccination series, plus boosters for a year or two afterward.

weeks of age. All the vaccinations are boostered when the dog is a year old and then every three years thereafter. Rabies vaccines are boosted as required by local and state law—usually every one or three years. Other vaccines, such as intranasal parainfluenza, *Bordetella,* and Lyme are recommended only for dogs at risk of these diseases and may need more frequent administration. For instance, intranasal *Bordetella*/parainfluenza should be used just prior to possible exposure to kennel cough—if your Beagle is going to a dog show or staying in a kennel, for instance. This vaccine can be repeated up to six times a year with no ill effects.

The risk of infectious disease varies throughout the country, and the vaccination program offered at CSU's small-animal clinic is designed specifically for that area and modified for pets with certain risk factors. Your veterinarian can help you tailor a vaccination program that's appropriate for your Beagle, based on his current health and the incidence of infectious disease in your locale. Keep in mind that if you travel and must board your Beagle, many kennels require proof of vaccination within the past year. You may be able to persuade the kennel to accept a statement from your veterinarian that the vaccination protocol you are using is effective.

Canine Infectious Diseases

The most common diseases that threaten dogs are primarily viral in origin: canine distemper, canine parvovirus, canine hepatitis, canine cough, canine herpesvirus, and rabies. A virus is a parasitical agent that survives by preying on the living cells of a suitable host, in this case, dogs. The occupation of a cell by a virus is destructive to that cell, often resulting in disease, which can range from mild to severe or even fatal. Except for rabies, none of these canine viral diseases are transmissible to people, but they can be carried from people—on shoes, for instance—to dogs.

Viral diseases don't respond to medications such as antibiotics, but supportive therapy such as fluids and antibiotics for prevention of secondary bacterial infections can help pull the dog through once a virus has taken hold. For all these diseases, vaccinations are the most effective form of prevention.

Canine Distemper Around the world, canine distemper is the disease that poses the greatest threat to dogs. Puppies and young dogs are most likely to be infected with this highly contagious virus, although it can also affect older dogs.

The canine distemper virus kills more than 50 percent of the adult dogs that contract it, and in puppies the death rate often reaches 80 percent, thanks to other opportunistic diseases, such as pneumonia and bronchitis, which strike the already weakened dogs. Even if a dog survives distemper, his nervous system and senses of smell, hearing, and sight can be irreparably damaged, and he may be partially or totally paralyzed.

The distemper virus makes its way from dog to dog through that most canine of actions: sniffing. The virus is contained in mucous and watery secretions from an infected dog's eyes and nose as well as in his urine and feces, so a healthy dog need not even come in contact with one that's infected to pick up the disease. The virus can be spread by air or carried in on shoes or other inanimate objects. Unless you and your Beagle live in total isolation, it's impossible to prevent exposure to this ubiquitous virus.

A dog with distemper may appear to have a severe head cold. Signs include squinting, fever, stuffiness, and a pus-like discharge from the eyes. The dog may lose weight, cough, vomit, and have diarrhea. Some dogs with distemper develop severe stomach and intestinal inflammation. Seizures are common, and indicate infection of the central nervous system, which is often fatal. Occasionally, the virus causes the tough keratin cells on the footpad to grow rapidly, resulting in a hardened pad—the origin of distemper's old-time name of hardpad disease. In mild cases, these signs may go unnoticed, or the dog may only have a slight fever for a couple of weeks.

If you suspect distemper, even if your dog doesn't have these exact signs, don't delay treatment. Distemper manifests itself in many different forms, but the earlier it's caught, the better chance your Beagle has of pulling through. Recovery takes much longer if secondary bacterial infections are given time to develop. Even after physical recovery, nervous problems may continue for many weeks.

Did You Know?

A dog's heart beats between 70 and 120 times per minute, compared with 70 to 80 times per minute for humans.

Canine Parvovirus Parvovirus emerged in 1978 and is found worldwide. It's a deadly and highly contagious disease that attacks the intestinal tract, white blood cells, and sometimes the heart muscle. It lurks in an infected dog's feces and hops a ride on shoes, paws, or any other moving object. High heat and sub-zero temperatures have no effect on it.

Parvovirus is most often spread wherever dogs are found in numbers, such as dog shows, boarding kennels, animal shelters, pet shops, parks, and playgrounds. Puppies between 6 weeks and 6 months of age are most at risk. A Beagle that spends most of his time at home is less likely to be exposed to it, but of course lack of socialization brings its own problems. If you suspect that you've walked through an infected area, use a solution of one part bleach to 30 parts water to clean your shoes and any areas or objects—such as kennel runs or crates—that may be contaminated.

> Parvovirus is most often spread wherever dogs are found in numbers, such as dog shows, boarding kennels, animal shelters, pet shops, parks, and playgrounds.

Signs of parvovirus are vomiting, severe bloody diarrhea, depression, fever, and loss of appetite. Feces may appear light gray or yellow gray, or may be streaked with blood. If you see these signs in your Beagle, run, don't walk, to the veterinarian. Signs of infection usually show up within a week of exposure. Parvovirus is diagnosed based on the dog's signs or through a fecal exam.

The vomiting and diarrhea of parvovirus lead to severe dehydration, so fluid therapy is crucial. A course of antibiotics won't kill the virus but will help prevent secondary infections, which are quite common. Dogs that die usually do so two to three days after signs appear.

Parvovirus can also cause the heart to become inflamed, a condition called myocarditis. This occurs most often in pups younger than three months. Diarrhea isn't common in this form of parvovirus; instead, puppies act depressed, stop nursing, then collapse, gasping for breath. They may die within minutes of this collapse. If they survive, their hearts are usually permanently damaged, and death from heart failure can occur weeks or even months after apparent recovery.

Vaccinations are the first line of defense against parvovirus. To further safeguard your Beagle, don't let him sniff or otherwise come in contact with the feces of other dogs until he's at least six months old. Pick up after your dog, and urge your friends and neighbors to pick up after their dogs. Your veterinarian can advise you about the incidence of parvovirus in your area.

Infectious Canine Hepatitis The type of bug that causes canine hepatitis is an adenovirus, which tends to be resistant to common detergents and disinfectants. It is found worldwide and is spread by direct contact between dogs.

When the ICH virus is inhaled or ingested by a dog, it travels first to the tonsils, which are a great launching site for disseminating the virus to the lymph nodes and then to the bloodstream, which takes it to the liver, kidneys, eyes, and the cells lining the inner surface of the blood vessels.

Classic signs of hepatitis are fever, lethargy, reddened membranes, enlarged lymph nodes, and inflamed tonsils. Some dogs may have enlarged livers, jaundice, or small hemorrhages of the skin and mucous membranes. Treatment is aimed at preventing shock and hemorrhage, managing neurological disease, and preventing secondary infections. A dog with hepatitis may need intravenous fluids, corticosteroids, blood transfusions, and antibiotics.

Within a week of infection, the body's immune response kicks in and bounces the virus out of most areas of the body, but it can survive for a while in the kidneys, so a dog can still be excreting the virus in its urine for six to nine months. A lingering reminder of the infection is a clouding of the cornea, a condition sometimes called blue eye. It usually disappears after a few weeks. As with all these diseases, vaccination is the best form of prevention.

Canine Infectious Tracheobronchitis More commonly known as kennel cough or canine cough, this highly contagious disease causes inflammation of the upper throat, trachea, and bronchi, the tubes leading to each lung. It has a number of bacterial and viral causes: the *Bordetella bronchiseptica* bacterium; canine parainfluenza virus; canine adenovirus-2; mycoplasmas, which are closely related to bacteria; canine distemper virus; canine herpesvirus; and *Pasteurella multocida,* a bacterium. Like parvovirus, kennel cough is airborne and spreads most often where many dogs are gathered, as at dog shows, field trials, and boarding kennels—hence its name of kennel cough.

Kennel cough usually takes four to six days to incubate and is identified by the loud, honking cough that develops. The tonsils and back of the throat may appear reddened and foamy. The sound of the cough changes from moist to dry and harsh, and gets worse when the dog is excited or after it drinks water. Pressure on the trachea—from pulling on a leash, for instance—can also cause coughing. Kennel cough usually lasts for a week or two, but sometimes it continues for five or six weeks, a long time to listen to a dog cough.

Rest and freedom from stress are the usual prescription for kennel cough. Your veterinarian may prescribe antibiotics to ward off secondary infections, a cough suppressant to keep you and the dog from going crazy, a bronchodilator to relieve clogged airways, or fluid therapy to prevent dehydration.

There is a vaccine for kennel cough, and most boarding kennels require proof that it has been given within the past 6 months or a year. Unlike other vaccinations, the kennel cough vaccine can be given up to six times a year without ill effects.

Canine Herpesvirus This disease is found in dogs around the world and is responsible for fading-death syndrome in young puppies, who can acquire it as they pass through the birth canal or from nasal contact with an infected dog, usually their mother or littermates. CHV can also lie dormant in the mucous membranes and genital tracts of healthy dogs, just waiting for a stressful situation to activate it. Fortunately, it's less resistant than some other viruses to soaps, detergents, and disinfectants.

Canine herpesvirus spreads through the body via the bloodstream and targets the lymph nodes, spleen, kidneys, liver, lungs, gastrointestinal tract, adrenal glands, and brain, killing their cells and causing localized hemorrhaging. In puppies more than five weeks old, canine herpesvirus may appear as a mild respiratory infection. Younger puppies suffer more severe cases, and those that are only a week or two old usually die. Signs of a severe infection include depression, lethargy, lack of appetite, persistent crying, abdominal pain, and a soft, odorless, yellow-green stool.

This disease proceeds rapidly and, by the time the dog is taken to the vet, is often too far along for treatment to do any good. No fully effective vaccine is available.

Rabies Humans have feared rabies for thousands of years, and for good reason. The bullet-shaped virus brings death wherever it goes, although people are fortunate enough to have a treatment available that is effective if given immediately after exposure to the virus. In this country, rabies is carried primarily by wild animals, such as skunks, bats, foxes, and raccoons, and by domestic dogs and cats. It's spread through the bite or saliva of an infected animal.

Signs of rabies vary greatly and include restlessness, nervousness, bizarre behaviors, and increasing viciousness. An affected animal may also be sensitive to light. In some cases, heavy, rapid breathing through the mouth causes the dog's saliva to froth—the classic image of an animal suffering from rabies. This stage, called the furious stage, lasts one to seven days. The disease can move into the paralytic stage, which usually lasts only a day or two. The animal has difficulty swallowing and soon suffers paralysis, followed by coma and death. Virtually 100 percent of animals that show signs of rabies will be dead within 10 days. Because the saliva becomes infectious only shortly before clinical signs appear, even apparently healthy animals that bite or scratch a person should be monitored closely for 10 days. If no abnormal signs are seen by the end of this period, the animal was not infectious at the time of the bite.

As Beagles love being outdoors and are hunting dogs at heart, their risk of rabies infection is potentially high. All states require rabies vaccination annually, biennially, or triennially. Even if you manage to confine your Beagle to your yard, vaccination is a worthwhile precaution in case a rabid skunk or raccoon invades the yard. Wild animals have even been known to enter homes through pet doors.

Leptospirosis and Other Vaccine Reactions

Leptospirosis is a bacterial infection that can be spread between dogs and people. The bacteria are found in the droppings of animals such as rats, mice, and cattle, and infection usually results from drinking contaminated water.

Many dogs, including Beagles, have adverse reactions to the vaccine for this disease. Rarely are the reactions to the vaccine so severe that the dog dies. Nevertheless, many veterinarians no longer give the leptospirosis vaccine to dogs. Veterinarians at Kansas State University's College of Veterinary Medicine say that the risks of the vaccine have begun to outweigh the benefits. There are more reactions to the leptospirosis vaccine than to most other vaccines, and it doesn't do a very good job of protecting dogs, says William Fortney, D.V.M. The disease is uncommon so, in this case, a vaccine can do more harm than good.

Young dogs are more susceptible to reactions from any vaccine, not just leptospirosis. Signs of a reaction are usually a low-grade fever or muscle aches and pain. Your Beagle may feel like sleeping a lot and not eating much for a day or two afterward. A more severe reaction—which is usually seen in response to a leptospirosis vaccine or a killed vaccine (which carries inactivated disease agents)—may involve hives, facial swelling, or vomiting. A dog can even go into anaphylactic shock, usually within 20 minutes of vaccination.

Report any reaction to your veterinarian, who can notify the U.S. Pharmacopeia, a private organization that operates a reporting program in conjunction with the American Veterinary Medical Association. You can find USP's Web site at www.usp.org or call (800) 487-7776.

If your Beagle has had a vaccination reaction, don't give up on vaccinations. Your veterinarian can pre-treat the dog with an antihistamine or take other steps to prevent a recurrence. The risk from a vaccine reaction is much less serious than that of contracting a potentially fatal disease.

Spaying and Neutering

Animals age about five times as quickly as people do. By the time a male or female Beagle reaches six to nine months of age, the hormones have kicked in and the dog is able to reproduce, even though it isn't fully mature emotionally or physically.

In females, the reproductive cycle begins when they enter estrus, or heat. Estrus usually occurs every six months. It starts with a bleeding phase called proestrus, and is followed by estrus, during which your female is quite attractive to male dogs and eagerly seeks their advances, twitching her tail in invitation. The estrus cycle can also initiate a temporary personality change. It's not unusual for dogs to seem cross or agitated while in heat. The length of the estrus cycle depends on the individual. It may last for only a few days or for as long as a month.

When male dogs become sexually mature, their desire and ability to mate is not confined to a certain period. They are ready, willing, and able at any time, as long as they have access to a receptive female. Just like any other dog, if not more so, a male Beagle will have the urge to roam in search of romance as well as to mark his territory just in case a willing female might be around to sniff his message. Intact males that are not bred lead a life of frustration. If a female isn't available, the Beagle may well satisfy his urges by humping pillows, legs, or anything else he can find that seems suitable. Not an attractive habit by any means.

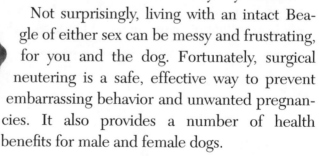

Not surprisingly, living with an intact Beagle of either sex can be messy and frustrating, for you and the dog. Fortunately, surgical neutering is a safe, effective way to prevent embarrassing behavior and unwanted pregnancies. It also provides a number of health benefits for male and female dogs.

Spay surgery, which your veterinarian may refer to as an ovariohysterectomy, is the removal of the ovaries, fallopian tubes, and uterus, thus ending heat cycles and mood swings. A spayed Beagle won't drip blood on your newly cleaned carpet and won't have to be kept away from males while she's in heat. Nor will you have to do the hard work of finding good homes for any puppies she might produce. A spayed Beagle is protected from uterine infections, which can be fatal if not caught early, and the possibility of a difficult or dangerous pregnancy. If your Beagle is spayed before her first heat cycle, her chances of developing mammary cancer plummet. Fifty percent of mammary cancers are malignant in dogs, but studies show that fewer than one percent of females spayed before their first heat cycle develop mammary cancer. The risk increases to 25 percent after they have one heat cycle. These are risks hardly worth taking for a beloved Beagle that is not intended for breeding.

The neutering of a male dog simply involves removing his testicles, an operation called an orchiectomy. After this surgery, your Beagle's desire to mark his territory will be diminished or even eliminated, and he'll no longer be at risk of testicular cancer. (If one or both testicles are retained inside the body, the risk of this cancer is higher, so neutering becomes even more important.) Altered males are also less prone to prostate disease, a potentially life-threatening condition characterized by blood in the urine, straining or inability to urinate or defecate, prostatic abscesses, and painful perianal adenomas, growths or tumors that occur around the anal area.

Did You Know?

Tests conducted at the Institute for the Study of Animal Problems in Washington, D.C., revealed that dogs and cats, like humans, are either right- or left-handed.

Is Anesthesia Safe?

Penny is a six-month-old Beagle puppy who is close to sexual maturity. Her owner, Susie, doesn't plan to breed Penny and is aware of the health benefits of spaying, but she's fearful about Penny being anesthetized. When Susie was a little girl, her dog had to have surgery and died under anesthesia.

While Susie's concerns are understandable, she has little to fear for Penny's safety. Anesthesia drugs and techniques are much advanced from 20 years ago. Veterinarians today can tailor anesthesia to each dog's needs, using different protocols depending on the dog's age and health status, as well as the type of procedure being done. The dog's body can process the drugs used in modern veterinary medicine more quickly and efficiently than it could the old-style, long-acting barbiturate anesthetics; today's drugs are also less likely to depress the cardiovascular system or cause irregularities in the heart rhythm.

The amount of anesthetic given is calculated based on the dog's weight, and relative amounts of body fat, lean muscle, and bone. The veterinarian also uses a presurgical blood test to gain important information about how the body's organs are functioning. All of these factors help the veterinarian determine how much and what type of anesthesia to use to safely operate on your dog.

Altered Beagles of both sexes are more focused on their people instead of on fulfilling sexual desires. License fees are also less expensive for a dog that can't reproduce, since the county is assured that the pet won't be contributing to the cost of caring for unwanted shelter animals.

Spay/neuter surgery can take place when your Beagle is four to six months old. The surgery is painless, although your dog may be a bit sore for a few days afterward. Your veterinarian can provide medication to keep the dog comfortable during the healing process.

Myths about Spaying and Neutering

○ My Beagle will get fat. It's true that some animals start to put on weight after they've been altered, but this is attributed to the change in metabolism brought about by the slowing of the rapid growth phase, which usually occurs at just about the same time as sexual maturity. The secret to keeping your Beagle sleek is to make sure he gets plenty of exercise and doesn't eat too much.

○ My Beagle's personality will change. That's true, and for the better. Your Beagle will be more interested in paying attention to you than in running after a mate.

○ My Beagle will be healthier if she goes through heat first or even has a litter of puppies. Just the opposite is true. Malignant mammary tumors are most common in female dogs who are unspayed or were allowed to go through one or more heats before being spayed. Spaying before the first heat virtually eliminates the risk of mammary tumors. And giving birth to a litter of puppies comes with its own risks, including bleeding to death, infection, or the need for a Cesarean section if things don't go right.

○ My Beagle won't be macho anymore. Neutering a dog does not take away his "manhood." While your male Beagle won't be able to sire puppies, his underlying personality will remain the same.

The cost for spay or neuter surgery varies widely, with an average of about $110 for females, $100 for males. A cryptorchid male—a dog with one or more retained testicles—usually costs more. This fee covers the veterinarian's time for the surgery, the anesthesia, and suture removal. The cost for surgery may be more or less depending on the economics of maintaining a veterinary hospital in your particular area as well as the size, age, and health of your Beagle. Given all the health and behavioral

Myths about Breeding

○ Purebred Beagles are expensive; I can breed my dog and make back the money I spent to purchase her, plus a little profit. Well-bred Beagles are expensive because of all the money the breeder puts into producing a litter. There are veterinary checks of the bitch's health and condition before she's bred, the cost of the stud fee, and expenses for transporting her to and from the stud. Then there's an ultrasound exam to confirm the pregnancy and number of puppies. If whelping doesn't go as expected, your Beagle may need an emergency Cesarean section in the middle of the night. You could lose her and all the puppies. If the puppies do make it safely into the world, they'll need to be dewormed and vaccinated—several times. Finally, there's the expense and time involved in advertising the litter and screening the buyers.

○ Purebred Beagles are expensive; I can make back the money I spent to purchase him by using him as a stud dog. Unless your dog has proven himself in the show ring and has passed all his health clearances with flying colors, not very many people are going to want to pay big bucks to use him as a stud.

benefits that result from this permanent surgery, the expense is well worth it and may even save you money over the years, since you won't have to board your female during heat cycles, pay for the cost of a litter, or spend several hundred dollars on emergency surgery for a raging uterine infection.

"I would advise pet owners to have their pets spayed or neutered. The medical advantages have been proven, and serious complications to the procedure are uncommon," says Kathy Gaughan, D.V.M., of Kansas State University's College of Veterinary Medicine. "Pets recover from surgery very quickly. Usually the day after surgery, most pets are bouncing around as if nothing ever happened."

Sick Calls and Emergencies

You want to give your Beagle the best of care, but you can't afford to run to the veterinarian every time she sneezes. By developing good observation skills and cultivating a good relationship with your veterinarian, you can solve some problems by phone and learn when your dog really needs to get to the vet fast and when it's okay to take a wait-and-see stance.

When to Call the Vet

When your Beagle is well, you know it. Her eyes are bright and shiny, her tail is wagging at the sound of your keys, signifying a car ride, and a sweet hound smile splits her face from side to side. Her coat shines, and her energy level is set at "Go!" But even the healthiest of Beagles can experience the occasional health problem, so you'll want to be prepared for any contingency.

How can you know if your Beagle isn't feeling well? Many signs indicate illness, such as lethargy or vomiting, but with Beagles the sure tip-off is lack of appetite. "Our Beagles have eaten everything from a pile of used charcoal to the shelled pecans I needed to bake pies at Thanksgiving, without ill effects," says Janiece Harrison. "It's not unheard of for Beagles to eat pantyhose. I once heard someone say that if a Beagle won't eat, get to a vet as soon as possible. I've always used that as a good barometer of their health."

Once you get to know your Beagle's routine, it will be pretty obvious when she's not feeling well. Paying close attention to her habits will train you to notice when something isn't right. To ensure your Beagle's continuing well-being, take her to the veterinarian if you notice any of the following signs:

○ Abnormal behavior, sudden viciousness, or lethargy. Pets often manifest physical problems through what appears to be misbehavior. Lethargy is a common sign of many diseases.

○ Abnormal discharges from the nose, eyes, or other body openings. Discharges often indicate irritation or infection.

○ Abnormal lumps, limping, or difficulty getting up or lying down. A lump can be a simple swelling from injury, or a benign or malignant tumor. A soft, hot, or painful swelling is probably an abscess. Limping or difficulty moving may be the result of an injury or a painful joint condition such as arthritis.

○ Bad breath or heavy tartar deposits on teeth; red or swollen gums. Severe dental disease.

○ Dandruff, hair loss, open sores, a ragged or dull coat. Poor coat condition can indicate a diet that's nutritionally deficient, skin disease, or other problems.

○ Difficult, abnormal, or uncontrolled urination or defecation. One of the signs of diabetes or kidney disease is frequent or excessive urination. A dog who urinates frequently but doesn't produce more than a few drops may have a bladder infection or blockage. Diarrhea that lasts for more than a day can signal any number of problems.

○ Excessive head shaking, scratching, and licking or biting any part of the body. Parasites, an infection, or skin disease may have taken hold.

○ Increased sensitivity. Depending on where the dog is sensitive, she may have neck or back pain, an internal infection or injury, an abscess, or allergic dermatitis.

○ Loss of appetite for more than a day, marked weight loss or gain, or excessive water consumption. The causes for continued lack of interest in food can range from dental disease to cancer. If your Beagle suddenly loses interest in food, it's a good bet that something's wrong. Rapid or unexpected weight loss or gain is almost always significant. Diabetes or kidney disease can cause your Beagle to drink much more water than usual.

○ Repeated coughing, gagging, sneezing, or vomiting. Your Beagle may have something stuck in her throat, a collapsed trachea, or heart disease.

○ Vulvar discharge. A sign of pyometra, a serious uterine infection.

What to Expect If Your Beagle Is Sick

There are some situations, such as the need for intravenous feeding or medication, that might require your Beagle to be hospitalized, but in most instances you can take care of her at home after the veterinarian has done her work. Being able to care for your sick Beagle at home is a plus. Your dog will feel more secure and recover more quickly if she's being nursed by loving hands in a familiar place. One of the most important skills you'll need is the ability to successfully give medications.

How to Administer Medication and Pills

It's good to know how to give a pill or other medication. An effective technique ensures that your dog gets the right amount of medication each time, helping her to get well faster. Be sure you give all the medication your veterinarian prescribes. Some bugs are hardy and will come back if they don't get the one-two punch of the complete prescription.

Down the Hatch Your Beagle is most likely to receive medication in the form of a pill. Many Beagles will simply swallow the pill if you mix it in with their food. Others require more cunning. Hide the pill in something special, such as cream cheese or peanut butter. If your Beagle is sneaky enough to eat around the pill and then spit it out, or if her appetite has gone south, you'll have to try a more direct method.

To give a pill manually, kneel or sit with the dog held firmly between your knees. Hold the pill in your right hand. Using the first and middle fingers of your left hand, gently pry your dog's jaws open, and place the pill far back on the center of her tongue. (If you're a lefty, simply reverse these directions.) To make sure the pill goes down, hold her mouth closed and lightly stroke her throat until you see her swallow.

One of the most important skills you'll need is the ability to successfully give medications.

You can also try grasping the dog's head in your left hand and tilting it back until she's looking straight up. With the pill in your right hand, firmly between the thumb and forefinger, open the mouth using the middle finger of your right hand. As you drop the pill into the mouth, use your right index finger to push it over the tongue. Hold your dog's muzzle closed and gently blow into her nose. The sensation will make her lick and swallow, and down the pill will go. Whichever method you use, remember that some pills taste nasty if they're broken, so don't break the pill unless it's just too big to get down in one attempt.

To give liquid medications, prepare the appropriate amount of medication and restrain your Beagle between your knees as described above. Using the technique in the previous paragraph, tilt the head up, open the mouth, and aim the syringe at the cheek pouch. Make sure the mouth is closed around the syringe, and slowly squeeze out the liquid. When it reaches the back of the mouth, your dog should automatically swallow. If she doesn't, try gently blowing into her nose to make her lick and swallow. Avoid fast, hard squirts of liquid to the back of the throat—your dog could choke.

Medicating Eyes and Ears A Beagle in the field or playing outdoors may suffer an eye injury from running through foliage or underbrush, so it's important to know how to administer eye drops and ointments. A good, firm head-hold is a must; you don't want your dog to shake her head and cause you to poke her in the eye. Hold the eye drops in your right hand, tilt the head upward, and place the drops directly on the eyeball. Try not to let the applicator tip touch the eye. To make sure the eye drops are distributed evenly, close and open the eyelids.

To apply an eye ointment, gently pull down the lower lid, and apply the ointment to the inside lower lid, avoiding direct contact with the eyeball. You can also pull the upper lid back and apply the ointment to the white of the eye. Close and open the eyelids to evenly distribute the medication.

If you scrupulously keep your Beagle's ears clean and dry, she shouldn't have too many ear problems. This breed is prone to ear infections, however, so you may have to administer ear drops or ointment. To do this, tilt the head slightly to the side and apply the appropriate amount of medication. Then use your fingers to gently massage the medication into the ear. Your Beagle is sure to shake her head after you're done, and less of the medication will fly out of the ears if you've rubbed it in first. Unless your dog's ears are unusually painful or sensitive, she'll probably enjoy the massage.

Costs

Sometimes it seems as if we spend more on veterinary care than we do on medical care for ourselves. Who would imagine that a dog could run up such high veterinary bills? But if we compare the costs of veterinary and medical care, we soon find that we're actually getting a pretty good deal.

Why Does It Cost So Much?

Americans spend about $10 billion annually on veterinary care. The leading-edge medical care that we've come to expect for ourselves is now available for our animals as well. Dogs can receive blood transfusions, ultrasound, MRI, CT scans, open-heart surgery, pacemakers, cataract surgery, chemotherapy, radiation, acupuncture, chiropractic, and more. Every day, people who 10 years ago would have had no alternative but euthanasia are being faced with the possibility of extending or saving a pet's life through new techniques, technologies, and treatments. But those are for major medical situations. What about day-to-day health care?

> The leading-edge medical care that we've come to expect for ourselves is now available for our animals as well.

The fees your veterinarian charges reflect the costs of facility upkeep, equipment, employee salaries and benefits, advertising, continuing education, and fees for professional memberships, not to mention her own bread and butter. While veterinarians generally enter their profession because they love animals, they are also concerned with making a living. They spent as much time in veterinary school as your doctor did in medical school and face high student loan and practice start-up payments; but compared to doctors, they make very little indeed, considering that they serve as your Beagle's general physician, surgeon, radiologist, dentist, dermatologist, neurologist, ophthalmologist, psychiatrist, ear, nose and throat specialist, and pharmacist. Although your veterinarian may care deeply about your Beagle's welfare, she would quickly go bankrupt if she provided diagnosis, care, and medication at no charge or for less than her costs, just as your doctor would in a similar situation.

You should also keep in mind that your health insurance pays for a big chunk of your medical expenses. If it didn't, your doctor bill would vastly outweigh your veterinary bill, comparatively speaking.

Your veterinarian's job, after diagnosis, is to make you aware of the alternatives for your Beagle's treatment. The decision about the extent of care must rest with you and your financial situation. That doesn't mean, however, that your veterinarian won't be willing to work with you to arrange a payment plan that will allow you to give your dog the care he needs.

How to Discuss Finances with Your Vet

Most of us are brought up with the notion that it is impolite to talk about money in any way, shape, or form, but when it comes to dealing with a professional about your Beagle's care, there's no shame in discussing how best to cover the treatment financially. Your veterinarian has a mortgage and orthodontist bills for the kids, too, so she'll understand that you might not be able to make the entire payment in one lump sum.

Some veterinary clinics offer financing, while others may be willing to work with you on a more informal basis, especially if you're a long-standing client with a good history of

How to Make an Insurance Claim

It's your responsibility as a policyholder to make the best use of your insurance plan. Take these steps to get the most for your money:

1. Designate a file for pet insurance forms.

2. Always take a claim form with you to the veterinarian's office. Many companies require a veterinarian's signature.

3. Make copies of receipts. A receipt must accompany every claim form. Some companies require only copies; others require originals. Keep a copy for your records.

4. Make copies of completed claim forms. If a question or payment issue arises, a copy to review on your end of the phone line will be reassuring.

5. Note an acceptable payment period on your calendar. Reimbursement may slip your mind, and it may be delayed in cases where a problem is encountered and you forget to inquire about the payment's status.

6. Mark claims paid and date received. Leave a paper trail that's easy to understand. Looking back a year later, you'll be glad for the notations.

©1999 Solveig Fredrickson

paying your bills. Not every veterinarian is willing or able to work with clients in this manner, but if you don't ask you won't know.

Savings Plans and Insurance Plans—How They Can Help

According to a 1997 survey by the American Animal Hospital Association, only one percent of pet owners surveyed carried insurance for their pets, but if you're concerned about being able to provide care for your Beagle in case of an emergency or a major medical situation, pet insurance is something to consider.

Ten Questions to Ask Every Provider

Before choosing a pet insurance or membership plan, be sure to get straight-forward answers to all your questions. If it makes you more comfortable, get the answers in writing.

1. Does your policy follow fee/benefits schedules? If so, please send me your detailed coverage limits. In the meantime, please give me examples of coverage limits for three common canine procedures so I can compare them to my current veterinary charges.

2. Does your policy cover basic wellness care, or does it cover only accidents and illnesses? Do you offer a wellness care endorsement that I can purchase on top of my basic plan for an additional fee? What other endorsements do you offer, and how much do they cost?

3. Under your policy's rules, can I continue taking my Beagle to its current veterinarian, or do I need to switch to another veterinarian?

4. Does your policy cover hereditary conditions, congenital conditions or pre-existing conditions? Please explain each coverage or exclusion as it pertains specifically to my dog. Is there a feature where pre-existing conditions will be covered if my dog's pre-existing condition requires no treatment after a specified period? What is that period?

5. What happens to my premium and to my Beagle's policy if your company goes out of business? What guarantees do I have that I won't be throwing my money away?

6. How quickly do you pay claims?

7. What is your policy's deductible? Does the deductible apply per incident or annually? How does the deductible differ per plan?

8. Does the policy have payment limits over a year's period or during my pet's lifetime? How do the payment limits differ per plan?

9. What is the A.M. Best Co. rating of your insurance underwriter, and what does that rating mean?

10. Is there a cancellation period after I receive my policy or membership? How long do I have to review all my materials once I receive them, and what is the cancellation procedure?

©1999 Solveig Fredrickson

Pet insurance doesn't cover routine care such as vaccinations or annual exams, or elective surgery such as a spay or neuter, but if your Beagle breaks a leg or develops a tumor and requires surgery, insurance will cover many of the costs. Other conditions that may be covered include ear infections, skin rashes, gastrointestinal upsets, and treatment for diabetes or heart conditions. Coverage may also include prescriptions, laboratory fees, and x rays.

Preexisting conditions are not covered unless the pet has been considered cured and has not required treatment for six months. Policy holders can take their pets to any veterinarian, anywhere in the country, which is useful if your Beagle is injured on a trip or at an out-of-town dog show.

Some insurance providers and veterinary clinics offer HMOs or wellness plans for pets, which include vaccinations, heartworm preventive, flea preventive, teeth cleaning, and microchipping at reduced rates.

Just as with human health insurance, the owner pays a deductible before coverage kicks in. The amount of the deductible varies depending on the plan chosen. In general, expect a policy to pay 80 percent of the veterinary expenses up to a given amount, and 100 percent after that, up to the plan limit. Different plans have different benefit levels.

The average annual cost of pet insurance reported by the AAHA survey respondents was $141, with a low of $30 and a high of $500. Rates for pet insurance depend on the animal's age at the time he's insured and the plan chosen. Discounts are available for multiple pets and puppies. Even older pets can be covered, at a higher rate.

Common Health Concerns

5

In This Chapter

- ○ Parasites, Inside and Out
- ○ Illnesses and Emergencies
- ○ Genetic Disease and Disorders

B esides regular veterinary exams and vaccinations, ensuring your Beagle's physical well-being includes keeping him free of parasites and protecting him from accidents, as far as is possible. In this chapter, you'll learn what problems can affect him and how to handle them.

Parasites, Inside and Out

External and internal parasites are the bane of every dog and dog owner. The outdoorsy Beagle is frequently exposed to these critters, so you need to take precautions against them. Besides being irritating, fleas, ticks, and worms carry disease, cause physical problems such as bloody diarrhea and secondary bacterial infections, and can even help transmit other parasites, such as tapeworms. They may also lead to allergic conditions. More than 50 percent of the skin problems seen by veterinarians are flea related. Keeping your Beagle free of parasites is one of the tenets of good health.

What Every Owner Needs to Know

Parasites are organisms that rely on other life forms, such as your Beagle, for their existence. Internal parasites may make a cozy home inside your dog's gut, and external parasites may feast on his blood, like little vampires. These hardy devils can survive for long periods without food, sometimes even in extreme environments. In the past, parasites were often difficult to get rid of, no matter how fastidious a housekeeper one was, but advances in parasite control have made the job almost trouble free.

External Parasites

Among the external parasites that can affect your Beagle are fleas, ticks, and mites. If your dog is scratching frequently or has bald spots or inflamed skin, there's a good chance that external parasites are the culprits.

Fleas These annoying parasites plague dogs just about everywhere. The most common flea is *Ctenocephalides felis,* or the cat flea, although it certainly doesn't discriminate among the canine, feline, and human species.

Depending on where you live, flea season can be as short as four months or it can last year round. Fleas thrive in climates that are warm and moist, not too hot, too wet, or too cold. Unless you live in Antarctica or the Sahara, or above the flea-line in the thin atmosphere of parts of the Rocky Mountains, you're likely at some point to find your Beagle scratching an itch caused by the bite of the pesky flea, which lurks outdoors in grass and piles of leafy debris. Indoor environments are hospitable to fleas as well. They delight in wall-to-wall carpeting, pet bedding, and upholstered furniture.

C. felis is perfectly formed for its mission, which is to latch onto a warm body and suck its blood. The entomological image of Superman, the flea can leap tall dogs in a single bound. A Beagle is hardly a challenge at all. The flea's six legs are fitted with claws that enable it to cling tenaciously to its prey. Attached to its large oval head is a beaky proboscis from which juts a drill-like feeding tube, which the flea drives

If your dog is scratching frequently or has bald spots or inflamed skin, there's a good chance that external parasites are the culprits.

into the body, injecting an anticoagulant that makes it easier to siphon out the blood and, incidentally, causes that ferocious itching. Some dogs are so sensitive to this substance that a single fleabite can result in an orgy of biting and scratching. This agonizing condition is called flea allergy dermatitis (FAD) and produces severe itching, crusty sores, thickened skin, and even bacterial skin infections. Beagles tend to be prone to FAD, and it can make them miserable.

How does the flea know when and where to strike? It reacts to the vibrations caused by footfalls, changes in light caused by the shadow of an approaching body, and the scent of exhaled carbon monoxide. But even more pernicious than the flea's ability to find and attack its victim is its reproductive capability. In a typical life span of six to eight weeks, a single female flea can lay about 2,000 eggs. Assuming that your Beagle is hosting quite a few more than one female flea, the result could be a staggering number of flea eggs, all waiting for the optimum moment to hatch into larvae and begin the life cycle all over again.

Depending on conditions such as temperature and humidity, the flea's life cycle can be as short as 16 days or as long as 21 months. Female fleas lay their eggs on your Beagle. The eggs then fall off the dog and onto carpet or bedding. After incubating for 2 to 12 days, larvae hatch from the eggs and undergo a series of molts over a one- to two-week period. During the final molt, the larvae spin cocoons, inside which they make the transformation to pupae. When conditions are right, they emerge from their cocoons as adult fleas, ready to feast on your dog.

To find out if your Beagle is hosting a colony of fleas, search his coat using a fine-tooth metal flea comb. His medium-short coat offers fleas few hiding places, so you shouldn't have difficulty spotting them. As few as one or two fleas can be evidence that an entire army of the pests is lying in wait throughout your home. Even if you don't find fleas on your dog, there may be more subtle evidence of an infestation: flea dirt, or excreted blood, on his skin. You can identify flea dirt by combing or brushing your Beagle while he's standing on a white towel or piece of paper. If dark flecks fall onto the white area, moisten them to see if they turn red—a sure sign of flea dirt. If so, you then need to treat your dog for fleas.

Fortunately, flea control is easier and safer than ever. New developments include insect growth regulators, or IGRs, which prevent flea larvae from reaching maturity, and pills and topical treatments that are dangerous only to fleas, not your dog. They work by destroying the flea's nervous system or reproductive ability. Some of these products are given only on a monthly or quarterly basis and have made flea control foolproof.

Flea control is available through a pill given monthly or topical solutions applied monthly or quarterly. These products are available from your veterinarian and are the most effective anti-flea weapons you can buy. Some of them are so advanced that they can kill fleas within 2 to 24 hours, and are also effective against ticks, mites, hookworm, and heartworm. Depending on which product your veterinarian recommends, the protection lasts for one to three months and is not affected by sunlight, rain, or shampooing. The topical solutions are an especially good choice for dogs who suffer from FAD, because they work even before the flea bites the dog.

But no matter how safe a product is promised to be, it's still important to read the directions carefully so you understand exactly what it does and how it should be used. For instance, some topicals require you to wear gloves when applying them.

Whatever treatment is recommended by your veterinarian, ask her to explain how it works and why she thinks it's the best choice for your Beagle. In most cases, her recommendation will be based on the climate in your area, the status of your Beagle's health, and whether you are already experiencing an infestation.

If for some reason you decide against using one of the new topical or oral treatments, or if you just want to make sure your home is really free of fleas, you'll need to follow a three-step program of flea control.

Start with a thorough housecleaning. To get rid of eggs, larvae, and pupae,

Did You Know?

Dogs have extremely sensitive hearing and a sense of smell up to 1000 times better than humans to compensate for their relatively poor eyesight.

vacuum every inch of carpeting, curtains, and upholstered furniture—especially under the cushions—and throw away the bag when you're finished. To really give fleas a one-two punch, have the carpet and furniture cleaned professionally and then treated with a nontoxic powder containing borax, which kills fleas by drying them out. This powder is available at pet stores, or you can have it professionally applied. Launder your bedding and that of your dog in hot water. Don't forget to treat the inside of your car or any other place your dog has been. If the fleas at your house are out of control, you may need to use a premise spray around baseboards or beneath furniture, or even a flea "bomb" that permeates the entire living area. Naturally, you and your Beagle (as well as any other pets) need to vacate the house for several hours while the bomb does its work.

You need to treat your yard as well. You can probably get by with spraying around the house, along the fence line, and under and around decks or patios. Keep the yard well raked so fleas won't have piles of debris in which to lay their eggs. If you hire an exterminator, be sure the products he employs are safe for use around pets; double-check his information with your veterinarian before the yard is treated.

Finish the process by applying the topical preventive or by bathing your dog with a flea-control shampoo and treating him with an appropriate flea-control spray or mousse. Do not use veterinary topical treatments with over-the-counter products.

If you're using an over-the-counter flea-control method, choose pyrethrin-based products that are formulated to work together, and read the directions carefully before applying any product. Pyrethrins, derived from chrysanthemums, are the least toxic of the different types of flea-control products you can buy over the counter. Be sure that the product you're using is safe for your dog's life stage. Puppies and old dogs are especially prone to reactions from the toxins in flea-control products, so don't assume that more is better.

Flea control products are formulated for specific uses, which are spelled out in the directions. For instance, never use a premise spray (one made for use in the home or yard) directly on your dog. Most important, be sure you're not mixing two or more products that are dangerous if used together. When in doubt, check with your veterinarian.

The best flea control is prevention, so talk tactics with your veterinarian before a problem begins. Fortunately, systemic treatments such as Advantage, Frontline, Program, Revolution, and TopSpot have made bombing and spraying obsolete except in extreme cases.

Ticks Ticks belong to the arachnid family, which also includes spiders. They have eight legs attached to brown or black tear-shaped bodies and can be as small as a sesame seed or larger, especially if they're engorged with blood. Ticks aren't as widespread as fleas, but they can bring with them more serious problems including: Lyme disease; Rocky Mountain spotted fever (an infection characterized by fever, depression, vomiting, diarrhea, enlarged lymph nodes, discharge from the eyes and nose, and muscle or joint pain); ehrlichiosis (an illness characterized by

> Examine your Beagle for ticks any time he's been outdoors, especially if you live in a tick-infested locale or have been playing in a heavily wooded area.

fever, loss of appetite, eye and nose discharge, and swollen limbs; it can look similar to RMSF or Lyme disease); tularemia (a bacterial disease with signs that include skin lesions, swollen lymph nodes, pneumonia, and weak hindquarters); and babesiosis (a

What Is Lyme Disease?

This tick-borne ailment first made its appearance in 1975 in Lyme, Connecticut, from whence it takes its name. Since then, Lyme disease has been reported in 45 states, with 94 percent of the human cases occurring in California, Connecticut, Massachusetts, Minnesota, New Jersey, New York, Pennsylvania, and Wisconsin. New Mexico, on the other hand, has very few cases of Lyme disease.

The ticks that carry Lyme disease harbor <u>Borrelia burgdorferi</u>, a type of bacterium called a spirochete, which is spread to people and animals through the bite of the tick. The ticks are most active—and the risk of infection is greatest—from late spring to early fall, generally the months of May to September.

As Lyme disease has a variety of symptoms, which may not develop until some time after the bite, it is sometimes difficult to diagnose. People may develop a characteristic skin rash that resembles a bull's-eye, hives, flu-like symptoms, achy muscles and joints, swollen glands, fever, and headaches. Left undiagnosed or untreated, Lyme disease can eventually affect the central nervous system and cause joint damage, heart complications, and kidney problems.

Dogs are as vulnerable to Lyme disease as humans are, and the disease is more difficult to pin down since dogs rarely develop the skin rash seen in people. Common canine signs of Lyme disease are high fever, lack of appetite, and sudden lameness for no apparent reason.

For both people and dogs, antibiotics are the treatment of choice, especially if the disease is caught in its early stages. With later diagnosis, Lyme disease takes longer to respond to treatment.

If you and your Beagle will be venturing through a tick-infested area, protect yourself by wearing clothing that protects your arms, legs, and feet. Tuck pants into socks so ticks won't have access to your skin. Try to keep your Beagle on the trail and away from tall grasses. Checking for and removing ticks promptly will reduce the chance of disease transmission.

protozoal infection characterized by fever, lethargy, and loss of appetite). All of these diseases can be transmitted from ticks to people as well as dogs. If a large number of ticks attach to a dog, they can cause severe anemia or tick paralysis.

North America is home to five main species of ticks: the deer tick, the western blacklegged tick, the Lone Star tick, the Rocky Mountain wood tick, and the American dog tick. The deer tick and the western blacklegged tick transmit Lyme disease, babesiosis, and ehrlichiosis. Rocky Mountain wood ticks and American dog ticks transmit Rocky Mountain spotted fever and tularemia, while the Lone Star tick carries ehrlichiosis and tularemia. These diseases are unpleasant for people and dogs, and serious cases can even be fatal, so don't take these bloodsuckers lightly.

Ticks operate by attaching themselves to the skin, digging in with their sharp mouthpieces. They most commonly attach around a dog's head, neck, ears, feet, and in the folds between the legs and body. When full, they appear bloated and round. Spring and summer are the tick's favorite seasons.

Examine your Beagle for ticks any time he's been outdoors, especially if you live in a tick-infested locale or have been playing in a heavily wooded area. Protect your hands with gloves, then part the fur, and check all the way down to the skin. Ticks can be hard to spot unless they're already swollen with blood, especially if they're on dark areas of your Beagle's coat.

If you find a tick, use tweezers to remove it. The spirochete that causes Lyme disease can enter through your skin, so never touch or crush a tick with your bare hands. Veterinarians at the University of California at Davis School of Veterinary Medicine suggest spraying the tick with a flea-and-tick insecticide to loosen its hold. Then grasp it by the head with the tweezers and pull slowly yet firmly. Try not to leave any of it behind, but don't worry if you do. Just trim the hair around it and bathe the area for a few days with alcohol, hydrogen peroxide, or soap and water. Old wives' tales recommend burning ticks off or covering them with nail polish, petroleum jelly, kerosene, or gasoline, but these methods are all harmful to your dog and should be avoided.

After the tick is removed, drop it in alcohol to kill it. If Lyme disease or some other tick-borne ailment is prevalent in your area, you may want to note in your pet diary the date it was found. Knowing when a tick bit your dog can help your veterinarian make an accurate diagnosis if your Beagle later develops signs of disease.

With his love of the outdoors, your Beagle is likely to be exposed to ticks often. If they're a serious problem in your area, ask your veterinarian to recommend a spray, shampoo, dip, or other treatment against the little bloodsuckers. As noted previously, some new topical products protect against a variety of internal and external parasites, including ticks. Spraying your yard and shrubbery can also help eliminate ticks.

Mites Mites are microscopic members of the arachnid family. Dogs can become infested with any of four species of mites: *Demodex canis,* which causes canine demodicosis, also known as demodectic mange or red mange; *Sarcoptes scabei* var. *canis,* the cause of canine scabies, or sarcoptic mange; *Cheyletiella,* which causes a mild but itchy skin disease; and *Otodectes cynotis,* more commonly known as ear mites.

Demodex mites are characterized by their cigar shape, visible under a microscope. They usually coexist harmlessly with dogs, making their home inside the hair follicles of the skin. Demodicosis develops when the *Demodex* population rages out of control, often in response to stress or illness, and most commonly in puppies, although adults can also develop the disease.

Reddened, scaly skin and patchy hair loss are the classic signs of demodicosis. In puppies, demodicosis is usually localized, occurring on the head—around the eyes and mouth—and on the front legs. Itchiness is uncommon. Your veterinarian can confirm the presence of *Demodex* mites through skin scrapings or a skin biopsy.

Small patches of localized demodicosis rarely require treatment. By the time the dog is about a year old, the condition usually disappears on its own, taken in hand by the immune system. Demodicosis is not contagious, but young Beagles who develop it should be spayed or neutered since veterinary researchers suspect that the disease is related to a genetic defect in immune function and may be heritable.

"When we first got our Beagle puppy, she had some little patches of fur missing on her head," says Jen William. "The breeder, who turned out not to be very reputable, claimed that the pup had just gotten 'a little beat up' by the other dogs since she was the runt of the litter. A trip to the veterinarian confirmed that it was actually mange. She responded well to the treatment of regular baths with a medicated shampoo, a topical medication, and some antibiotic pills."

Demodicosis can become generalized, spreading over the entire body. Dogs with generalized demodicosis show the same signs that characterize localized demodicosis, but the condition is more widespread and severe, especially on the feet, and chronic inflammation causes the skin to become darker and thicker.

Unlike localized demodicosis, the generalized form requires drastic treatment involving frequent dips to kill the mites and antibiotics to stave off secondary bacterial infections. Generalized demodicosis isn't fun for any dog, but it's

Did You Know?

An average of 800 dogs and cats are euthanized every hour in the United States.

especially debilitating to older Beagles, whose immune systems may not be strong enough to fight it off.

Canine Scabies Also known as sarcoptic mange, this skin disease develops when the *Sarcoptes* mite tunnels under your Beagle's skin. The result is intense itching, crusty sores, hair loss, and self-inflicted wounds produced by the dog scratching and biting at the itchy spots. These signs, plus skin scrapings, can help your veterinarian diagnose sarcoptic mange.

Scabies is highly contagious to other dogs and sometimes even spreads to people and cats. If you have a Beagle with scabies, keep him separated from other pets. Any animals that have been in contact with a scabies-infested dog should be treated as well, even if they don't show signs.

Treatment requires a course of medicated baths, usually once a week (most commonly) over a six-week period, using products prescribed by your veterinarian. Short-term use of corticosteroids can help control the itching. Some veterinarians also offer oral medication, which is repeated every two weeks for a minimum of two to three treatments.

Cheyletiella This mildly itchy skin disease occurs most often in puppies and adolescent dogs and is contagious to other animals and people. Fortunately, an infestation of *Cheyletiella* mites isn't very common, especially if you have a good flea-control program. The mites are usually killed by the same treatments that work on fleas.

Cheyletiella mites look like small white specks and are large enough to be seen with the naked eye on the dog's skin or fur. Mild itching and dandruff along the dog's back are indications of *Cheyletiella* infestation. Your veterinarian can confirm the presence of the mites through a skin scraping or just by looking at the dandruff under a microscope. As with other mite infestations, a series of medicated baths and dips is the usual treatment. To rid your home of the mites, perform a thorough housecleaning and be sure other pets are treated if they were exposed to a mite-infested dog.

Ear Mites When these mites house-hunt, they look for the nice, warm moistness of an ear canal. Cats provide their preferred habitat, but they won't turn their noses up at a dog, especially if he has nice floppy ears like the Beagle. Put ear mites on your list of suspects if your dog has dry, reddish-brown or black earwax and frequently shakes his head or paws at his ears. If you carefully scrape out some of the wax with a Q-tip or a tissue wrapped around your finger and look closely at it, you might be able to see the white, pinpoint-size mites moving around.

Unless ears are checked and cleaned regularly, an ear mite infestation can reach the severe stage before it's noticed. A bad case of ear mites can cause hair loss from scratching, bleeding sores around the ears, and can block the entire ear canal. Left untreated, an infestation can eventually lead to serious bacterial or yeast infections.

Treatment is less drastic than for other mite infestations. Your veterinarian will clean the ear canals and prescribe eardrops to kill the mites. The drops must be administered in cycles for at least a month to make sure all the mites are eliminated. In case any of them escape from the ear, a bath is also a good idea.

Ringworm Unlike the previous external parasites, which all belong to the insect family, ringworm is a fungal infection caused by *Microsporum canis,* a plantlike parasite rather than a true worm. Often mistaken for other skin conditions, ringworm is characterized by dry, scaly

skin, hair loss, and sometimes draining sores or itching. Discolored, ring-shaped patches on the skin give it its name. Ringworm is common and contagious, spread through contact with an infected person or pet. It affects dogs, other domestic animals, and people.

The ringworm fungi, or dermatophytes, invade the outer layers of the skin, hair, and nails, where they find sustenance from keratin, a protein derived from dead skin cells. Warmth and high humidity are ideal growth conditions for this fungus, which can be detected by your veterinarian through skin scrapings and fungus cultures.

Ringworm may resolve on its own in one to three months, but meanwhile the dog is shedding spores that can infect all of your other pets—and you. Untreated dogs are also likely to become carriers and may shed spores for months and years even though they look healthy. Rather than partial treatments of lesions, veterinarians recommend whole-body treatment with shampoos or oral antifungal agents to control or eliminate the infection. Topical antibiotic ointment may be needed to treat infected sores. Pets and people who have been in contact with affected dogs should also be treated. To prevent a recurrence, disinfect household surfaces and vacuum thoroughly.

Internal Parasites

Just as nasty as external parasites are internal parasites, which include roundworms, hookworms, tapeworms, whipworms, heartworms, and parasitic protozoa such as *Coccidia* and *Giardia*. Through various methods, they make their way inside your dog, usually settling in his intestines, where they gorge on blood or tissues, robbing your Beagle of vital nutrients, and damaging or killing cells and tissues. Some reproduce inside the dog, eventu-

Collecting a Fecal Sample

When you take your dog outside to eliminate, bring along a plastic sandwich bag and a container in which to store the sample. A clean plastic dish with a lid, such as an empty margarine tub, is ideal.

Place the plastic bag over your hand, pick up the sample, and place it in the container. It should be collected no more than 12 hours before being examined by the veterinarian. Refrigerate it until you can get to the veterinary clinic.

ally resulting in serious physical problems, such as heart blockages (heartworms). Others hitch a ride out via the feces so they can infect other dogs.

Signs of internal parasites include lack of appetite, weight loss, coughing, bloody diarrhea, a low energy level, and anemia. Roundworms and tapeworms can often be seen in feces. Infected puppies may appear potbellied, with rough, dull fur. Fortunately, internal parasites are easily diagnosed, treated, and prevented. Most heartworm preventives, which are given on a monthly basis, also kill roundworms, hookworms, and whipworms. A good flea control program helps prevent tapeworm infection.

When you take your new Beagle puppy to the veterinarian for the first time, the vet will want a fecal sample to examine for parasites or their eggs. Thereafter, an annual fecal exam for intestinal parasites and a blood test for heartworm are a good idea, to make sure your Beagle stays worm free.

If parasites are identified, your veterinarian will prescribe the appropriate medication. Each parasite requires a specific treatment. Your veterinarian can also suggest preventive medication so your dog won't get reinfected. In some cases, you may need to disinfect your home as well. Several weeks after treatment, your veterinarian will want to recheck a stool sample to make sure all the parasites have been killed.

To prevent reinfection, start your dog on preventive medication and keep him away from feces deposited by other animals. No sniffing allowed. Keep your own yard clean by picking up after him as soon as possible, especially if you have young children. Although it's rare, some internal parasites can be transmitted to people, and the most common occurrences involve children who come in contact with feces.

Roundworms These are the most common of the internal parasites. *Toxocara canis* are present in most dogs at birth, having been transmitted through the placenta, or shortly after birth, from the mother's milk. Roundworms are rarely a problem for adult dogs, but a heavy load of them can make a puppy very sick or even kill him.

> Roundworms are rarely a problem for adult dogs, but a heavy load of them can make a puppy very sick or even kill him.

A roundworm-ridden puppy has the potbelly of a seasoned beer drinker, but elsewhere his body looks thin and scrawny and is covered by a dull, rough coat. Other common signs of roundworm infection are vomiting and diarrhea, coughing, or even pneumonia. No matter how sorry for him you may feel, don't buy a Beagle puppy with these signs. Internal parasites are easily treated, but their presence doesn't say much for the breeder's care of the dogs. If you already have a puppy with these signs, take him to your veterinarian for deworming.

It doesn't happen very often, but roundworms can be transmitted to people. Dog-to-human transmission usually occurs when young children touch egg-laden feces or play in dirt or grassy areas where roundworm eggs have been deposited, and then put their hands in their mouths. Prevent roundworm infection by keeping your yard feces free and taking a fecal sample to your vet annually so your dog can be treated for any worms that may be present.

Hookworms Hookworms *(Ancylostoma caninum)* prefer a warm, humid climate, such as that found in the southern United States, but live just about anywhere. They hook up with your dog by penetrating the skin, usually through the feet, or by being transmitted to pups through their mother's milk. Once inside, hookworms travel through the body to the small intestine, where they attach to the intestinal wall and begin sucking out blood. A really heavy load of them can lead to severe anemia. Other signs of hookworm infection include diarrhea, weakness, and weight loss. Hookworms are diagnosed through a stool sample and can be treated with medication, but reinfection occurs quickly if feces aren't picked up daily.

Whipworms These parasites *(Trichuris vulpis)* worm their way inside your dog when he eats something that's been in contact with infective larvae or contaminated soil. They migrate to the large intestine where, like the hookworm, they feed on blood. Dogs can coexist with a small number of whipworms, but too many of them can lead to anemia, diarrhea, and weight loss. Whipworms don't pass eggs on a regular basis, so they are sometimes difficult to diagnose. Your veterinarian may need to run several fecal exams before hitting the jackpot. To prevent reinfection, pick up feces regularly.

Tapeworms Tapeworms *(Dipylydium caninum)* are one of the few internal parasites that can be identified with the naked eye. Tapeworm segments look like small pieces of rice and are often seen clinging to the fur around your dog's rear end or crawling through feces. If you notice either of these situations, take a stool sample to your vet for examination to make sure other worms aren't involved as well.

Fleas and tapeworms work together in infecting your dog. Fleas carry tapeworm eggs, which remain in the flea's intestine until a dog eats the flea. The tapeworm then continues its life cycle inside the dog. Thus, controlling fleas reduces your dog's risk of acquiring tapeworms.

Heartworm This parasite *(Dirofilaria immitis)* is one of the most deadly that can infect your Beagle. Like the tapeworm, the heartworm relies on a partner—in this case, the female mosquito—to complete its life cycle, which begins in the blood of a dog infected with microfilariae, or immature heartworms. When a mosquito bites this dog, it takes in the heartworm larvae, which spend several weeks developing inside the mosquito. The next time the mosquito bites a dog, the infective larvae are injected into his body, where they migrate through the bloodstream to the right side of the heart. There, they grow to adulthood and reproduce, bringing forth more microfilariae to start the process all over again. Adult heartworms can reach a length of up to 14 inches, and large numbers of them will eventually block the heart, causing disease and death. If you live in an area where mosquitoes are common, your Beagle is at risk of heartworm disease. Infected dogs can carry the disease to areas where it normally isn't found.

Signs of heartworm disease include weight loss, a low energy level, and coughing after exertion. A simple blood test or sometimes x rays are needed to confirm the diagnosis. If the disease progresses far enough, the result is congestive heart failure. Treatment, which is lengthy and expensive, involves several doses of a powerful drug to kill the mature heartworms. The body absorbs the worms after they die. In severe cases, the worms must be removed surgically. Several weeks later, the dog receives medication to kill any immature heartworms.

You'll want to get your puppy tested as soon as he's old enough to take preventive medication, which is prescribed only for dogs that are free of heartworm. Depending on where you live, your veterinarian may recommend that you give your dog heartworm preventive year round or only during mosquito season. The medication can be given daily or monthly, depending on your preference. If your dog takes heartworm preventive only part of the year, he will need to be retested annually before going back on the medication. Treatment for heartworms is expensive, not to mention dangerous for your dog, so prevention is the way to go.

Coccidia This protozoal parasite is fairly common, especially in puppies that come from crowded conditions, such as poorly run animal shelters, pet stores, or puppy mills.

There are many forms of *Coccidia,* but the one that usually infects dogs is called *Isospora.* It's diagnosed through a fecal sample that contains the organism's eggs, or oocysts. Diarrhea is one sign of infection especially in puppies, but many adult dogs don't have any outward symptoms. It can be treated with medication, which also helps prevent development of secondary bacterial infections. Reinfection is unlikely as long as your Beagle is removed from the contaminated environment, or if you can effectively

Did You Know?

Dogs and humans are the only animals with prostates.

clean infected kennels or yards. Once established, the coccidial cysts in the environment can be extremely hard to kill.

Giardia Another protozoal parasite, *Giardia,* is also unlikely to infect your Beagle, unless he comes in contact with contaminated drinking water. Unless your dog is backpacking with you in the wilderness and drinking out of streams, you probably don't have to worry about it.

Signs of *Giardia* infection include mild stomach upset and diarrhea. Stools may be light-colored or covered in mucus. Your veterinarian will need a stool sample for a definite diagnosis and can then prescribe appropriate medication.

Illnesses and Emergencies

Being able to care for your Beagle in the event of an emergency could mean the difference between life and death. Of course, you'll want to get her to the veterinarian as soon as possible, but if it's the middle of the night or the clinic is far away, you may need to take matters into your own hands until help is available. Knowing what to do for the following conditions and injuries can allow you to stabilize the situation and prevent further damage.

> Being able to care for your Beagle in the event of an emergency could mean the difference between life and death.

Insect Bites and Stings

Just like people, dogs can be sensitive to the bites and stings of insects such as bees, wasps, and mosquitoes. If your Beagle shows signs of a reaction, such as hives, itching, or swelling, use tweezers to remove the stinger (if it's a bee sting) and apply a soothing paste made with baking soda and water. An ice pack can reduce swelling, and calamine lotion relieves itching. An antihistamine such as Benadryl is useful for treating hives. The amount given is determined by weight. Ask your veterinarian how much to give your dog in case of a reaction. Multiple stings, especially in the head area, can cause more serious reactions, such as swelling around the throat that inhibits breathing, or even shock. If this is the case, get your dog to the veterinarian right away.

Vomiting

Throwing up is a common reaction in dogs, and something as simple as overeating or eating grass or as serious as poisoning can cause it. Occasional vomiting with no other signs generally indicates mild stomach upset and is usually not a problem, but if your dog vomits repeatedly or forcefully (projectile vomiting), or you see blood or fecal material in the vomit, it's time to schedule an immediate trip to the veterinarian. Sporadic vomiting combined with poor appetite and coat condition is also a sign of illness and should be checked out.

Diarrhea

Like vomiting, diarrhea can be a sign of a lot of different things, and it may or may not be serious. Diarrhea often occurs when a dog's diet is changed too abruptly, when she's exposed to different drinking water—on a trip, for instance—or as a result of emotional upset or excitement. Usually, this is a mild form of diarrhea that can be treated by withholding food for a day, then giving a bland diet of chicken and rice for a couple of days to soothe the intestinal tract.

Diarrhea may signal something more serious if it lasts for more than a day, if there's blood in the stool, and/or if it's accompanied by vomiting or fever. Be prepared to tell your veterinarian the color of the diarrhea (yellow or greenish, black and tarry, light-colored, bloody), its consistency (watery, foamy, greasy or mucus-covered), how it smells (rancid, like food or sour milk, or just plain putrid), and its frequency (several times a day or several times an hour).

Choking

Most Beagles will eat anything, just on the off chance that it might be a treat. If your dog chows down on something that gets stuck in his throat, you'll need to take quick action. Signs of choking include coughing, gagging, retching, and pawing at the mouth. If you see this, try to keep the dog calm while you look inside his mouth, opening it by pressing your thumb and forefingers into the upper cheeks. If you can do so safely, try to remove the object by hooking it out with a finger, but take care not to push it in further. Take the dog to the veterinarian right away if you're not successful.

> Most Beagles will eat anything, just on the off chance that it might be a treat.

Bleeding

If your dog is bleeding heavily, you need to get it under control—fast! Put pressure on the wound and keep it there, using a towel or whatever you have available. A sanitary napkin also works well.

Performing the Heimlich Maneuver

Knowing how to do this can save your Beagle's life if she's not getting enough air. Place her on her side, put your palms just behind the last rib, partially covering the rib, and give four quick thrusts to dislodge the object, moving your palms no more than ½ to 1″ with each thrust to avoid breaking ribs or internal organs. Repeat until you're successful. Then take her to the veterinarian to make sure no injury has been done.

Maintain pressure until the bleeding stops or until you can get help. The ears, footpads, and penis bleed more freely than other areas of the body. It may be awkward, but keep pressure on them just as you would any other body part. If the blood is coming from an artery—you can tell if it's spurting bright red—you may need to apply pressure over the artery in the groin to get the bleeding under control so a bandage can be applied. Ask your veterinarian to show you where to press in the event this happens.

Scratches and scrapes aren't life threatening, but it's still a good idea to get the bleeding under control. If the wound is very shallow, you can clean it with three-percent hydrogen peroxide, and apply antibiotic ointment after the bleeding stops. Later, if it is extensive or deep, let your veterinarian take a look at the wound before you use peroxide or ointments. Limit your help to stopping bleeding; flushing with warm water; and seeing the vet within a few hours.

Fractures

The most common causes of fractures are unexpected leaps or falls, gunshot wounds, or being hit by a car. Hunting dogs, of

What Is Shock?

When the body sustains serious injury, its response is to shut down. There's not enough blood flow to meet the needs of all the organs, so they can't function properly. Situations that can induce shock include being hit by a car, blood loss from an injury, poisoning, or dehydration from severe vomiting and diarrhea. Signs of shock are a fast, weak pulse; dry gums; pale or gray lips; rapid, shallow breathing; low body temperature; weakness; and lethargy. If your Beagle is in shock, control any bleeding, keep him still and warm, and seek immediate veterinary help.

course, run the risk of being shot accidentally, and Beagles are frequently hit by cars, with the result being a broken bone or two. If your dog breaks a bone, shock is a very real danger. Keep her as still and warm as possible until you can get to the veterinary clinic. Treating for shock is even more important than splinting the leg.

There are several types of bone fractures. A greenstick fracture is a crack in the bone, which you won't be able to identify by observation. A simple fracture is a complete break, and a compound fracture is a complete break in which the bone actually pokes through the skin. Most veterinarians prefer to see the dog before you treat with at-home splints, which may cause more damage and pain to the dog. If you are tempted to splint, call your vet and ask the best way to apply the splint. Be prepared to tell him where the break appears to be.

How the veterinarian treats a fracture depends on the type and location of the fracture, the dog's size and age, the facilities and abilities of the veterinarian, and the cost of treatment. For instance, minor pelvic fractures may heal well simply with rest. A splint or cast is all that's needed for some greenstick fractures, but more serious cases may require complicated surgery.

Hit by Car

This is a traumatic event, and even a glancing blow can be enough to cause your dog serious harm. As with any other such injury, shock is the main thing you need to be concerned about. Gently place your Beagle on a large tray or some other item that can serve as a stretcher. Try not to move her head or neck in case there's spinal damage. Stop any bleeding, and make sure she's well wrapped up so she'll stay warm. Then get to the veterinary clinic on the double.

Heatstroke/Exhaustion

When temperatures rise to body level or higher, heatstroke or heat exhaustion is a real possibility. For a Beagle, that means about 101°F or more, heat levels that are common in the Midwest, South, and Southwest during the summer. In regions of high humidity, heatstroke can occur with temperatures as low as the mid '80s, especially if the dog is exercising. Your dog should not be out in the heat of the day when temperatures are this high. Dogs cool themselves by panting, and this simply isn't an efficient method when it's hot outside. Nor should you leave your dog in the car on a sunny day, even if it doesn't seem very hot out. The inside of a car heats up rapidly and can reach 130°F in a matter of minutes. Every summer, many dogs die from overheating, even though their owners left them in the car "for only a few minutes." Be extra careful with a very young or old Beagle or one who is overweight or sick;

How to Take Your Dog's Temperature

This is one of those indignities that your Beagle won't enjoy, but it doesn't take long and you can reward him with a treat afterward. It can be helpful to have an assistant to hold the dog so he won't squirm. Lubricate a digital rectal thermometer using K-Y Jelly or petroleum jelly. Gently insert it into the rectum, where it should remain for one minute. The normal canine temperature ranges from 100°F to 102.5°F. Call your veterinarian if your dog's temperature is more than 104°F or less than 100°F.

she's more prone to heat exhaustion or heatstroke than a healthy dog in good condition.

Panting, breathing in through the nose and out through the mouth, facilitates cooling by directing air over the mucous membranes of the tongue, throat, and windpipe, causing evaporation of fluid on the membranes, explains Kathy Gaughan, a veterinarian at Kansas State University's College of Veterinary Medicine. The canine cooling system also dissipates heat by dilating the blood vessels in the skin of the face, ears, and feet.

When dogs become overheated—that is, their temperature rises to more than 102.5°F—they are prone to heat exhaustion or heatstroke. Heat exhaustion usually occurs when a dog overexerts herself on a hot day. The signs of heat exhaustion include a body temperature of 105°F or 106°F, failure to salivate, a dry mouth, lethargy, lack of responsiveness, and loss of appetite. The skin on the inside of her ears may appear flushed and red. If your Beagle shows these signs, get him out of the sun immediately, and bathe her with cool water to reduce her temperature. Be careful not to shock her body with ice water. Set up a fan to blow on her, and encourage her to drink plenty of water. She should be examined by a veterinarian as soon as possible to treat any serious complications.

Dogs with heatstroke become weak or wobbly and may even lose consciousness. They have an extremely high body temperature. "If the body temperature rises to 107 degrees, the dog has entered the dangerous zone of heatstroke," Dr. Gaughan says. The body of a dog with heatstroke is hot to the touch, and the dog may even have seizures. "With heatstroke, the damage that can be done is irreversible. Organs start to shut down, and the veterinarian should be called immediately." Start cooling the dog off, and get her to the veterinarian as soon as possible.

> Remember, only mad dogs and Englishmen go out in the noonday sun.

Heatstroke and heat exhaustion are easy to prevent by making sure your Beagle keeps cool in the dog days of summer. Keep her indoors on hot days, and run the air conditioner or a fan. Don't leave her inside the car on hot days, even with the windows rolled down. Make sure she has a shady area in the yard and access to plenty of fresh, cool water. Set up a child's wading pool so she can take a refreshing dip every now and then. Limit playtime in the heat, and walk her in the morning or evening. Remember, only mad dogs and Englishmen go out in the noonday sun.

Seizures

Some of the reasons a Beagle might suffer a seizure include epilepsy, a blow to the head, or a bee sting. Poisoning, heatstroke, or kidney or liver failure can also bring on seizures.

A seizure is defined as a sudden uncontrolled burst of activity such as jerking legs, foaming at the mouth, making snapping motions, or collapse. The dog may also lose control of her bladder or bowels. A seizure may last only a few seconds or as long as a few minutes, with the dog gradually returning to normal.

If your Beagle has a seizure, simply cover her with something to prevent injury and wait until the seizure ends. There's no danger of your dog swallowing her tongue, so don't try to stick your fingers in her mouth; you'll risk getting bitten. Call your veterinarian to report the seizure and ask what to do. She'll need to perform an exam to determine the cause. Some seizures, such as those caused by epilepsy, can be controlled with medication.

Poisoning

Homes, garages, and yards are full of potential poisons. Even some of the products we use on our dogs, such as flea sprays and dips, are poisons. From antifreeze to aspirin, chocolate to cigarettes, there are a number of items in every home that can kill or seriously affect a Beagle. If your dog shows any signs of poisoning, call your veterinarian or a poison control hotline immediately. You will aid the diagnosis if you know what your dog swallowed and can provide the packaging or a sample of the substance.

Poisons that attack the neurological system include organophosphates and carbamates, which are found in some flea and tick products and lawn and garden pesticides. You may also know them by the names diazinon, fenthion, malathion, carbaryl, and carbofuran. A dog who has gotten into this type of poison seems apprehensive and exhibits high levels of drooling, urination, defecation, vomiting, and diarrhea. Her pupils are the size of pinpoints.

Other neurological poisons include pyrethrins and pyrethroids, also found in flea control products. They are less toxic than organophosphates and carbamates, but the situation is still serious. Excessive salivation, vomiting, diarrhea, and tremors are signs of this type of poisoning, as are extreme excitability or depression.

Some rat and mouse poisons prevent the blood from clotting. If you think your Beagle has eaten any of this kind of poison, rush her to the veterinarian. Labored breathing, refusal to eat, nosebleeds, bloody urine or feces, and tiny hemorrhages on the gums are all indications of this type of poisoning, but you shouldn't wait until you see them to get to the veterinarian.

Your Beagle may not be a smoker, but chomping on cigarettes, cigars, chewing tobacco, or marijuana can still be the death of her. Signs of marijuana or tobacco poisoning are excitement, drooling, vomiting, and muscle weakness, all of which develop in minutes after ingestion. Large amounts lead to coma or death.

Pain relievers such as aspirin, acetaminophen, and ibuprofen aren't safe for your Beagle either. Although a veterinarian may prescribe a small amount of aspirin for pain relief, too much can cause anemia and gastric hemorrhage. And a single 200-mg tablet of ibuprofen is toxic to a small dog, causing painful stomach ulcers. Acetaminophen will severely depress your Beagle as well as cause abdominal pain. If treatment isn't provided, your dog could be dead within 24 hours, just from ingesting a few extra-strength tablets. Other medications that can be harmful to your dog include cold pills, antidepressants, and vitamins.

Luisa Fallon had to take her Beagle, Floyd, to the veterinarian because he was passing bloody urine and seemed in pain. When she thought back to the previous evening, she remembered that Floyd had been particularly interested in a guest's jacket pocket. She had found some strange powder on the kitchen floor the next morning and an unidentified

> ## Did You Know?
> Dogs see color less vividly than humans but are not actually color-blind.

chewed-up wrapper behind the couch later in the afternoon. It turned out that Floyd had stolen and eaten a hangover remedy that contained 500 mg of paracetamol and caffeine. Floyd recovered well after treatment but is scheduled for tests to make sure his liver and kidneys aren't damaged.

Don't forget cleaning agents and automotive products. If swallowed, cleaning products can cause problems ranging from mild stomach upset to severe burns of the tongue, mouth, and stomach. Less than a tablespoon of antifreeze (ethylene glycol) can be deadly. Other common household items that can cause poisoning include mothballs, pennies, potpourri oils, fabric softener sheets, batteries, homemade salt dough, and alcoholic drinks.

Most Beagles aren't choosy about what they eat, so contaminated food foraged from the trash can cause problems, too. If your Beagle suddenly starts vomiting or has bloody diarrhea, a painful and distended abdomen, or shows signs of shock, food poisoning is something to consider. Get her to the veterinarian right away.

To prevent poisoning, keep a tight lid on anything potentially dangerous and store it well out of reach. Whenever possible, don't use or keep anything in your home that you wouldn't want your dog to eat, such as rat poison or snail bait. Graduate to the use of humane traps and release the pests where they won't bother anyone. Use natural deterrents for snails and other garden annoyances (consult a book on organic gardening for ideas), and keep compost heaps enclosed so your dog can't get to them. Wash your dog's feet with mild soap and water if she walks on a yard that's been treated with pesticides. Never give your Beagle

> Never give your Beagle any medication meant for people unless your veterinarian specifically advises it and recommends an appropriate amount.

any medication meant for people unless your veterinarian specifically advises it and recommends an appropriate amount.

Fish Hooks

A Beagle is a great catch, but she doesn't need to be caught on a hook. If your dog tangles with one of these sharp objects and you can't get to a veterinarian quickly for removal, figure out which way the barb is pointing. Then grit your teeth and push it on through the soft tissue. Once it's free, you can use wire cutters to cut the shank next to the barb and remove each piece separately. Your veterinarian may recommend antibiotics to ward off any infection.

Burns

Bathe a burn caused by flame with cool water or cover the area with a cool compress. Avoid treating burns with butter, ointment, or ice. Butter and ointment hold the heat in, and ice damages the skin. Keep the dog warm to prevent shock, and take her to a veterinarian right away.

For chemical burns caused by substances such as battery acid or toilet bowl cleaners, consult the National Animal Poison Control Center for quick advice (or the packaging label). Prevent your pet from licking herself and get her to the vet immediately.

Allergic Reactions

Frantic scratching and biting at the skin is a sure sign that your Beagle is suffering from an allergy of some sort. Allergies can also manifest themselves in

First-Aid Kit Essentials

- ○ Your veterinarian's phone number
- ○ An after-hours emergency clinic's phone number
- ○ The National Animal Poison Control Center's hotline number: (800) 548-2423 or (900) 680-0000
- ○ Rectal thermometer
- ○ Tweezers
- ○ Scissors
- ○ Penlight flashlight
- ○ Rubbing alcohol
- ○ Hydrogen peroxide (three percent)

- ○ Syrup of ipecac and activated charcoal liquid or tablets (poisoning antidotes)
- ○ Anti-diarrheal medicine
- ○ Dosing syringe
- ○ Nonstick wound pads, gauze squares, and roll cotton to control bleeding
- ○ Adhesive tape
- ○ Elastic bandage
- ○ Styptic powder (in case nails are cut too short)

other ways, from skin problems such as rashes and hot spots to sneezing, coughing, face rubbing, and foot licking. When no other cause is present, suspect allergies if your Beagle develops ear infections, vomiting, loose stools, or gas.

Allergies can develop in response to inhaled substances, such as pollen; to particular types of food, most commonly corn, wheat, soy, beef, or dairy products; or to materials with which the animal comes in contact, such as wool or carpet; to fleas, or even to cats. The scratching, biting, licking, and rubbing at that ever-persistent itch lead to infection characterized by red bumps and pimples. If you've ever had allergies, you know how uncomfortable they can be, so get veterinary advice as soon as possible.

Inhalant allergies, also known as atopy or allergic inhalant dermatitis, are usually diagnosed after fleas or other possible causes have been eliminated, but sometimes skin tests are necessary. Treatment can range from dietary supplements and medicated shampoos to drugs such as antihistamines and steroids to regular allergy shots. This can be a very frustrating condition to treat; rarely is there a quick solution.

In the same vein, food allergies are usually diagnosed after other possible conditions are ruled out. Again, treatment is long term, beginning with feeding a hypoallergenic diet for six weeks. This type of diet contains ingredients to which the dog has never been exposed. Because the variety of proteins used in dog foods has greatly increased over the years, today's hypoallergenic diets often contain unusual ingredients such as catfish or herring. If signs of the allergy disappear, ingredients are added back to the dog's diet, one at a time, until it's discovered which one causes the reaction. Then that substance is eliminated from the dog's menu.

The diagnosis of contact allergies, or irritant contact dermatitis, is based on owner observations or sometimes skin tests. Washing the exposed areas to remove the irritant is helpful, but the main thrust of treatment is to prevent reexposure.

The degree of allergy is indicated by the degree of itching and subsequent damage the dog does to his skin, says William Fortney, D.V.M., a veterinarian at the Kansas State University Veterinary Medical Teaching Hospital. "A mild case will produce a mild reaction, but a more intense allergic reaction will cause more scratching." Some dogs inherit atopic allergies. When you're looking at puppies, check out the parents to make sure they don't seem to be scratching excessively for no apparent reason.

> Frantic scratching and biting at the skin is a sure sign that your Beagle is suffering from an allergy of some sort.

Eye Problems and Injuries

When we wake up, one of the first things we do is rub our eyes to get the "sleepies" out. That dried, crusty stuff accumulates in the corners of our eyes while we sleep, but it's not harmful and it's easy to get rid of. Very mildly goopy eyes are a common affliction of dogs as well. Like people, dogs produce tears—a combination of mucus and water—as a way of cleansing and lubricating the eye. As the tears drain, the result is a watery or mucus-like discharge that can be clear, whitish, cloudy, light yellow, brownish, or reddish. A small amount in the corner of the eye in the morning is normal and can simply be wiped away with a dampened tissue, paper towel, or soft washcloth (use warm water but no soap). Heavier discharges often indicate low grade or chronic infections and need to be treated by your vet.

Some eye discharge, though, can be a sign of serious injury or disease. Thick, greenish gunk or heavy amounts of normal discharge are a clue that a visit to the veterinarian is in order. It's especially important if the eye is red or swollen or the dog is squinting or pawing at his eye. A normal eye is bright and shiny. Your dog should look out of it at you without pain. If squinting is persistent and painful, or associated with redness, cloudiness, or discharge, your veterinarian needs to have a look right away. Early diagnosis and treatment could save your dog's vision.

Eye problems can run the gamut from irritation or injuries to allergies, inflammation, or infection, and dry eye. A swipe from a cranky cat or a brush with sharp-edged foliage can scratch your Beagle's cornea. Blowing dust, dirt, or debris can also injure a dog's eyes when she hangs her head out the car window. Grass seeds or particles can enter the eye when she runs through tall grass.

During the pollen season, many dogs have mild allergies, which are manifested in red, itchy, watery eyes.

Conjunctivitis, also known as pink eye, occurs when the eye's normal population of bacteria and fungi get out of control. The viruses that cause distemper and canine hepatitis can also cause conjunctivitis. Some forms of conjunctivitis are highly contagious between dogs. Keratitis, or inflammation of the cornea, results from injury or infection.

A thick, sticky discharge is often a sign of a condition called keratoconjunctivitis sicca, more commonly called dry eye. The eyes become dry and irritated, because the dog isn't producing enough tears. Dry eye typically affects older dogs.

When irritation occurs from a speck of dust or dirt, blinking usually produces tears that clean the eye. You can also bathe the eyes with preservative-free saline solution, such as that used for rinsing contact lenses. Never use any ointments or eyedrops without checking first with your veterinarian. Drops containing any type of steroid that are put on an eye with a scratch or puncture can permanently damage the eye.

If an irritated eye doesn't improve within a day, or your dog is reluctant to open his eye, take him in for a veterinary exam. Be sure you don't clean the eyes before the visit. The veterinarian needs to see the discharge to get an idea of the disease and treatment course. If you treated the eye with saline solution or some other mixture, be sure to tell the vet what you used. All the information you can provide is helpful. Once your vet diagnoses the problem, she will prescribe eyedrops or ointments containing antibiotics or anti-inflammatories.

Did You Know?

The tallest dog on record was 42 inches tall at the shoulders and weighed 238 pounds.

Electric Shock

Like all young dogs, Beagle puppies are explorers. Lacking hands, they use their mouths to discover the world around them. Chomping down on an electrical cord isn't the best sort of discovery, though. It can lead to electrical burns on the corners of the mouth or on the tongue and palate, or even electrical shock.

Signs of electric shock are convulsions, loss of consciousness, and slow respiration. Severe shock can cause the heart to stop beating. Before you touch a dog that has suffered electrical shock, switch off the electrical source. Then scoop her up and get to the veterinarian right away. If the heart has stopped, you may need to perform cardiopulmonary resuscitation first. Ask your veterinarian to show you how so you'll be prepared.

Frostbite and Hypothermia

Prolonged exposure to cold temperatures can cause frostbite or hypothermia. Frostbite is most common in dogs that are young, old, or ill, especially if they have short coats. It usually affects the feet, tail, and ear tips. Signs of frostbite are pale skin which later reddens and becomes hot and painful to the touch, swelling, and peeling. Don't cause further damage by massaging the skin or applying hot compresses; instead, thaw the areas slowly with warm, moist towels that you change frequently. Stop warming the skin as soon as it regains its normal color. Treat the dog for shock and get veterinary help quickly.

Hypothermia is a dangerous reduction in body temperature, which occurs after prolonged exposure to cold temperatures. If your Beagle is shivering exces-

Skin Disease

The skin is the body's largest external organ, and it's a good overall indicator of your Beagle's health. Nice pink skin that's odor free, unblemished, and covered with shiny fur is a mark of great health. When your dog isn't doing too well, though, the signs are often mirrored in his coat. You may notice rough, dull fur, hair loss, or a bad smell. Once begun, skin problems can be difficult to treat, especially if the underlying problem isn't identified. Besides parasites and allergies, some of the problems that can cause poor skin condition are bacterial infection, hypothyroidism, and autoimmune disease.

Bacterial infections rarely occur on their own. They usually attack once an allergy or other underlying disease has made the first penetration. That's why veterinarians often prescribe antibiotics in addition to other treatments—to stop bacteria in their tracks. Hot spots and pyodermas are other forms of infection, which are usually treated with shampoos and topical antibiotics. Keeping the dog from biting or scratching at the area is also important and may require the use of an Elizabethan collar (which resembles a lampshade) to prevent contact.

Hypothyroidism is a deficiency of thyroid hormone, which often manifests itself in symmetrical hair loss, a dull, dry coat, weight gain without an increase in appetite, intolerance to cold, and scaly skin. It's a common problem in Beagles.

Autoimmune disease, such as lupus, immune-mediated arthritis, and pemphigus, occurs when the body mistakenly attacks itself. There are several autoimmune skin diseases, which are usually diagnosed through biopsy. Diet, immune-mediating drugs, and the judicious use of steroids all play a role in treatment.

sively or seems unusually inactive or lethargic, warm her up quickly. Dry her off if she's wet from snow, and wrap her in a blanket, preferably one that's straight out of the dryer so it's extra warm. Take her to the veterinarian if she doesn't seem to recognize you or loses consciousness.

Genetic Disease and Disorders

Like every breed, the Beagle suffers from several health problems that are hereditary in nature. A careful breeder works hard to eliminate these problems from her line, but there's no such thing as a perfect dog. No matter how much testing or how careful the breeding, sometimes these diseases just pop up and must be dealt with. The most common hereditary problems found in Beagles are cherry eye, chondrodysplasia, epilepsy, and hypothyroidism. Also seen in Beagles, although less frequently, are eye problems such as glaucoma, cataracts, retinal dysplasia, and progressive retinal atrophy; hip dysplasia; luxating patellas; intervertebral disk disease; pyruvate kinase deficiency, polycystic kidney disease, beagle pain syndrome, and pulmonic stenosis, a heart defect. Naturally, Beagles with any of these conditions should never be bred (although exceptions are made for cherry eye because it is easily repaired). It would be cruel and unethical to pass on health problems to another generation of dogs and dog owners.

Cherry Eye

This swelling of the gland of the third eyelid (nictitating membrane), also known as glandular hypertrophy, is common in Beagles. It occurs when the tear gland at the base of the third eyelid becomes enlarged, protruding from the edge of the eyelid. This protrusion looks like a round, red mass, hence the name. It can occur in one or both eyes, and sometimes affects every puppy in a litter. Occasionally the gland can be repositioned manually and the problem treated with anti-inflammatory medication, but more commonly surgery is required to suture the gland in place. It's important to retain the gland rather than simply remove it because otherwise the dog could become prone to dry eye (keratoconjunctivitis sicca). Cherry eye isn't very pretty to look at, but it's not necessarily painful for the dog.

Other Eye Problems

Beagles have been known to develop dry eye, glaucoma, cataracts, retinal dysplasia, and progressive retinal atrophy. The best breeders have their breeding stock certified clear of eye problems by the Canine Eye Registry Foundation (CERF).

Dry eye is the result of decreased tear production and is most common in older dogs. The eye looks dull and may have a thick, stringy discharge. Infection gives the conjunctiva—the mucous membrane that lines the eyelids and covers the white surface of the eyeball—a red, inflamed appearance. Dry eye should be treated with medication so that there's no permanent damage. In some cases, the dog requires regular application of artificial tears.

Glaucoma, another disease of old dogs, is an increase in fluid pressure inside the eye. It often occurs when the lens is displaced, blocking the outflow of fluid from the eye. If the pressure from the fluid buildup isn't relieved, the condition becomes painful and eventually destroys the retina (the light-sensitive layer of cells at the back of the eye), and the dog is blinded. Glaucoma can be treated with medication, which must be given for the rest of the dog's life.

Cataracts, or clouding of the eye lens, are most common in dogs older than five years of age. Some cataracts are hereditary while others are acquired. For example, cataracts commonly develop in old dogs, simply as a result of the aging process. Many dogs with cataracts still retain enough vision to get around without a problem. Most dogs compensate for decreased vision with their sense of smell, an easy trick for a Beagle. Cataracts can also be removed surgically with excellent results.

Retinal dysplasia, the abnormal development of the retina through folding or displacement, is a congenital disorder, meaning that it's present at birth. It may or may not be hereditary. Dogs with retinal dysplasia can have very mild, almost undetectable, visual problems, or they can become blind. No treatment is available.

> Most dogs compensate for decreased vision with their sense of smell, an easy trick for a Beagle.

Progressive retinal atrophy (PRA) is an inherited retinal degeneration. Dogs with PRA have trouble seeing in dim light and eventually lose their vision altogether. Early signs of PRA are a dog's reluctance to move around in dimly lit areas or go down stairs, or staying unusually close to his owner. No treatment is available, but blind dogs can learn to get around quite well by relying on their sense of smell.

Chondrodysplasia

Also known as chondrodystrophy or multiple epiphyseal dysplasia, this condition of the long bones and vertebral bodies occurs when there is a failure in the growth centers within the cartilage precursors (precursors are a substance from which another substance—in this case, cartilage—is formed) and bones. The result is a Beagle with short, crooked legs as well as shortened, misshapen vertebrae, which can contribute to intervertebral disk disease. Essentially, this condition is a form of dwarfism. Besides being small, chondrodysplastic Beagles have crooked front legs, cow hocks in the rear, and a roached, or hunched, back. They sometimes walk with a limp.

Chondrodysplasia is identified by these physical signs and can be confirmed with x rays at three to eight weeks of age. The x rays show tiny areas of calcification that look like stippling or mottling. Some puppies with chondrodysplasia fail to thrive and don't live very long, but those who survive make fine, loving—if funny-looking—pets, and should have the same life expectancy as any other Beagle. Owners of chondrodysplastic Beagles need to protect their dogs from injury and may need to give aspirin or other pain relievers (as prescribed by the veterinarian) to relieve achy bones.

Judy Watts' Beagles, Hannah and Virginia, are both chondrodysplastic. Their looks give them the appearance of puppies, even though they're eight years old, and they're both highly social, which seems to be characteristic of dogs with this condition. "It's a trait that breeders have told me a lot of chondrodystrophic Beagles have," Watts says. "At the national specialty last year, several breeders told me that their favorite dogs of all time were affected dogs, because along with the chondrodystrophy seems to come a gene making them very sweet and gentle and kind dogs."

Orthopedic problems can affect chondrodystrophic Beagles, especially as they age. "They each have some disk problems that seem to be seasonal—this is the second fall that Hannah has had an inflammation in her disks, and Virginia had one as well this fall," Watts says. "They seemed to be fine after their course of prednisone. If they have to go on prednisone once a year for the rest of their lives, and that will help keep them from having to have surgery, then it's not such a bad thing. Virginia had surgery two years ago for a partially ruptured cervical disk. It was completely successful, but of course that doesn't preclude disks in other areas of the spine from having problems."

Watts gives Hannah and Virginia chondroitin and glucosamine supplements, which she hopes will help stave off arthritis related to the chondrodystrophy. Her veterinarian agrees that it may well help them and certainly won't hurt them.

Epilepsy

Epilepsy is a seizure disorder. Seizures are mysterious, the result of a temporary dysfunction of the brain. They can occur only once in a dog's life or on a frequent basis. Seizures can result from an injury to the head or from bacterial infections of the brain, or be inherited. Recurring seizures or convulsions without other cause are characterized as epilepsy. Beagles are among the breeds known to have an inherited, or idiopathic, form of epilepsy. The term idiopathic means "of unknown cause" and it's applied to seizures in dogs who have no other discernible disease or abnormality that could cause seizures. (For more about seizures, see page 171 in this chapter.) Epilepsy usually appears between one and five years of age, although it can develop as early as three weeks or as late as nine years. Anxiety, excitement, fatigue, or noise can trigger seizures. In females, seizures can be brought on by estrus. Epilepsy is often treatable with medication, but there is no cure for the disease.

Hypothyroidism

This is the most common hormonal disorder affecting dogs, and it's especially common in Beagles. Hypothyroidism is a decrease in thyroid function, caused by low levels of thyroid hormone (T_3 and T_4). Thyroid hormone is important for the entire body, so a decrease can cause many different types of problems. Dogs with hypothyroidism often display poor skin and coat condition, such as a dull, dry, or scaly coat and symmetrical hair loss on the tail and trunk; weight gain for no apparent reason; lack of energy or unwillingness to exercise; and mental dullness, becoming forgetful or having a shorter attention span. Sometimes the reproductive system is affected.

If your Beagle shows these signs, your veterinarian will recommend a blood test to determine the level of circulating thyroid hormone. If it's lower than normal, the problem can be treated with synthetic thyroid hormone, given in the form of a pill. This is not a cure because it must be given for the rest of the dog's life, but it will most likely restore your Beagle to his normal self. Hypothyroidism is most common in middle-aged or older dogs, but it can show up between two and six years of age.

Samantha was five years old when her owners took her to the veterinarian because of the hair loss on her rear end. A blood test showed that her thyroid hormone levels were indeed lower than normal, a problem that was easily solved with the addition of a tiny pill to her food at each meal. She gobbled it down without even noticing it.

Intervertebral Disk Disease

Veterinary neurologist Cleta Sue Bailey defines the intervertebral disks as fibrous, gelatinous "pillows" that cushion the vertebrae (blocklike bones through which the spinal cord runs) and absorb the stresses and shocks of movement. When these disks degenerate, or rupture, the result is severe neck and back pain. You may also hear this condition referred to as a herniated disk or a slipped disk. Dachshunds are most often associated with intervertebral disk disease, but Beagles are next in frequency.

Disk disease can be gradual in nature, brought on by repetitive stress such as jumping off furniture, or it can strike suddenly. Your Beagle will act as if his back is hurting him, limping or walking hunched over, perhaps panting, with a look of pain on his face. Severe disk disease can even cause paralysis of the rear legs. If a neck disk is affected, the dog may carry his head rigidly or be unable to lower his head to eat. That's when you really know there's something wrong with your Beagle. Patting him on his head causes him to cry out in pain.

Rest and anti-inflammatory medications can help ease the pain and reduce swelling. Sometimes hospitalization is required to keep the dog quiet and still. In some cases, surgery is the only answer. Judy Watts' Beagle Virginia had one cervical disk partially rupture. "If she hadn't had surgery, she would have been in pain for the rest of her life and might have become paralyzed," Watts says. "I had no intention of putting her to sleep when a surgical alternative was available. It was expensive and very stressful, but she's had no further problems with that part of her spine."

Hip Dysplasia

This condition is primarily thought of as affecting dogs weighing more than 35 pounds, but it can occur in smaller breeds as well. Hip dysplasia occurs when the head of the femur (thighbone) doesn't fit properly in the cup (acetabulum) of the hip joint. When the cup is too shallow, the joint is lax, meaning that the bone can slip around inside it instead of fitting solidly.

Hip dysplasia is diagnosed through x rays. It can range from mild to severe, with some dogs never showing signs and others developing lameness at an early age. Take your Beagle to the veterinarian if you see him limping after exercise, walking with a waddling gait, having trouble getting up or lying down, or showing reluctance to move.

Mild cases can be treated with anti-inflammatories, plus moderate exercise to encourage muscle mass and tone. Sometimes, surgery—which ranges from making minor changes in the shape of the femur to total hip replacement—is the only way to relieve the dog's pain.

The development of hip dysplasia depends on multiple factors, both genetic and environmental. If both parents are free of hip dysplasia, there is a much greater chance of their offspring not having hip problems, says James Roush, DVM, associate professor of small-animal surgery at Kansas State University School of Veterinary Medicine. In addition, keeping a dog on the proper diet and minimizing weight gain can reduce the risk of developing hip problems. Most puppy foods contain 0.5 to 1.5 percent calcium, which is the ideal amount, Dr. Roush says. Dog foods containing more than three percent calcium are more likely to lead to hip dysplasia or other skeletal problems.

Luxating Patella

Luxating patella is a fancy way of saying dislocated kneecap. You may also hear the condition referred to as patellar luxation or slipped stifle. When the patella, or knee, luxates, it slips out of the socket. The condition can occur in one or both knees.

Dogs that are prone to patellar luxation usually have weak ligaments, misaligned tendons, or grooves that are too shallow or narrow to hold the knee in place. When the knee pops out, usually toward the body, your Beagle may hop like a bunny or have a hard time straightening the knee. The knee can do the hokey-pokey, slipping in and out of place, or it can slip out and stay

Did You Know?

The average gestation period for a dog is 63 days.

out. The severity of patellar luxation is graded from one to four, with one being the least serious and four being the most severe.

If your Beagle has grade one or two patellar luxation, you should be able to keep the problem under control by keeping his weight at a normal level and strengthening the muscles around the knee with mild uphill exercise. A veterinarian may recommend dietary supplements such as glycoflex or glucosamine to rebuild cartilage. Surgery is an option for dogs with grade three or four luxation. After surgery, encourage use of the joint with slow exercise on leash and on level ground. Keep the pace at a walk so your dog doesn't "cheat" by skipping on his bum knee.

Pyruvate Kinase Deficiency

Beagles with this problem are born with a lack of pyruvate kinase, an enzyme that is required to maintain the health of red blood cells. Affected dogs develop anemia, and you may notice pale gums, weakness and reluctance to exercise. They may also have a fast heart beat, enlarged spleen and heart murmurs. Your veterinarian can diagnose the disease by measuring PK activity of the red blood cells.

The only cure for the problem is bone marrow transplant, which is usually too costly to be reasonable for most owners. PKD is inherited as an autosomal recessive, which means both parents must carry the gene to produce a PK deficient puppy. The affected dog and his parents should not be bred.

Polycystic Kidney Disease

In some Beagles, the kidneys are damaged by the formation of cysts—fluid filled pockets—that destroy kidney tissue. The cysts often start small and enlarge slowly. Both kidneys will almost invariably become affected. While one or two cysts may do no serious harm, when they become numerous or very large they can destroy so much tissue that the kidney can no longer function and kidney failure results.

There is no treatment for the disease, although cysts that become infected require rapid and aggressive antibiotic therapy to avoid fatal body-wide infection which can follow. Affected Beagles can live well for many years, but PKD is considered fatal in the long run. The disease is inherited, and dogs with it should not be bred.

Beagle Pain Syndrome

This problem has most often been reported in colonies of research Beagles, but it is occasionally found in pets. Affected Beagles have sore, stiff necks and will cry in pain if the neck is patted or manipulated. They may run a fever, lose their appetite and stand in a hunched position. This pain is caused by a sterile meningitis (inflammation of the lining of the spinal cord and brain) and by inflammation of small blood vessels in the neck. The problem is not caused by infection, and most dogs recover well with steroid therapy. By 18 to 24 months of age, the painful episodes usually end and the dog can lead a normal life. No one knows exactly why this occurs, but it is thought to be due to an inherited immune system disorder.

Pulmonic Stenosis

It's not especially common in the breed, but Beagles occasionally develop pulmonic stenosis, which occurs when the connection narrows between the right ventricle and the pulmonary artery. The result is an increased resistance to blood flow, which makes it more difficult for the right ventricle to pump blood. The muscle tissue in the heart thickens and becomes enlarged.

A Beagle with pulmonic stenosis may show few outward signs. The problem is usually discovered when the veterinarian hears a murmur through the stethoscope and confirms the diagnosis with a chest x ray and electrocardiogram. Heart failure from this condition is rare, but if your dog has a severe form of it, surgery can usually correct the problem.

By knowing how to recognize and care for the various problems that can affect your Beagle, you'll be better prepared than most dog owners to give him a safe and healthy life.

6

Basic Training for Beagles

By Liz Palika

In This Chapter

- When to Begin Training
- The Teaching Process
- What Every Good Beagle Needs to Know

All dogs, including Beagles, need training to learn how to behave themselves. When your Beagle learns to greet people by sitting still, he won't jump up on them. When he learns what the word "quiet" means, you can control his howling so neighbors won't complain about the noise. By learning how to teach your dog, you can train him so that he learns the important rules necessary for good behavior.

Does your Beagle howl? Does he try to escape from your yard? If he gets out of the yard, does he refuse to come when you call him? Does he raid the trashcan? Does he jump on your guests? These are not unusual behaviors for a young, untrained dog, but they are unnecessary, annoying, and potentially dangerous behaviors that can be changed (or at least controlled) through training.

Your Beagle howls because his breed was designed to call (or howl) while hunting. By the dogs' howls, the hunter then knew where his hounds were and where the chase was going. A Beagle's howl is loud and, in a suburban neighborhood, that howl can be very annoying!

Just as howling is a natural behavior, so are some of your Beagle's other unwanted actions. He likes to escape from the yard so that he can play with the neighborhood kids. He may also try to escape because he's alone; Beagles are pack animals used to hunting and living in a pack and a Beagle alone is an unhappy dog. He may raid the trashcan because he finds food in it or because it's fun. He jumps on guests because he's excited to see them and they are much taller than he is.

With training, your Beagle can learn to control himself, so he's not reacting to every impulse. He can learn to sit while greeting people, instead of covering them with muddy paw prints or ripping their clothes. He can learn to restrain some of his vocalizations and to ignore the trashcans.

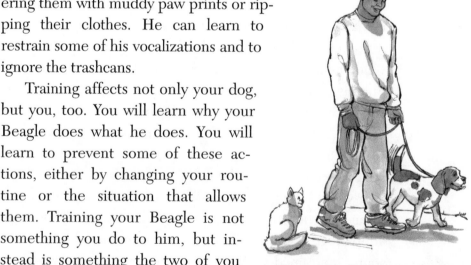

Training affects not only your dog, but you, too. You will learn why your Beagle does what he does. You will learn to prevent some of these actions, either by changing your routine or the situation that allows them. Training your Beagle is not something you do to him, but instead is something the two of you do together.

A well-trained dog will accept your guidance even when he would rather be doing something else.

Basic Commands
Every Dog Should Know

Sit: Your dog's hips move to the ground while his shoulders remain upright.

Down: Your dog lies down on the ground or floor and is still.

Stay: Your dog remains in position (sit or down) while you walk away from him. He holds the stay until you give him permission to move.

Come: Your dog comes to you on the first call, despite any distractions.

Walk on the leash: Your dog can walk ahead of you on the leash but does not pull the leash tight.

Heel: Your dog walks by your left side with his shoulders by your left leg.

Buster is a one-and-a-half-year-old Beagle owned by Joan Fritz and her family, of Oceanside, California. Buster is a very active young dog. As is normal for Beagles, his nose is always busy, sniffing here and sniffing there, searching for ever more exciting scents. Joan enrolled Buster in training class while he was still a puppy. "I realized that I needed help training Buster when I called him to come and he acted as if he couldn't hear me. He never even twitched an ear!" Joan feared that if Buster were off leash outside the yard, he would ignore her and end up running away or being hit by a car. With training, Buster has matured into a very nice dog who behaves quite well and is participating in advanced training, including off leash agility training.

Training is an ongoing process. As you learn how to teach your dog, you can apply the training to every aspect of your dog's life. He can learn how to behave at home, to ignore the trashcans, to restrain himself from chasing the cat, and to chew on his own toys instead of your shoes. He can also learn how to behave while

What a Trained Dog Knows

A trained dog knows:

❍ The appropriate behaviors allowed with people (no biting, no mouthing, no rough play, and no mounting).

❍ Where to relieve himself and how to ask to go outside.

❍ How to greet people properly without jumping on them.

❍ To wait for permission to greet people, other dogs, and other pets.

❍ How to walk nicely on a leash so that walks are enjoyable.

❍ To leave trashcans alone.

❍ To leave food that is not his (on the counters or coffee table) alone.

❍ Not to beg.

❍ To chew on his toys and not things belonging to people.

❍ That destructive behavior is not acceptable.

❍ To wait for permission to go through doorways.

A trained dog is a happy dog who is secure in his place in the family.

out in public, including greeting people while sitting instead of jumping up. Your dog will learn, through practice and repetition, that the training applies to his behavior everywhere he goes and all the time—not just at home and not just during training sessions.

When to Begin Training

Ideally, training should begin as soon as you bring your new Beagle home. If you have an eight- to ten-week-old puppy, that's okay. Your new puppy can begin learning that biting isn't allowed, that she should sit for treats, petting, and meals, and where she should go to relieve herself. By 10 weeks of age, you can attach a

Puppy Kindergarten

The ideal time to begin group training is as soon as your Beagle puppy has had at least two sets of vaccinations, usually between 10 and 12 weeks of age. Many veterinarians recommend that you wait even longer. Ask your vet what she thinks. Puppy kindergarten classes introduce the basic obedience commands—sit, down, stay, and come—all geared for a puppy's short attention span. Puppy classes also spend time socializing the puppy to other people and other puppies.

small leash to her collar and let her drag it around for a few minutes at a time so she gets used to it. Always watch her closely, of course, so that she doesn't get the leash tangled in something and choke herself. Young puppies have a very short attention span, but are capable of learning and are eager students.

Don't let your Beagle pup do anything now that you don't want her to do later when she is full grown. For example, if you don't want her up on your lap when she's 20 pounds of rough paws and hard elbows, don't let her on your lap now. It will be that much harder to change the habit later. Keep in mind as you begin your dog's training that, although Beagles are not large dogs, they are strong-willed, sturdy dogs with a forceful personality.

Start training early so that your puppy learns good behavior instead of bad habits.

Basic Obedience Class

Most obedience instructors invite puppies to begin the basic obedience class after they have graduated from a puppy class or after a puppy has reached four months of age. Dogs (or older puppies) over four months of age who have not attended a puppy class still go to a basic obedience class. This class teaches the traditional obedience commands—sit, down, stay, come, and heel. In addition, most instructors spend time discussing problem behaviors such as jumping on people, barking, digging, chewing, and other destructive activity. A group class such as this helps your Beagle learn to control himself around other dogs and people.

If you have adopted a Beagle who is an older puppy or an adult, you can still begin training right away. Your new dog will need time to get used to you and her new home; however, training will help her learn what you expect of her and, as a result, make the adjustment easier.

Start teaching your Beagle the household rules right away. If you don't want her on the furniture, never allow her on it, and don't make any excuses or explain away her actions—"Oh, it's cold tonight so I'll let her come up and cuddle!" If you aren't consistent, she won't be either!

Is It Ever Too Late?

Although training is most effective when started early in the dog's life and practiced consistently while she grows up, that doesn't mean it's too late to train an adult Beagle. The down side to starting training later in the dog's life is that you then have to break bad habits as well as teach new commands. With a young puppy,

Private Training

Private training is normally recommended for Beagles with severe behavior problems, such as biting, growling, dog aggression, or uncontrolled behavior. Private training is conducted one-on-one, either at your home or at the trainer's facility. The trainer can usually tailor sessions to your dog's individual needs.

you're starting with a blank slate and you can teach new behaviors before she learns bad habits. If you've ever had to break a bad habit (smoking, for example), you know it can be difficult. With the majority of Beagles up to about eight years of age, however, you can control most bad habits with consistent training and lots of patience.

If your dog is older than eight years of age, your success at changing bad habits is going to be more limited. You can teach new commands—sit, down, stay, and heel—and your dog will be able to learn these without too much trouble. But trying to stop a problem howler will be far more difficult, and Beagles who have not learned to come reliably on command by eight years of age will probably never be trustworthy.

Sometimes there are behavioral problems that are just too severe and impossible to solve. A habit may be too deeply ingrained or the stimulus causing the behavior is too strong. For example, if your dog has been raiding the trashcans, he has learned there is food in them. If he is motivated by food (as most Beagles are!), then each time he finds food he is rewarded. You will have a hard time changing this behavior because the reward is too strong an incentive. Instead of fighting it, simply prevent it from happening by making the trashcans inaccessible to your dog.

Basic Dog Psychology

Archeologists have found evidence that humans and the ancestors of today's dogs, wolves, shared a history dating back thousands of years. At some point, humans and individual wolves decided to cooperate. Why? We don't know. Perhaps the wolves, being themselves efficient hunters, aided the human hunters. Perhaps the wolves took advantage of the human's garbage heap. Though we don't know why this cooperation occurred, we know that it did and the result was domesticated dogs.

Families and Packs

In the wild, wolves live in packs. The pack is made up of a dominant male, a dominant female, several subordinate adults, a juvenile or two, and the latest litter of pups. Only the two dominant animals breed, while the others all help protect and provide for the youngsters. In addition to the breeding restriction, the pack has other important social rules, and these rules are seldom broken. If a youngster breaks a rule inadvertently or on purpose, an adult corrects him fairly but firmly. The correction of the errant youngster may consist of a growl, posturing over him, or even the physical correction of pinning him to the ground. If an adult breaks a rule, the correction given by the dominant male or female is much stronger. After all, an adult is expected to know the rules and follow them. An adult that continually creates havoc by breaking the rules may be exiled from the pack.

Packs are usually fairly harmonious. Each member knows his or her place and keeps to it. If an adult dies, becomes disabled, or leaves the pack, however, there may be some posturing or fighting until the new pack order is established.

Dogs fit into our family life because they have this pack history. Our family is a social organization similar to a pack, although our families have significant differences from a wolf pack and vary from each other depending upon our culture. We do normally have an adult male and female, although today there may be just one adult. Unlike in the wolf pack, the rules of our family are often quite chaotic. In the pack, the leaders always eat first, while in our families, people often eat any time and in no specific order. These family rules, or lack of rules, can be quite confusing to our dogs.

Beagles, more so than many other breeds, are secure in a pack situation. Bred to hunt in packs—both large and small—social order is very important to Beagles. A Beagle feels secure and comfortable in a pack, a group of other beings just like him. A Beagle alone can be unhappy and quite insecure. Since Beagles thrive in a pack, it's important that the Beagle have company. If everyone in your family works or is gone all day, get your Beagle some company, either another Beagle or even a cat.

What Does It Mean to Be Top Dog?

"Top dog" is a slang term for the leader of the pack. In the wolf pack, the top dog is the dominant male or dominant female, often called the alpha male or alpha female. In your family, there should be no confusion; you, the dog's owner, are the top dog, and your dog should maintain a subordinate position to any additional human family members as well.

Don't let your dog use his body language to show dominance. Your dog should recognize you (and your children) as above him in the family pack.

You Are the Top Dog!

- Always eat first!
- Go through doors and openings first; block your dog from charging through ahead of you.
- Go up stairs first; don't let him charge ahead of you and then look down on you.
- Give your dog permission to do something, even if he was going to do it anyway. If he picks up his ball, tell him, "Get your ball! Good boy to get your ball!"
- Practice your training regularly.
- Have your dog roll over for a tummy rub daily.
- Do not play rough games with your Beagle; no wrestling, no tug-of-war.
- Never let your dog stand above you or put his paws on your shoulders. These are dominant positions.

Often during adolescence, a Beagle with a particularly bold personality may make a bid for leadership of the family. Adolescence strikes at sexual maturity, usually between eight and 12 months of age. Luckily, however, most Beagles do have a more pack-oriented personality and strive only to get along instead of to create strife.

Since most Beagles are fairly eager to maintain pack harmony, it is usually fairly easy for most owners to maintain leadership of the family pack. As eating first is the leader's prerogative and an action the dog readily understands, you should always eat before feeding your dog. You should also go through all doorways first and have your dog follow you. Make sure you can roll your Beagle over to give him a tummy rub without any fussing on his part. A dog who takes over leadership of the home can make life miserable for all concerned—this is when growling, barking, biting, and mounting behaviors become apparent—so make sure you maintain your position as top dog.

Although it is very important that your dog regard you as the leader or top dog, don't look upon every action your dog makes as a dominance challenge. Most of the time, your Beagle won't care about his position in the family pack; he knows you're in charge. During the dog's adolescence and for more dominant personalities, however, training is extra important.

The Teaching Process

Teaching your dog is not a difficult project, although at times it may seem to be nearly impossible. Most dogs, especially most Beagles, do want to be good—they just need to learn what you do and do not want them to do. Therefore, most of the teaching process consists of communication. You need to reward the behaviors you want your dog to continue doing and you need to interrupt the behaviors you wish to stop. For example, let's use the kitchen trashcan again. If you're in the kitchen fixing dinner and your Beagle comes in, watch her out of the corner of your eye. When her sniffing nose moves towards the trashcan, use a deep, growling tone of voice and tell her, "Leave it alone!" When she reacts to that tone of voice by backing away, tell her in a higher pitched, happy tone of voice, "Good girl to leave it alone!"

Did you notice I emphasized two different tones of voice? Dogs are verbal animals and, as such, are very aware of different tones of voice. When the leader of a wolf pack lets a subordinate know that he or she made a mistake, the leader uses a deep growl to convey that message. When things are fine, the pack has

> Most dogs, especially most Beagles, do want to be good—they just need to learn what you do and do not want them to do.

A treat can be a wonderful training tool to help teach your dog to pay attention to you. When he looks at you, praise him, give him the treat, and then follow through with other training.

hunted, and all is well with the world, the leader may convey that with higher pitched barks or yelps. When you copy this technique—using a deep, growling voice for letting the dog know she's made a mistake and a higher pitched tone of voice to reinforce good behavior—your dog doesn't have to stop and translate that information. She just understands.

Don't confuse high and low tones of voice with volume, though. Your dog can hear very well—much better than you can—and it's not necessary to yell at her. Instead, simply sound as though you mean what you say.

As you begin teaching your dog, remember that human words have no meaning to her until she's taught that they do. She's probably already begun learning some words. She may know treat, cookie, ball, toy, walk, car, and bed. She may even know leash, outside, go potty, inside, and no bite! But other words are just sounds, just so much gobbledy-gook that has no meaning. As you teach her, you will teach her that words like sit, down, come, and heel have specific meanings that are important to her.

So how can you teach your dog that these words have meanings? First, repeat the word as you help your dog perform the act. As you help your dog to sit, say, "Sweetie, sit!" You can reinforce it by praising the dog after she has done as you asked, telling her, "Good girl to sit!" With you repeatedly using the word, your dog will learn that it has meaning, that she should pay attention when she hears that word, and she should do whatever the word requires her to do.

Corrections should be given as the dog is making the mistake, not after the fact.

Just as communication is a big part of the training process, so is your timing. You must use your voice to praise your dog as she is doing something right—AS she is doing it, not after the fact. The same thing applies to letting your dog know that she's making a mistake. Use your voice to let her know she's making as mistake as her nose goes into the trashcan. Don't wait until she's got the trash pulled out onto the floor. Instead, correct her with a firm, "No! Leave it alone!" AS the nose goes to the trashcan. When your timing is correct, there is no misunderstanding; your dog knows exactly what message you are trying to convey.

Don't rely on corrections (verbal or otherwise) to train your dog. We all, dogs and people alike, learn just as much from our successes as we do from our mistakes and we are more likely to repeat our successes! Don't hesitate to set your dog up for success so that you can praise and reward her. If you want to keep your Beagle off the furniture, have her lie down at your feet and hand her a toy to keep her busy *before* she jumps up on the furniture. You can then reward her for good behavior instead of correcting her for bad.

A properly timed correction lets your dog know she's making a mistake, but it doesn't tell her what to do instead. If your Beagle is chewing on your leather shoes and you simply correct her, you convey to her that chewing on your shoes is wrong, but you don't teach her what she can chew on. Since chewing is important for dogs, that's an important message. So instead of just correcting her, correct her (to show her what is wrong), then take her to her toys, hand her something of hers to chew on (to show

Training Vocabulary

Listed below are some basic vocabulary terms you will need to understand in order to train your Beagle.

Positive reinforcement: Anything your dog likes that you can use to reward good behavior, including treats, praise, toys, tennis balls, and petting.

Praise: Words spoken in a higher than normal tone of voice to reward your dog for something he did right; part of positive reinforcement.

Lure: A food treat or a toy used to help position the dog as you want him, or to gain his cooperation as you teach him.

Interruption: The moment when you catch your dog in the act of doing something and you stop him. An interruption can be verbal, using a deeper than normal tone of voice, or it can be a sharp sound such as dropping a book on the floor. An interruption stops the behavior as it is happening.

Correction: Usually a deep, growling verbal sound or words to let your dog know that he has made a mistake, as he is doing it. A correction can serve as an interruption, but you can also let your dog know that you dislike what he is doing. This can be a snap and release of the leash. A correction should be firm enough to get your dog's attention and stop the behavior at that moment and that's all.

her what is right), and then praise her when she picks up one of her toys (to reinforce a good choice).

Teaching Your Dog to Be Handled

Although some Beagles have a very independent personality, they still cannot care for themselves. You must be able to brush her, comb her, bathe her, trim her toenails, and clean her ears. When she is sick or has hurt herself, you must be able to take care of her, whether it's administering eardrops when she has an infection, caring for her stitches after neutering, or washing out her eyes if dirt gets in them.

It's important to teach your Beagle to accept handling of her body before there's an emergency. If you teach her this early (as a puppy or as soon as you bring her home), then when she has a problem that requires special care, you will have already built that bond of trust and she will know to relax and let you care for her.

To introduce this notion, sit on the floor and invite your Beagle to lie down on the floor between your legs, on your lap or in front of you. Start giving her a tummy rub to relax her. When she's relaxed, start giving her a massage. Begin massaging at her muzzle, rubbing your fingers gently over the skin, and at the same time, check her teeth. Move up her head, touching the skin around her eyes, then move on to her ears. Handle each ear flap, look in each ear, and massage around each ear's base. As you massage, look for any problems. Look for discharge from the eyes or nose. Look for dirt, excess wax, or redness in the ears. Let your fingers feel for lumps, bumps, or bruises on the skin.

Continue in this same manner all over your Beagle's body. If she protests at any time, go back to the tummy rub for a moment, let her relax, and then continue. Do not let her turn this into a wrestling match; instead, keep it calm, relaxing, and gentle.

Do this exercise daily and incorporate your grooming regime into it. Even though a Beagle has a very short coat, she still needs daily grooming. A daily brushing can greatly lessen the hair she sheds in the house. In addition, if you groom her daily, you can

A tummy rub can help relax your dog if he's over-stimulated. You can also follow through with any needed grooming. In addition, this is a wonderful time for bonding with your dog.

discover potential problems (such as fleas or ticks) before they become full-blown. If your dog needs medication or first aid treatments, you can do that while massaging, too. Simply make it part of the massage and don't let it turn into a fight.

There is a side effect of this massage you will enjoy. When you're finished massaging your Beagle, she will be totally relaxed, like a limp noodle. So plan ahead and do it when you want your dog to be quiet and relaxed. If she's hyperactive and overstimulated in the evening when you would like to watch a favorite television show, sit on the floor, massage her, and then let her sleep while you watch your show!

The Importance of Good Socialization

Socialization is a vital part of raising a healthy, mentally sound Beagle. A young Beagle who has been introduced to a variety of people of different ages and ethnic backgrounds will be a social dog, one who is happy to meet people and is unafraid. A Beagle who has been kept in the backyard too much will be fearful. He may grow up afraid of children, or of senior citizens. A dog who has never met people of a different ethnic background than his owners may be afraid of different people. A Beagle who is afraid can become aggressive out of fear. These so-called "fear biters" are dangerous; a dog who bites out of fear often doesn't think before he acts. Most of these fear-biters eventually have to be destroyed because of their danger to people.

Socialization also refers to meeting other dogs and pets. Your Bea-

Introduce your dog to other friendly, well-behaved, healthy dogs. Avoid rowdy, poorly behaved, aggressive dogs; they could scare your dog and ruin the socialization you've done so far.

gle should have opportunities to play with other well-behaved dogs so that he learns what it is to be a dog and how to behave around other dogs. Ideally, your Beagle should also meet friendly cats, rabbits, ferrets, and other pets. Always protect your Beagle by introducing him to pets that you know are friendly to dogs, and protect those pets from your Beagle. Don't let him chase them.

Socialization also includes the sights, sounds, and smells of the world around your Beagle. Let him see and hear the trash truck that comes by each week. If he's afraid of it, have him on leash when the truck comes by and let the driver offer your Beagle a good dog treat. Let him watch the neighborhood kids go by on inline skates; just don't let him bark at or chase them. Walk your Beagle past the construction crew mending the potholes in the road. He can smell the hot asphalt as he watches the men work. Take your Beagle to different places so that he can smell new smells and see new sights. The more he sees, hears, and smells, the better his coping skills.

> Take your Beagle to different places so that he can smell new smells and see new sights. The more he sees, hears, and smells, the better his coping skills.

Don't overload him, though, by trying to introduce him to everything all at once. You can start socialization when your puppy is nine to ten weeks of age by introducing him to calm, friendly family members and neighbors. Let these people pet him and cuddle him, but don't allow rough games; keep the experiences very positive. Week by week, you can introduce your puppy to more people and different things.

Should your Beagle puppy be frightened of something, don't hug him, pet him, and try to reassure him; your puppy will assume those comforting words are praise for being afraid. Instead, use a happy tone of voice, "What was that?" and walk up to whatever scared him. Don't force him to walk up to it—just let him see you do it. For example, if your puppy sees a trashcan rolling in the street after the wind has blown it over, and he appears worried by it, hold on to your puppy's leash (to keep him from running away) and walk up to the trashcan. Ask your puppy (in an upbeat tone of voice) "What's this?" Touch the trashcan. Pat it several times so your puppy can see you touch it. If he walks up to it, praise him for his bravery!

Beagles are by nature social dogs. Bred to hunt in a pack, they are pack oriented and social. This doesn't mean that socialization training is not important for them. It is. A Beagle who grows up alone, without a pack, can be isolated, lonely, and afraid, so you should consciously try to arrange socialization outings for your Beagle. In addition, puppy kindergarten is a wonderful place for your Beagle to meet other people and puppies.

A Crate Can Help Your Training

Originally designed as travel cages, crates have become popular training tools for a variety of reasons.

Using a crate to confine your baby Beagle during the night and for short periods during the day helps him learn and develop more bowel and bladder control since his instincts tell him to keep his bed clean. He is not going to want to relieve himself in his crate.

Using the crate to confine your Beagle when you cannot supervise him also helps prevent problems from occurring. Your Beagle can't chew up your shoes, raid the trash, or shred the sofa cushions if he's confined to the crate. By preventing problems from occurring, you also prevent bad habits from developing. As he grows up, you can gradually give him more freedom; but not until he's mature mentally—about two years old for most Beagles.

Many first-time dog owners resist the idea of a crate, saying it's too much like a jail. But dogs like small secure places, especially when sleeping. Most dogs quickly learn to like their crate and it becomes a special place for them. My dogs continue to use their crates (voluntarily) into old age because each dog's crate is his personal space where he can retreat to when tired, overwhelmed, or not feeling well.

Introduce the crate by opening the door and tossing a treat or toy inside. As the dog goes in, say the command phrase you wish to use, such as "Sweetie, go to bed!" or "Sweetie, kennel!" When he grabs the treat or toy, praise him, "Good boy to go to bed! Yeah!" Repeat this several times. When mealtime comes around, feed your dog in the crate, placing the food to the back, but don't close the door on him yet. Let him go in and come out on his own.

At night, put the crate in your bedroom next to your bed so that your Beagle can smell you, hear you, and know that you are close by. He will be less apt to fuss during the night when he's near you. You will also be able to hear him if he needs to go outside during the night. In addition, by sleeping in your room, your dog gets to spend eight hours with you. In our busy lives, this is precious time!

Let your Beagle spend the night along with a few hours here and there during the day in his crate. Other than at night, your Beagle should not spend more than three to four hours at a stretch in the crate; he needs time to run and play during the day.

A crate helps your puppy develop bowel and bladder control, prevents accidents from happening, and becomes your puppy's special place.

Choosing the Right Crate

Crates come in two basic types. There are plastic crates with solid sides that were originally designed for traveling with the dog, and there are wire crates that look more like cages. Each style has its pros and cons. The plastic crates give the dog more security because of their solid sides. The solid sides make the crates bulky, however, and they don't break down much for storage. The wire-sided cages usually fold down into a smaller, flat package, although they are still quite heavy. The wire sides provide more ventilation for the dog, but are open and don't provide much security.

To choose the right crate, consider your needs. Are you going to have to move the crate much? Are you short of storage space? Do you need to move the crate often? Also consider your dog's needs. Is greater airflow or an increased sense of security more important for him? Choose a crate that will give your Beagle room to stand up, move around, lie down, and stretch out.

What Every Good Beagle Needs to Know

Beagles live by their own pack rules and those rules are not necessarily the same as yours. In a Beagle pack, it's normal to sniff each other's rear end, for example, whereas we (people) consider that extremely poor manners—even when a dog does it! Your Beagle needs to learn the social rules that you will require of her, so that your life together is enjoyable rather than embarrassing or difficult.

No Jumping

Beagles are not big dogs, but they are strong for their size. Although a Beagle jumping up on an adult is not going to knock anyone over, this behavior can still rip pantyhose and put muddy paw prints on clothing. A Beagle jumping on a child or a senior citizen with poor balance can cause harm. Therefore, it's usually a good idea to teach your Beagle not to jump on people as greeting.

If you teach your Beagle to sit each time she greets people (anyone, including you, your family, guests, and people on the street), sitting becomes a replacement action for jumping up. She cannot jump on them and sit at the same time. Later in this chapter, we'll talk about the mechanics of teaching your dog to sit.

There are several different ways you can use the sit to stop the jumping up. First, if your dog doesn't have her leash on—such as when you come home from work—make sure you greet her with empty hands. As your dog dashes up to you, grab her buckle collar (which should be on her with her ID tags) and tell her, "Sweetie, no jump! Sit!" With your hand on her collar, help her sit. Keep your hands on her as you praise her for sitting. If she tries to jump up, your hands are on her to prevent it and you can continue to teach her.

The leash is also a good training tool to help you control your dog. When guests come over, ask them to wait outside for a moment (weather permitting, of course!) while you leash your dog. Once your Beagle is leashed, let your guests in. Make sure your dog sits before your guests pet her. If she jumps up, correct her, "No jump!" and have her sit again. Don't let your guests pet your dog while she's jumping up and misbehaving; if they do, they are rewarding her for bad behavior.

You can do the same thing when you and your dog are out in public. Have her sit before anyone pets her. If she's too excited and cannot hold still, don't let people pet her until you make her sit. If people protest, "Oh, I don't mind if she jumps!" explain that you are trying to teach her good social manners.

Anti-Bark Collars

Several different types of bark control collars are available to dog owners. Some give the dog an electric shock or jolt when he barks, some make a high-pitched sound, and one delivers a squirt of citronella. The citronella works on the same principle as the vinegar/water squirt bottle: the smell disrupts the dog's concentration and is annoying enough that he stops barking. This is the collar I recommend for most Beagles; it is effective for most dogs and is a humane training tool.

Beagles Do Howl!

All dogs bark; it's their way of communicating. Beagles, though, do not simply bark—they can also howl! The original purpose of that howl was for hunters to hear where their dogs were. Each hunter knew his dogs' howls and could tell by the tone of voice whether the dogs were searching for prey, chasing their prey, or had lost it. Unfortunately, in a suburban neighborhood, that howl can be highly annoying.

The first thing you need to do is teach your Beagle a command that means "quiet" and enforce it while you're at home. Ask a neighbor to help you. Have her come over to your house and ring the doorbell. When your dog goes dashing to the door, making noise, tell her, "Sweetie, quiet!" as you grab her collar. If she stops making noise, praise her, "Good girl to be quiet!" If she continues making noise, gently close her muzzle with your hand as you tell her to be quiet. When she stops, praise her.

Many Beagles will learn this command with repeated training. Some are a little more persistent about making noise, however. With these dogs, the correction needs to be a little stronger. Take a spray bottle and fill it with one part vinegar to seven parts water. There should be just enough vinegar to smell. If it smells too strong (to your nose), dilute it a little more.

Then, when your Beagle charges to the door barking or howling, follow her, and quietly tell her, "Sweetie, quiet!" If she stops, praise her. If she doesn't, spray the water/vinegar towards her nose. She will be disgusted by the vinegar smell and will stop barking to think about it. As soon as she stops barking, praise her. The squirt bottle works as an interruption because your dog has a very sensitive sense of smell and she's going to dislike the smell of the vinegar. Therefore, it can stop the bad behavior (the barking or howling) without resorting to an overly harsh correction.

Use the same training techniques (verbal correction, collar, closing the muzzle, or the squirt bottle) to teach your Beagle to be quiet around the house. When she is reliable in the house, move the training outside. If she barks at the gate when kids are playing in front of the house, go outside the gate, and correct her with a verbal command and a squirt from the bottle. Always, of course, praise her when she's quiet.

If your Beagle makes a lot of noise and doesn't seem to understand your "quiet" corrections, she may not realize that she is making noise. With some Beagles, the howls just seem to come from somewhere inside them and the dogs have no idea (consciously) that they are doing something! For these dogs, teaching them to speak on command and praising them for speaking makes them more aware of the noise they're making. Set up a situation where your dog will make noise. For example, tease her with a favorite toy. When she barks or howls, tell her, "Sweetie, speak!" and praise her. Repeat this several times a day for a couple of weeks. Then tell her "Sweetie, speak!" without the teaser and praise her when she makes noise. Repeat this for a week or two. When the speak command is well understood, then you can start teaching "No speak!" in those situations in which you want her to be quiet!

No Begging

Beagles are very quick to pick up on a person who is an easy mark. With those large soulful brown eyes, who can resist a Beagle? You should! There is no reason any Beagle should beg for food from people who are eating. Begging is a bad habit and one that usually escalates to worse behavior. The dog may start by picking up food that has fallen on the floor, then progress to pawing at a hand or leg, trying to solicit a handout. Eventually, the dog is actively begging and making a nuisance of herself. Sometimes it goes so far that the dog steals food from the kids' hands or off the table.

Fortunately, this is an easy habit to break although it requires consistency from all family members. Later in this chapter, you will learn how to teach the down-stay command. When your Beagle has learned the down-stay, simply have her down-stay in a particular spot away from the table (or where people are eating) and make her hold her position until people are finished eating. By teaching her to lie down and stay in a corner of the room, so that she's not underfoot, and so that she cannot beg under the table, you are breaking the bad habit. When

Teach your dog to hold a down–stay while you're eating. He will learn that he gets to eat when you are finished so he must be patient.

everyone has finished eating, the dog can then be given her meal or a treat in her bowl away from the table.

When you begin teaching this new rule, use the leash and collar on the dog. In this way, if she makes a mistake and tries to beg

No Exile

I don't like to exile dogs to the backyard while people are eating. Although this is much easier to do—just put the dog outside and close the door—compared to training the dog, it has a tendency to build up more frustration in the dog. He knows you're eating and he knows he's been exiled. That is enough right there to cause frustration. When the dog is let in the house later, he's going to be wild!

If the dog is allowed to remain in the house, however, and is required to behave himself, he learns self-control. He knows he will get something to eat after the people are finished so he learns to wait.

(and she will initially!), you can use the leash to take her back to the spot where you want her to lie down and stay. Correct her as many times as you must until she holds the position or, in a worst-case scenario, the meal is over.

No Biting

All it takes is one bite and your Beagle could be taken from you and euthanized. All dogs owners must take this issue seriously because at the present time the legal system works against dogs, not for them. There have been far too many dog bite cases in which people, especially children, have been seriously mauled or killed.

A dog bite is legally defined as the dog's open mouth touching skin. There need not be a puncture wound or even broken skin. Vicious intent is not necessary either. If your Beagle is in the backyard and decides to grab the neighbor's son (who has the dog's toy), that qualifies as a bite, even if the skin is not broken.

It's important to teach all dogs that teeth are not allowed to touch skin—ever! That means the dog is not to grab your hand

No Rough Games!

Beagles are not large dogs but they are tough, sturdy little dogs who like to play and love to play rough. Unfortunately, some rough games, like wrestling and tug-of-war, give the dog the wrong message about how he should regard or treat people. Wrestling teaches the dog to use his strength against you, to fight you, and to protest when you hold him tight. Tug-of-war teaches him to use the strength of his jaws and his body against you. Neither game teaches him to respect you or to be gentle with you.

After too many of these rough-and-tumble games, every time you try to trim his toenails, a wrestling game will ensue. Or when you try to have him hold still, he will fight you. When you attempt to take something out of his mouth, he may decide to play tug-of-war with it instead! Bad behavior!

Rather than playing these detrimental games, play hide-and-seek or retrieving games.

when she wants you to do something. Nor should she use her mouth to protest when you're taking a toy away from her. To keep your dog safe, never allow her to use her mouth in such a way that teeth (or the mouth itself) touch skin.

It's easy to teach young puppies that they should not use their mouth. Take your hand away as you correct the puppy verbally. A consistent, "No bite!" in a deep, growling tone of voice is usually all that is needed. If your Beagle puppy tries to use her mouth during playtime, tell her "no bite" and get up and walk away; end the game. If she bites hard, say "Ouch!" in a high-pitched, hurt tone of voice, followed by a deep, growling "No bite!" If the puppy is persistent about using her mouth, take hold of her collar with one hand while you close her mouth with the other hand and tell her, "No bite!"

Time-Out!

Sometimes when puppies are corrected for what is natural behavior to them (such as mouthing), they throw a temper tantrum. If your puppy throws himself around, flailing and acting like a cornered wild animal, don't mess with him or try to stop it. Simply put him in his crate and give him a time-out. Don't yell at him, don't scold him, don't try and reassure him—just put him in his crate, close the door, and walk away. In 15 or 20 minutes, if he's quiet and calm, let him out, but don't make a big fuss over him—just open the door and let him out.

Most puppies—just like most human children—will throw one or two tantrums sometime during their puppyhood. If you give in to it, your puppy will learn that this horrible behavior works. If you give him a time-out, however, he'll learn that this behavior doesn't work and is not rewarding.

If you are having trouble teaching your Beagle to stop using her mouth, if your Beagle seems intent on mouthing you, or if you have a gut feeling that you may be bitten by the dog one day, call a professional trainer or behaviorist to help you. Don't wait until a bite happens.

Digging

Dogs dig for a number of reasons, all of which are very natural to the dog. As pack den animals, Beagles like a tight, snug place to cuddle up in, and a hole in the ground is just right. As hunting animals, Beagles like to follow a scent and that might be a beetle digging in your grass or a mouse under the pile of firewood.

Since digging is so natural, you should offer your Beagle a spot where she can dig to her heart's content—maybe out behind the garage where it won't be too obvious to you. Dig up this area and make the dirt soft. Bury a few dog toys and treats and invite your dog to dig here.

In the rest of the yard, fill in the holes and spread some grass seed. If she goes back to one or two holes and redigs them, crumple up some hardware cloth (wire mesh), place it in the hole, and fill the hole with dirt. When she tries to redig that hole, the wire mesh will prevent her from doing so and will not feel at all comfortable on her paws.

Destructive Chewing

As with many other undesirable activities, destructive chewing is a natural behavior for puppies. Most Beagle puppies begin to chew when they're teething—losing their baby teeth and getting in adult teeth. The gums are sore, and chewing seems to help relieve the discomfort. At this point, many puppies learn that chewing is fun. Unfortunately, while it may be fun for the puppy, chewing can be incredibly destructive and costly. In addition, the puppy who chews will inevitably swallow something she shouldn't, so chewing also becomes dangerous. Therefore, this bad habit needs to be controlled.

You can prevent a lot of bad behavior by keeping your puppy close to you when she's in the house. Close doors or put up baby gates; don't let her have free run of the house. Under your supervision, you can teach her what is right to chew on and what is wrong. When she picks up one of her toys, praise her, "Good girl to have a toy! Good toy!" When she picks up something she shouldn't, correct her by taking it away, walking her to one of her toys, and saying, "Here, this is yours." When she picks up her toy, praise her.

As with many other problem behaviors, prevention is very important. Keep your Beagle close to you, close closet doors, keep the dirty clothes picked up, and empty the trashcans. If you can prevent her from getting into trouble as a puppy, when she grows up, she won't have any bad habits and won't be tempted to try them.

Other Bad Habits

Beagles are usually pretty good dogs. Their biggest problems are generally howling and barking, jumping on people, and not coming when called. Training can help all three of these problems if you are consistent with it.

If your Beagle has some other behavioral problems, you can approach them in the same manner as we did these. What is your dog doing? Why is she doing it? When does she do it? Can you use your training to teach her? Can you prevent it from happening?

If you are unable to solve this problem yourself, don't hesitate to call a professional trainer or behaviorist for help. Ask your veterinarian for a recommendation.

House-Training

House-training your Beagle is primarily a matter of taking him outside when he needs to go, making sure he does relieve himself while out there, teaching him a phrase that tells him to try to go, and then restricting his freedom until he is reliably trained.

Using a Crate to House-Train

When I introduced the crate earlier, I said that a crate is a wonderful tool to help you house-train your Beagle. Since dogs are born with an instinct to keep their bed clean and will toddle away from their bed as soon as their legs will support them, the crate

House-Training Timetable

Your Beagle will need to relieve himself after:

○ waking up

○ eating

○ drinking

○ playtime

○ every two to three hours in between.

Be alert; when your puppy is sniffing the floor and circling, grab him quick, and take him outside!

helps the puppy develop bowel and bladder control. You, of course, must never leave the dog in the crate too long; if you do, he will have to relieve himself and will be upset at doing so in such a confined space.

House-Training Guidelines

Using a crate is not all that needs to be done to house-train a baby puppy, older puppy, or adult Beagle. He needs to be taught to go outside, to relieve himself where you want him to outside, and what the phrase is that signals this activity.

Just sending the dog outside won't work. If you just send him out there alone, how do you know whether or not he's relieved himself when you let him back in? He may have spent the time sniffing for rabbits rather than relieving himself and once you let him in, he may remember his bladder is full and then—whoosh! It's all over your floor!

You need to go outside with him. When he's sniffing and circling, tell him quietly, "Go potty!" (Use whatever word or phrase works for you.) When he does what he needs to do, praise him,

"Good boy to go potty!" Once he's relieved himself, bring him inside with you, but still restrict his freedom. Close doors or put up baby gates to keep him close. Do not consider him reliably housetrained until he's eight or nine months of age and hasn't had an accident in months! If he's younger and hasn't had any accidents, it just means you're doing everything right!

When Accidents Happen

If you catch your puppy in the act of relieving himself inside, you can let him know he's making a mistake, "Oh, no! Bad boy!" and take him outside. If you find a puddle and he's already moved away, however, don't correct him—it's too late.

Keep in mind that your Beagle must relieve himself; the act of urination or defecation is not wrong. When there is an accident, it is the place he did it that is wrong. If you correct him after the fact, he could easily misunderstand you and think that the act of urination or defection is what you're angry about. Then you'll have a dog that sneaks off behind the furniture to relieve himself.

In summary, go outside with him, praise him when he does it outside, supervise him in the house, and correct only those accidents that you catch happening.

Asking to Go Outside

Since so many Beagles have a hard time controlling their barking or howling, I do not like to teach Beagles to bark to go outside. Why emphasize a behavior that might already be a problem? Your dog does need a way to let you know he has to go outside, so we'll teach him to ring some bells instead.

Go to a craft store and get two or three bells (one to two inches in diameter). Hang them from the doorknob or handle of the door where the dog goes in and out. Make sure they hang at your dog's nose level. Cut a hot dog into tiny pieces and rub one piece on the bells. Invite your dog to sniff it. When the bell rings, praise him, take him outside, and give him a tiny piece of hot dog outside.

Repeat this three or four times per session for a few days. When he starts ringing the bells on his own, praise him enthusiastically and let him outside!

Five Basic Obedience Commands

Every dog should know these five basic obedience commands. They form the foundation of good behavior and, with these commands, your Beagle can learn self-control and to be well behaved at home and in public.

Sit

The sit exercise teaches your Beagle to hold still—a hard concept for many young Beagles! When he sits, he isn't jumping on people; you can feed him without him knocking the bowl out of your hands; and you can get his attention so that he can do other things. Sitting is an important lesson in self-control.

There are several different ways to teach any dog to sit, and as long as the method is humane and works, that's fine. One of the easiest methods uses a treat as a lure. Tell your

Hold a treat in your hand and let your dog sniff it. Then take the treat up and back over his head. As his head comes up, his hips will go down.

Beagle, "Sweetie, sit!" as you hold a treat above his nose. Move your hand back toward his tail, over his head. As his head goes up to follow the treat, his hips will go down. As he sits, praise him, "Good boy to sit!" Then give him the treat.

When your dog sits and his hips are on the ground, praise him.

Another easy method involves shaping the dog into position. With your Beagle close to you, tell him, Sweetie, sit!" as you place one hand on his chest under his neck and push gently up and back as the other hand slides down his hips and tucks them under. Think of a teeter-totter—up and back at the front and down and under at the rear. As you position your Beagle in the sit, praise him, "Good boy to sit!"

With one hand on the front of the dog's chest under his neck, push gently up and back as you slide the other hand down his hips. At the same time, tell your dog to sit. Praise him when he does.

Down

When combined with the stay command (see below), the down teaches your Beagle to be still for gradually increased periods of time. You will be able to have him lie down and stay while people are eating, so he isn't begging under the table. You can have him lie at your feet while you're watching television in the evening, or you can have him lie quietly while guests are visiting. The down/stay is a very useful command.

Start by having your Beagle sit. Once he's sitting, show him a treat in your right hand. As you tell him, "Sweetie, down!" take the treat from his nose to the floor right in front of his front paws. Lead his nose to the floor. As his head follows the treat, your left hand can be resting on his shoulders to help him lie down. If he tries to pop back up, that hand can keep him down. Once he's down, praise him and give him the treat.

Have your dog sit and then show him a treat. Tell him to lie down as you take the treat from his nose down to the ground in front of his paws.

If he doesn't follow the treat down,

As your dog lies down, praise him.

gently pull his front legs forward and shape his body into the down position.

Try to help him do the command himself rather than physically positioning him.

Stay

If your dog doesn't lie down for the treat, just scoop his front legs out from under him and gently lay him down. Praise him even though you're helping him do it.

You want your Beagle to understand that stay means hold still. He will do this both in the sit and in the down, although you should never ask him to sit-stay nearly as long as you ask him to hold a down-stay, simply because the down-stay is an easier position to hold for longer periods of time. In either position, he should hold it until you give him permission to move.

Start by having your Beagle sit. With an open palm towards his nose, tell him, "Sweetie, stay!" At the same time, exert a little

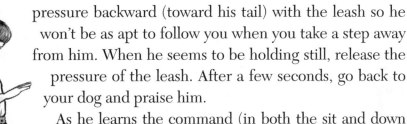

pressure backward (toward his tail) with the leash so he won't be as apt to follow you when you take a step away from him. When he seems to be holding still, release the pressure of the leash. After a few seconds, go back to your dog and praise him.

As he learns the command (in both the sit and down positions), you can gradually increase the time and distance away from him. For example, for the first few days, take one step away and have him hold the stay for 10 seconds. Later that week, have him hold the stay while you take three steps away and have him be still for 20 seconds. Increase it gradually, though; if your Beagle makes a few mistakes, you're moving too fast.

The signal for stay is an open-palmed gesture right in front of the dog's face.

Walking Nicely on the Leash

It's no fun to take a walk with a dog who chokes himself on the leash and pulls so hard your shoulder hurts. That's torture, not fun! When your dog learns to walk nicely, without pulling, and pays attention to you when you talk to him, then walks become fun.

Hook the leash up to your Beagle's collar and hold the leash in one hand. Have some good dog treats in your other hand. Show your dog the treats and then back away from him so that it appears you are leading your dog by his nose. When he

Use a treat and your happy verbal praise to encourage the dog to follow you on the leash as you back away from him. Praise him when he follows you.

follows you, praise him. When he's following you nicely, turn so that he ends up on your left side and you're both walking forward together. You can still use the treat to encourage him to pay attention to you. Stop, have him sit, and praise him! Practice this often and keep the walking distances very short, with lots of sits and praise. If, while you're walking, your dog gets distracted, simply back away from him again and start all over.

When your dog is following you nicely, turn so that the both of you are walking forward together. Keep a treat handy to pop in front of his nose should he get distracted. Praise him.

If your dog is too distracted to pay attention to the treats or is fighting the leash, use the leash to give him a snap and release correction. Back away from him, let him hit the end of the leash, and give him a snap and release correction at the same time you give him a verbal correction, "No pull!" When he reacts to the correction by looking at you, praise him for looking at you, "Hey, what happened? Good boy!"

Show your Beagle that when he walks with you nicely without pulling, good things happen (praise and treats), but if he pulls on the leash or ignores you, he gets a leash snap and verbal correction.

Come

It is very important that your Beagle understands that "come" means he should come directly to you, on the first call, every time you call him. He isn't to come just when he wants to, or when nothing else is very interesting, but instead is to come all the time, every time.

Have your Beagle on the leash and hold the leash in one hand. In your other hand, have a box of dog treats. Shake the dog treats and, as you back away from your dog (so he can chase you), call him to come, "Sweetie, come!" Let him catch up to you, have him sit, and then give him a treat as your praise him, "Good boy to come!"

Shaking the box of dog treats is a sound stimulus that makes your verbal command much more exciting. Since this command is so important, use the sound stimulus (shaking the box) often during your training.

Make sure your dog will come to you reliably all the time before you try it off leash.

When your dog is responding well on the leash, make up a long leash (20 to 30 feet in length), and repeat the training with the long leash. Continue using the box of treats, too. Don't be in a hurry to take the leash off your Beagle. Most Beagles aren't mentally mature and ready for off leash training until they are at least 2 years old. Some aren't ready for off leash training even then. Your training on leash must be very, very good, with few mistakes, before you ever try it off leash. When you do, only do so in a fenced, secure area.

Training Is an Ongoing Process

Training your Beagle can be a lot of work. You need to pay attention to your dog, respond to him, and teach him right from wrong. You may need to make some changes around the house, and other family members will have to cooperate.

The rewards are worth it, though. Buster's owner, Joan, is now doing advanced training with Buster, including off leash agility training. She says, "We are having so much fun with Buster. We could never have even thought of doing any of this unless he was reliably

A well–behaved dog is a joy to own and a pleasure to spend time with.

trained." A well-trained dog is a joy; you will want to spend time with him and, in return, he will be your best friend.

Grooming

In This Chapter

○ Why Grooming is Important
○ Routine Care Every Beagle Needs
○ Home Grooming Versus Professional Grooming

The bond between you and your Beagle is being strengthened in many ways, from mealtime to playtime. One step in the bonding process you shouldn't overlook is grooming, since it can be the most important in terms of getting to know a dog. Your Beagle's body is a topographical map to her well-being. By becoming familiar with its terrain—through regular brushing and eye, ear, and dental care—you will find that the road to good health is smoother and has fewer detours.

Why Grooming Is Important

Grooming has a number of benefits. It is a great way to spend time with your dog and it develops trust between you. A Beagle who is groomed regularly is more likely to be comfortable being handled by a veterinarian, trainer, dog judge, or professional groomer. Grooming is also an excellent way to keep tabs on what's going on with a dog's body. By establishing a grooming routine in early puppyhood, you quickly learn what's normal for your Beagle. Anything unusual stands out, often allowing you to catch problems such as ear infections, skin disease, parasitic infestations, and tumors before they become serious. Signs of problems you might notice during grooming sessions include itchiness, hair loss, redness, tenderness, or lumps, all of which you should report to your veterinarian.

A grooming session can also be relaxing—as good as a massage—for a dog who enjoys it. And dogs just feel better when they're clean and sweet-smelling. Many pet owners notice that their dogs are livelier and seem younger after being groomed.

> By establishing a grooming routine in early puppyhood, you quickly learn what's normal for your Beagle.

Happily, Beagles are a wash-and-go breed, with no need for fancy trimming. They don't drool a lot or have a heavy body odor, and their complete grooming needs can be met in only a few minutes each week. The close-lying, medium-length coat is easy to care for. A good brushing, a quick wipe of the ears, regular toenail trimming, and a bath every two or three months—or as needed—keeps this breed looking and feeling its best. The earlier you begin exposing your Beagle to the pleasures of being brushed and bathed, the easier it will be to keep her clean and well groomed.

Introducing Your Puppy to Grooming

Whether your Beagle loves grooming time or runs away yelping when you pull out a brush or draw a bath depends on her early experiences. The grooming session is something your puppy comes to look forward to if it is introduced properly. Keep grooming sessions short at first, and fun. Teach your puppy to open her mouth so you can look at her teeth, and offer plenty of praise when she complies. Avoid scaring the puppy in any way. Fondle her ears and paws while the two of you are watching television. Dogs are especially sensitive in those areas, so they need to learn that being handled can be pleasurable.

Establish a weekly routine so the puppy comes to expect grooming at a certain time and knows what grooming consists of; groom her the same way at each session. Plan grooming for a time when you won't be interrupted by anything else, and assemble grooming tools in advance so you don't have to leave the pup to go find something. Grooming is best done before a pup has eaten, so her tummy isn't full, and after she has relieved herself. Groom the dog on an elevated, nonskid surface, such as on a picnic table, on a rubber mat on a washer or dryer, or on a professional grooming table. Be sure you keep one hand on the pup at all times, and if you have to walk away, put the dog on the floor. Don't take the chance that she'll jump or fall off. Praise your Beagle when she sits still for grooming; you want to make the experience as pleasant as possible.

Routine Care Every Beagle Needs

The amount and frequency of grooming your Beagle needs depends on her lifestyle. Most Beagles need

only a weekly brushing to keep their coats shiny and in good condition. Beagles who spend their days getting down and dirty in the great outdoors may need to be brushed (and bathed) more often.

Brushing, Combing, and Optional Trimming

Brushing is the foundation of good grooming. It loosens and removes dirt, dead hair, and skin cells, and distributes the skin's natural oils through the coat. To brush your Beagle, use a bristle brush, hound mitt, or rubber curry. A bristle brush has natural or nylon bristles and a handle for an easy grip. Choose one with short, natural bristles. A hound mitt fits over your hand like a glove and has short, nubby bristles. A rubber curry is square or oval in shape with soft, short, flexible rubber nubs, and sometimes has a strap to slip your hand beneath for a better grip. These types of brushes remove loose or dead hair quickly and easily and polish smooth coats till they gleam. They also feel good to the dog when used properly, giving her a sensation much like a massage. Whichever you choose, be sure the brush fits your hand well so that grooming goes smoothly.

Start at the head and brush back toward the end of the body. Be sure you brush all the way down to the skin, not just over the surface of the coat. This helps loosen and remove dandruff flakes. Don't skip the stomach area, even if your dog resists lying on her side or back. Firmly insist that she submit politely to being groomed all over her body. While you brush, examine your Beagle for evidence of fleas and ticks (for what to do if you find evidence, see the section on external parasites in chapter 5, pages 146–158).

You'll also want to purchase a steel comb with fine- and wide-spaced teeth. Use the fine-tooth side when you're searching for fleas and the wide-tooth side to remove loose hairs after a bath. The fine-tooth side also helps remove dirt from the dog's coat. A high-quality metal comb should last your dog's lifetime.

To keep hair from flying all over your house while you're brushing your Beagle, do it outside if the weather is warm. Otherwise, put her on a sheet or towel that you can shake out and throw in the washing machine after the grooming session. This will help keep hair from getting in your carpet, on your bed, or lodging in corners.

Beagles shed year-round, so weekly brushing can help keep loose hair under control. Shedding is heaviest in the spring, when the Beagle loses his heavy winter coat, and in the fall, when he blows coat to make way for winter hair growth. Fortunately, most Beagle shedding isn't too noticeable because the hair is short. Regular brushing will help keep it off your clothes and furniture. A wire slicker brush is useful for getting out the dead hair and stimulating the skin, which promotes blood circulation and new hair growth. If shedding gets to be too much during the spring and fall, you can help keep it under control by bathing your dog more frequently and brushing her daily.

Pet Beagles don't need any trimming whatsoever. Some show dog owners trim (or have a professional groomer trim) the whiskers of their Beagle to soften his expression and give his face a cleaner look. Some also trim his tail with thinning shears so it is gently blunted and rounded at the tip. The brush on the underside of the tail isn't trimmed at all. If

Did You Know?

The pom-pom cut used on Poodles was originally developed to increase the breed's swimming abilitites as a retriever. The short haircut allowed for faster swimming but the pom-poms were left to keep the joints warm.

you like this look, a professional groomer can do it for you, or a breeder can show you how to achieve it at home. You can also give your dog's feet a neater look by using a pair of small straight scissors to trim any stray hairs between the pads.

Ear Care

After you've brushed the coat, move on to the ears and eyes. A Beagle's hanging ears trap debris and moisture, making him more prone to ear infections. To keep them healthy, look inside the ears to check for dirt, scratches, foxtails, parasites, or discharge, any of which may require a visit to the veterinarian. A small amount of honey-colored wax is nothing to worry about, but be concerned if you see a heavy, or dark buildup, large amounts of wax, or swollen tissues that are tender to the touch. If the ears look free of problems, give them a good sniff. There shouldn't be any unpleasant odor (a sign of infection).

Clean the ears by moistening a cotton ball, Q-tip, or cosmetic pad with mineral oil or a liquid ear cleaner recommended by your veterinarian, and gently wiping them out, going no deeper than you can see. Always start in the deepest part, and pull debris outward to the ear tip. This helps avoid dragging bacteria and dirt into the ear canal where it may cause infection or itching. Avoid using drying agents such as alcohol or cleansers that contain alcohol. They can sting if there's a slight abrasion in the dog's ear and, by drying the ear out, they can mask problems that should be treated. If the ear is oozing, there's a reason for it. Drying the ear up without discovering and treating the underlying problem simply begins a cycle of ear problems. Signs of ear infections are constant head shaking, scratching at the ears, and scratching just below the ears.

Eye Care

Check the eyes for redness or other signs of irritation. Healthy eyes are bright and clear, and the eyeball is white. A small amount of clear discharge in the corners of the eyes—like the "sleepies" we have when we wake up—is normal and can simply be wiped away with a damp tissue or cloth.

Tooth Care

Dental care is an aspect of grooming that many pet owners ignore, but it can pay off in fresh breath and better health. Gum disease caused by tartar buildup is a common problem in dogs, but regular brushing keeps it at bay. The American Animal Hospital Association recommends brushing a dog's teeth at least three times a week.

Gum disease begins when food particles and saliva accumulate on the teeth, forming a soft plaque that later hardens into tartar. The bacteria trapped in the plaque contribute to doggy breath and to the development of gingivitis—inflammation of the gums—and periodontal disease—inflammation of the lining of the tooth socket. Signs of periodontal disease are: a brownish buildup on teeth; gums that are swollen, red, or bleeding; bad breath; loose, broken, or missing teeth; pus between the gums and teeth; and any unusual growth in the mouth. Your Beagle may also have gum disease if she's reluctant to eat, frequently drops bits of food, doesn't want to drink cold water, or doesn't want to chew on her favorite toy.

Untreated teeth can also cause serious problems in your Beagle's overall health. Abscessed teeth or periodontal disease

> The American Animal Hospital Association recommends brushing a dog's teeth at least three times a week.

Essential Grooming Tools

- ○ Hound glove
- ○ Slicker brush
- ○ Shedding blade or rake
- ○ Greyhound comb
- ○ Flea comb
- ○ Quality dog shampoo and conditioner

- ○ Nail clippers or grinder
- ○ Styptic powder
- ○ Cotton balls
- ○ Ear cleaner
- ○ Dog toothbrush or thimble brush
- ○ Dog toothpaste

can lead to heart and kidney disease in dogs, because the bacteria from the mouth enter the bloodstream and travel throughout the body, potentially causing infection in various organs. By brushing your Beagle's teeth on a regular basis, you can decrease the need for veterinary cleanings, which require anesthetizing the dog.

Accustom your Beagle to having her teeth brushed during puppyhood by gently scrubbing them with a soft gauze pad. Puppy mouths are sensitive during teething, so be careful not to hurt her; you don't want to make her mouth shy, wary of having anyone touch or examine her mouth. Wrap some gauze or a soft washcloth around your finger, moisten it with water, and wipe all the teeth, front and back, with strokes from the gum line to the tip of the tooth. This familiarizes your Beagle with having her gums and teeth rubbed.

After the permanent teeth come in, you can graduate to a finger brush, one that fits over your finger, or a toothbrush and toothpaste. Be sure to use a brush and toothpaste made for dogs; toothbrushes should be soft so they don't damage gum tissue, and toothpaste needs to be formulated for the dog's system. Toothpaste made for people can cause an upset stomach if your dog swallows it. Teeth can also be cleaned with a paste made of baking soda and water.

Start by brushing the front teeth, then move to the upper and lower teeth in the back. Hold the brush so that the bristles are at a 45-degree angle to the tooth surface, and move the brush in an oval motion. Be sure you get down into the crevices where teeth and gums meet, because this is where odor and infection begin. For ease of brushing, hold the mouth shut with one hand, use your thumb to lift up the pet's lip, and brush with the other hand. Kansas State University veterinarian Linda DeBowes, who has advanced training in animal dentistry, says it's not necessary to brush the inside of the teeth. Simply getting the outside is helpful for overall dental care.

Veterinary teeth cleaning includes use of a short-lasting anesthetic that allows for gum-line probes, removal of tartar, and tooth polishing. In between brushings and cleanings, dry kibble or hard biscuits can help reduce tartar buildup, but don't rely on biscuits for all your Beagle's dental needs. They simply aren't up to the job. Special dental diets decrease plaque accumulation on teeth, but they aren't suitable for all dogs. Ask your veterinarian if this type of diet is appropriate for your Beagle.

Foot Care

If your Beagle spends a lot of time running on pavement, his nails will wear down naturally, but otherwise nails should be trimmed at least monthly. If you can hear the nails clicking on the floor, it's time for them to be trimmed. Overgrown nails snag easily on carpets, upholstery, and bed coverings. If they get too

The Joys of Peanut Butter

"Our biggest grooming aid has been peanut butter," says Janiece Harrison. "We did a terrible job of getting our Annie accustomed to handling, and nail cutting used to be an ordeal. We now have the following routine: the whole family (my husband, Annie, Bo [the other Beagle], and I) assemble in our small spare bathroom. I put a scoop of peanut butter on a jar lid. I hold Annie in my lap and let her begin licking the peanut butter while Bill does her nails. Bo's there for moral support. The whole process goes much more smoothly now. Peanut butter really does work any time we need to keep her occupied while we check her for ticks or apply Advantage. Luckily, Beagles don't need much grooming other than monthly nail cutting. Ours love to be brushed with Zoom Grooms and they get baths three or four times a year."

long, they can grow right into the footbed, which is extremely uncomfortable and can even impair the dog's ability to walk.

Puppies, especially, have sharp, fast-growing nails, so keep them trimmed regularly, both to accustom the dog to trimming and to prevent painful gouges in your skin. Get puppies used to nail trimming by "tipping" the nails every week, taking off just a little bit each time.

Nail trimming often involves much howling on the part of the dog and flinching on the part of the owner, but with care and early training, it can be accomplished without trauma for either party, especially if you can resist those soulful Beagle eyes and the pitiful Beagle whine. If your Beagle puts up a struggle, recruit your spouse or one of the kids to hold her. A good way for your assistant to immobilize the dog is to place her between the knees, facing outward, with the left hand supporting the dog's chest.

Once the dog is settled, you're ready to trim. Have your assistant firmly grip one of the legs at the elbow so the dog can't pull it back. The same technique works on the hind legs. Another method is to stand the dog on a table or other high surface and lift each foot up and back as you would if you were shoeing a horse. (If you don't have a grooming noose, you'll need an assistant to hold the dog still.) Then grasp the paw and clip just at the curve of the nail. As you clip, praise your Beagle if she's behaving nicely, and give a firm "No" to put a stop to squirming.

Clip only the tip of the nail; avoid clipping past the curve, or you risk hitting the quick, a blood vessel inside the nail. Being "quicked" is painful and produces bleeding. It's easier to avoid the quick in dogs with light-colored or clear nails, because you can see the vein. In case you clip too far, though, have some styptic powder on hand to stop the bleeding. You can find it at pet supply stores. If you run out or don't have any on hand, flour or cornmeal will work in a pinch.

Use pliers-style nail trimmers available at your local pet supply store. The clippers with the orange handles are highly regarded. Smooth the nails with a metal file after trimming.

If you can't stand the fuss your Beagle puts up—and if your budget allows—simply take the dog to a groomer or veterinarian to have nail clipping done. You'll both be happier.

Part of the grooming process should include examining the footpads for foreign objects or injuries. In winter, clean your Beagle's feet after he has gone outdoors; this removes de-icing chemicals, salt, snow, and ice, which can injure the feet or make the dog sick if he licks his paws.

Anal Gland Care

The anal glands are located on each side of the anus. If you imagine the anal area as a clock, the anal glands are found at about the 5:00 and 7:00 positions.

These scent glands produce a fluid that plays a role in territorial marking. This fluid is usually excreted when the dog defecates, but sometimes the glands become clogged, a common problem in Beagles. Scooting her rear on the floor or biting and licking at her rear are signs that your dog's anal glands might be clogged. If clogging isn't relieved, the glands can become impacted or infected, a situation that usually requires a veterinary cleaning and may require a course of antibiotics and hydrotherapy to clear up the problem. Some Beagle owners have been able to control the problem through diet and exercise, but others find that it's necessary to express, or empty, the glands on a regular basis.

If you notice your Beagle scooting or biting, you can ask your veterinarian or a groomer to express the glands. You can learn to do it yourself, but it's not a very pleasant process and you'll probably prefer to leave it to the professionals.

A Happy Ending

End each grooming session with a soothing massage and a treat. Clean equipment thoroughly after each use so that it's ready to go for the next time. And if you're ever tempted to skip a grooming, remember that we brush our hair and wash our faces every day— we owe it to our dogs to provide similarly consistent care.

Bathing

Conventional wisdom used to hold that dogs should be bathed only when dirty, but that was back when shampoos for dogs were much harsher than they are today. Regular bathing can improve coat condition and simply make a dog more pleasant to be around. If a gentle shampoo is used, a dog can be bathed weekly without drying out his coat. Most Beagle owners, however, find that their dogs only need a bath every two or three months—when they start developing doggy odor. A dull coat is another sign that a bath is in order. If your Beagle enjoys rolling in duck droppings or other stinky, dirty substances, he'll need to be bathed more frequently. When your Beagle does need a bath, he can easily fit in the kitchen sink (if you have a good-sized one), saving your back from the aches caused by bending over a bathtub.

It's not easy to give a Beagle a bath. They don't especially care for being wet, and you might as well prepare for the idea that you're going to get as wet as if you'd taken a bath with your dog. To make it less of an ordeal, gather everything you need for the bath—shampoo, towels, and cotton balls to place in his ears so water won't run into them—run the water, and then get the dog. If he sees you making preparations for a bath, he may slink around and attempt to escape, so be sure there's no hiding place or exit available.

> Regular bathing can improve coat condition and simply make a dog more pleasant to be around.

Before bathing, brush the dog thoroughly to remove dead hair. Put him in the sink, with a rubber mat beneath him to prevent slipping, and wet him to the skin with warm water, using a gentle spray. Lather with a gentle dog shampoo. It's important to use a shampoo specially formulated for dogs because their skin has a different pH level than ours does. A shampoo formulated for humans could strip away a dog's beneficial skin oils. Unless your Beagle has parasites or other skin problems, choose a gentle shampoo that doesn't contain flea- or tick-fighting insecticides. The fewer chemicals your dog is exposed to the better. Use a mild tearless shampoo for puppies and a deodorizing or conditioning shampoo for adults. If you do have a problem with fleas, you may want to try a shampoo that has natural flea-fighting ingredients such as citrus, eucalyptus, tea tree oil, pennyroyal, or citronella. Shampoos made with colloidal oatmeal are soothing for dry, itchy coats.

After lathering, rinse your Beagle thoroughly with warm water. (If you are using a medicated or flea shampoo, leave it on the skin for 15 minutes, or as directed on the label.) After rinsing, shampoo again if you're using a gentle shampoo, or as directed if you're using a medicated or flea shampoo. Rinse again. Thorough rinsing is a must if you don't want your Beagle to have dry, flaky skin. A 50/50 mixture of cider vinegar or lemon juice and water is a good final rinse that will help remove shampoo residue.

Apply a light conditioner and rinse again. (Leave-in conditioners can be sprayed on after the bath.) Conditioners leave the coat shiny. Again, use a product formulated for dogs.

Then towel-dry the dog thoroughly, absorbing as much water as possible. Keep the dog in a warm, draft-free place until he's completely dry. This also ensures that he doesn't immediately go roll in the mud or dirt, necessitating another bath. If you want to speed the process using a blow dryer—a good idea with puppies so as to prevent chilling—follow the procedure described below.

Use a low, gentle setting, never hot. Hold the dryer at least a foot away from the dog so you don't burn his skin. As you blow the coat dry, brush the dog out, moving the brush in the same direction as the coat grows.

If your Beagle's fur tends to develop a greasy feel between baths, rub in some dry oatmeal or cornmeal to absorb the oil. Then brush it all out, using the same brushing technique described in the brushing section above. A bristle brush is the best tool for this

How to De-skunk Your Beagle

If your Beagle has a run-in with a skunk and comes out on the losing side, you'll want to get rid of the powerful, irritating odor before you welcome him back indoors. Try bathing him with the following solution, developed by Karyl Brandon, an animal science technician at Kansas State University's College of Veterinary Medicine. You can find the ingredients at most drugstores or grocery stores.

Mix one quart of three-percent hydrogen peroxide, a quarter cup of baking soda (sodium bicarbonate), and one teaspoon of liquid soap. Wet your Beagle down to the skin, then apply the mixture, and work it through his fur. Leave it on for three or four minutes, then rinse thoroughly. Don't allow your Beagle to lick or drink the solution.

Throw out any of the mixture that you don't use. It's not safe to bottle and store this chemical combination.

dry bath. Greasy coats can signal various skin diseases, so a Beagle that doesn't stay clean between baths should be checked by her veterinarian.

Home Grooming
Versus Professional Grooming

While professional grooming isn't really necessary for a Beagle, if you're a busy owner of one or more Beagles, you may find that it's simply more convenient. The time saved by having a dog professionally groomed can be well worth it if you're trying to juggle a job, school, kids, and dog care.

Along with busy professionals, senior citizens figure prominently in the clientele of groomers. People who are elderly may be unable to do the work. Beagle owners benefit from professional grooming by being able to spend more time with a pet who looks nice and smells good, without having to worry about hair or odors getting on furniture and clothing.

If you plan to take your Beagle to a professional groomer, you'll probably want to schedule visits every two to three months—as often as you would normally bathe the dog. If you opt to have your Beagle professionally groomed, begin early, during puppyhood. It's much easier for a groomer to teach a youngster to accept the professional process than to persuade an older dog that grooming is fun. Early introductions give the groomer an opportunity to develop a good relationship with your Beagle that can last into his golden years.

> The time saved by having a dog professionally groomed can be well worth it if you're trying to juggle a job, school, kids, and dog care.

What to Look for in a Groomer

If you decide to have your Beagle professionally groomed, you'll want to take just as much care in the choice of a groomer as you do in choosing a veterinarian or other pet-care professional. Top-notch groomers not only treat their canine clients with love and respect, they also can spot potential health problems early on. Before you just choose a shop out of the *Yellow Pages* or simply plop your Beagle down on the counter of the grooming shop down the street, interview the groomer carefully to make sure this is someone to whom you're willing to entrust your dog.

The best way to start your search is through that old standby—word of mouth. Ask your veterinarian if there's a groomer he or she recommends to clients. Some veterinarians even have groomers on staff. Grooming brings pets in on a regular basis, and veterinary technicians who are trained as groomers—or groomers who are trained as veterinary technicians—can be the first line of defense against disease, able to identify looming skin or health problems perhaps before you might notice.

Your Beagle's breeder and pet-owning friends and neighbors are good sources of recommendations as well. Ask how long they've been taking their pets to the groomer and whether they're satisfied with the service they receive. Boarding kennel operators and pet store managers may be able to point you in the direction of a good groomer.

You can also contact professional grooming organizations for referrals. To find members of the National Dog Groomers Association of America in your area, call (412) 962-2711. You can contact the American Grooming Shop Association at (719) 570-7788.

When you have a list of names, call each groomer for information about the services offered, types of products used, pricing, and whether they offer pickup and delivery. Ask how long they've been in business and with what breeds they usually work.

Educational credentials are important as well. Groomers may learn on the job—by apprenticing with another groomer—or they may attend a grooming school. Following that, a groomer can further her education by getting certified by one of the national certifying organizations. Though law does not require certification, and there are good groomers who are not certified, it is a voluntary process that requires a groomer to be evaluated by her peers. The fact that a groomer is certified is a clue that she is dedicated to improving her own skills.

Did You Know?

Dalmatian puppies are born pure white; they don't start getting spots until they are three or four days old.

If your Beagle is a senior citizen or has a health problem, find out what steps the groomer takes to ensure the dog's comfort and safety. A shop that's associated with a boarding kennel may require proof that a dog's vaccinations are up to date or that he has received a *Bordetella* vaccine within the past six months.

Once you're satisfied with the responses you receive, visit the grooming shops that interest you. Before you walk in the door, note how long it took you to drive there and whether parking is easily available. Inside, the shop should be clean, neat, and well lit. Watch how the groomers handle the dogs in their care. Are they firm but gentle, or do they seem uninterested or hurried?

A good groomer will greet you with a smile and take the time to explain procedures, answer questions, and show you the kinds of brushes and combs you need to use at home to maintain your Beagle between grooming appointments. If you like what you see, make an appointment to bring your dog in for a bath and blowout.

Hopefully, your Beagle's good manners will permit the groomer to handle her without any problems. The socialization you've accomplished should ensure that she doesn't growl or shy away when a stranger touches her. If this is a problem, you need to warn the groomer ahead of time so she can avoid getting bitten. Training classes and regular handling by other people help your dog learn that being touched can feel good, especially if it also leaves her clean afterward.

Groomers are trained, skilled professionals. By choosing carefully, you're sure to be pleased with your Beagle's appearance and the care she receives.

Family Life

8

In This Chapter

○ Exercise
○ Playing Nicely with Children
○ Vacations: Traveling with and Boarding Your Beagle

Beagles are pack dogs, and they love to be with their people. The more company the better, as far as this breed is concerned. Whether that companionship involves exercise, play, or travel, your Beagle will be ready, willing, and able to participate. With early socialization and training, he can take part in numerous dog sports, accompany you on walks and hikes, do well with children and neighbors, and be an uncomplaining travel companion. With plenty of activity and companionship, your Beagle can't help but be a fine family friend.

Exercise

All dogs need exercise to keep them physically and mentally healthy. An inactive dog is a fat dog, with the accompanying likelihood of joint strain or torn ligaments. Inactive dogs, especially Beagles, are also prone to mischief—anything to relieve their boredom. This often leads to behavior problems such as chewing or barking. Regular daily exercise will help keep your Beagle slim, trim, and happy. For a Beagle, exercise can be as simple as going for a long walk or chasing a ball in the backyard or as demanding as participation in agility, obedience trials, tracking, and other dog sports.

> Inactive dogs, especially Beagles, are also prone to mischief—anything to relieve their boredom.

The American Animal Hospital Association recommends walking a younger or middle-aged dog for 10 to 15 minutes once or twice each day. This can begin when your Beagle is 12 weeks old as long as he is up to date on his vaccinations. A pup this young may only want to walk for five minutes at a time, but as your dog becomes conditioned, you can increase walks to whatever length or amount of time is comfortable for both of you. Remember that a Beagle is bred to go all day in the field, so his stamina may well outlast yours. If an extra-long walk isn't possible, you can meet his desire for activity by throwing a ball in the backyard or inventing other at-home games.

If your Beagle is older or overweight, consult your veterinarian about how much and what type of exercise to give. Usually, a 10- to 15-minute walk once a day is a good start. As the pounds start to drop off, your dog's energy level will rise, and you can increase the amount of daily exercise.

The Wheel Thing

Jennifer Davidson and Luna found inline skating to be a great way for both of them to get their exercise. Luna, of course, was on foot, kept under control with a 15-foot extendable leash. With Jennifer on skates, Luna was able to run at top speed, which she loved to do.

"Except for one particularly nasty mishap where we went in opposite directions around a pole, she was really great about making sure she was on the same side of obstacles as I was," Jennifer says. "I used the command 'This way' to make sure she was paying attention when I saw things like poles coming up.

"We were both fairly tired after a very fast mile, and if I slowed the pace considerably for the second mile, upon reaching home Luna would consume the entire contents of her water dish and immediately collapse for an extended nap. Not too different from my own plan of action."

Sports

Dog sports are not just fun, they also double as exercise. Challenge your Beagle's athletic abilities by introducing him to activities such as agility, field trials, flyball, tracking, and freestyle. Beagles are crowd pleasers in whatever arena they perform.

Agility The fast-paced sport of agility is a race against time. Dogs, with their people running alongside, must maneuver through a series of obstacles such as A-frames, hoops, weave poles, and tunnels. Scores are based on accuracy as well as speed. Beagles are built for agility, although their desire to thoroughly sniff the course can slow them down. Agility is a fun way to give your dog exercise and increase his self-confidence.

Sassy and her owner Sydney Armstrong joined a puppy class that combined elements of obedience and agility when Sassy was four months old. When they started competing in United Kennel Club agility trials, Sassy earned her AGI title in four trials. Then they went for the AGII title, which was quite a bit more difficult. To earn her AGI and AGII titles, Sassy had to complete three trials for each title with scores of 170 or higher. The next step is an Agility Champion (ACH) title.

Sassy has also competed in AKC agility trials, and last spring she was the #4 ranked Novice Beagle in one point system and was tied for seventh place overall in another. (Point systems, usually administered by publications such as *Front & Finish* or *Show Beagle Quarterly*, are how national rankings are determined in various dog sports.) Sassy is good at running the courses, but of course she loves to stop and sniff, which lowers her score because of the extra time she spends. Sydney says agility gives her lots of time with Sassy, and they both enjoy the interaction with other dogs.

To see if your Beagle might be interested in this fun sport, take him to a local agility event or class. If he's raring to go, sign him up for a class. Before starting agility training, your Beagle should know and respond to the commands sit, down, stay, and come. Make sure he's physically fit. Take him in for a veterinary exam to check for good range of motion and lack of back pain.

Beagle Field Trials Do you beagle? If you own a Beagle, you might want to give it a try. The sport of beagling—the tracking of rabbits or hares—has a long and honorable history. Beagling began in England many centuries ago and today has evolved into a competitive event enjoyed by more than 60,000 Beagles annually.

Beagles hunt in pairs or packs. Each pair or pack should present a unified appearance, being as near as possible to the same height, weight, conformation, and color. With flags (tails) up, the Beagles work cheerfully, directed by the "master" and "whips"(people who help the master).

The goal of a field trial is to demonstrate a dog's ability to perform its natural functions. In the case of the Beagle, that means finding and tracking rabbits or hares. Three types of field trials are open to Beagles. The first is the slow and precise brace trial, in which groups of two or three Beagles are judged on their accuracy in trailing a rabbit that's been flushed by a "beater." In this event, it's easy to keep up with the Beagles on foot. A separate option, gundog brace, is much the same but includes a test for gun-shyness (the test is simply a blank cartridge fired overhead while the dogs are working the scent).

In small pack option (SPO) trials, packs of four to seven Beagles pursue rabbits. There's no beater to flush the rabbit; the dogs must find their own. SPO trials have no time limit, so they demand Beagles with plenty of stamina, and include a test for gun-shyness.

Finally, there are the fast-paced, exciting large pack trials, the swift pursuit of large hares—which have a different running style than rabbits—by a pack of 30 to 60 Beagles, which must be able to run for at least eight hours. As in SPO trials, the pack must find the hare on its own. The pack moves so rapidly that even riders on horseback aren't always able to keep up. The dogs' progress is followed by the sound of their tonguing, or baying.

In any field trial, the dogs are divided into groups by sex and height and are judged on accuracy of trailing. Field trials are competitive events, and a Beagle who earns enough championship points

Did You Know?

According to the American Animal Hospital Association, more than 40 percent of pet owners talk to their pets on the phone or through the answering machine.

is entitled to carry the letters FC—Field Champion—in front of his name. Training for field trials can begin when a Beagle is about six months old. Desirable qualities include searching and pursuing ability, accuracy in trailing, proper use of voice, endurance, adaptability, patience, determination, independence, cooperation with other pack members, and intelligence. In case you're worried, beagling usually involves the rabbit or hare leading the Beagles on a merry chase and then escaping.

Flyball If your Beagle has a passion for balls, and some of them do, explore the possibility of flyball competition. Few dog sports are more fun—or more noisy—to watch. Dogs bark, handlers shout encouragement and instructions, and spectators cheer on their favorites.

Flyball is a team relay race, with four dogs on each team. One at a time, each dog must sprint over four hurdles (set four inches below the shoulder height of the smallest dog), trigger the release of a tennis ball by stepping on a lever, grab the ball, and take it back over the hurdles. The first team to run without errors—such as skipping one or more hurdles—wins the heat. Tournament play can be organized in double elimination or round-robin style.

To be successful at flyball, your Beagle should enjoy running, jumping, and playing with balls. He also needs to be physically fit (with no back, hip, or elbow problems) and under your control. Flyball dogs compete off leash, so your Beagle must respond reliably to voice commands. Be patient during training sessions and don't rush things. You want your dog to learn accuracy as well as speed.

Titles your dog can earn are based on the number of points he achieves in competition. They are Flyball Dog, Flyball Dog Excellent, Flyball Dog Champion, Flyball Master, Flyball Master Excellent, Flyball Master Champion, Onyx Award, and Flyball Grand Champion. For more information about flyball rules, equipment, or teams in your area, contact the North American Flyball Association (see the appendix). The rules are $10; all other information is free.

Tracking This is the ideal sport for a Beagle, a master at following his nose. A tracking trial is simply a test of whether a dog can follow a trail by scent. There's no competition, either against the clock or against other dogs. Of course, you can't just show up at a field trial and give it a go; your Beagle needs to learn the elements of tracking first. An obedience instructor or a tracking club can help you train for one of the following titles: tracking dog (TD), tracking dog excellent (TDX), and variable surface tracking (VST). A dog who earns all three titles is awarded the status of champion tracker (CT).

To pass a TD test, your Beagle must be able to follow a track 440 to 500 yards long, with at least two right-angle turns. The track is laid by someone unknown to the dog and is one or two hours old. The goal is for your dog to find the scented article dropped at the end of the track.

Things get a little tougher with the TDX test. The track is 800 to 1000 yards long and three to five hours old. It may take the dog through tall grass or ditches, and the track layer will try to trick him with dummy scent articles along the way.

City Beagles with street smarts can learn to follow a trail on such surfaces as asphalt, concrete, and linoleum, for a VST title. The VST track takes a dog over at least three types of surfaces for a distance of 600 to 800 yards. The track is three or four hours old with up to eight turns.

Freestyle A fusion of traditional obedience exercises and the equine sport of dressage, freestyle is a routine set to music that shows dog and handler working in harmony and expressing their creativity through costume and movement. To be successful in freestyle requires a Beagle who is athletic, attentive, flexible, and trainable.

Freestyle competitions take place across the United States. For more information, contact Pup-Peroni Canine Freestylers (see the appendix).

Obedience Trials

Another way for your Beagle to compete, besides in the various sports above, is in obedience trials. Every Beagle should learn basic obedience commands: sit, down, stay, heel, and come. But learning doesn't have to end there. Your Beagle can build on those commands to earn beginning and advanced obedience titles. As with any performance event, success breeds self-confidence.

While they don't resemble the dogs that traditionally take home high scores in obedience trials—Golden Retrievers, Shetland Sheepdogs, and Border Collies—Beagles are capable of earning obedience titles. The secret, trainers say, is positive reinforcement, preferably with something the Beagle loves—like food. In the ring, though, your Beagle will have to perform solely for love of you, because treats and coaxing aren't allowed. As Beagles are bred to be independent, their natural instincts don't predispose them to some of the requirements of obedience trials. With enough training and positive reinforcement, though, they can become some of the most reliable, animated, and happiest workers. Always keep training and showing fun. Beagles will find something better to do if they're not having a good time. And not every Beagle is cut out for obedience.

"When I tried showing Gopher in obedience, he was

offended that I would actually tell him what to do, so that didn't work," Janet Nieland says.

Obedience titles dogs can earn are companion dog (CD), companion dog excellent (CDX), utility dog (UD), and utility dog excellent (UDX). Overachievers can go for the title of obedience trial champion.

To earn a novice, or CD, title, your Beagle must heel on and off leash at an appropriate pace, sit nicely whenever you stop, stand politely for the judge's examination, perform a sit-stay and down-stay for an allotted period of time, and come when called. The dogs with the highest scores respond to these commands with alacrity and precision. A title is earned when a dog achieves passing scores at three obedience trials. More advanced titles require the dogs to perform off leash and for longer periods, as well as to complete jumping and retrieving exercises. Utility dogs must be proficient at scent discrimination, a piece of dog biscuit for Beagles.

Canine Good Citizen

If obedience work sounds too regimented, but you'd still like your Beagle to have a title, prepare him for the Canine Good Citizen test. The American Kennel Club sponsors this program, with tests administered by local dog clubs, private trainers, and 4-H clubs.

To earn a CGC title, your Beagle must be well groomed and demonstrate the manners that all good dogs should exhibit. The CGC test requires a dog to perform the sit, down, stay, and come commands, react appropriately to other dogs and distractions, allow a stranger to

Did You Know?

40 percent of dog and cat owners carry pictures of their pets in their wallets.

approach him, sit politely for petting, walk nicely on a loose lead, move through a crowd without going wild, calm down after play or praise, and sit still for examination by the judge.

Other Activities

If dog sports or obedience trials aren't your thing, consider participating in conformation shows or therapy work. These two very different activities each offer a special kind of satisfaction, whether it is the joy of a win in the show ring or the gratification of your dog bringing pleasure to people.

Conformation Showing We often think of dog shows as the Miss America pageants of the dog world, but their underlying purpose is to select those dogs that are most suited for breeding. With that in mind, each dog's structure (or conformation), movement, and attitude are judged against the breed standard, which purports to describe the perfect Beagle. The dogs that most closely meet the standard earn championships and are considered good breeding prospects. If your Beagle has what it takes to compete in this arena, you may enjoy conformation showing. It's an opportunity to travel, get together with other Beagle lovers, and see other nice dogs in the breed.

Your breeder can give you good advice about whether your Beagle is suited to the show ring, not only conformationally but also temperamentally. If you don't plan to use a professional handler, ring craft classes offered by a local dog club can teach you how to present your Beagle to best advantage.

> Your breeder can give you good advice about whether your Beagle is suited to the show ring, not only conformationally but also temperamentally.

All-breed dog shows are where your Beagle can earn points toward a championship. Each win brings one to five points, depending on the number of dogs defeated, and a three-, four- or five-point win is called a major. To earn a championship, your Beagle needs 15 points won under three different judges. Two of the wins must be majors, each won under a different judge.

Therapy Work

If you enjoy helping others, you and your Beagle can bring pleasure and laughter to people confined to hospitals and nursing homes. Therapy-dog visits are a wonderful way for you to share the joy of Beagle ownership with others. Petting your dog can ease the loneliness of a widower in a nursing home, lower the blood pressure of a hospital patient, and bring big smiles and shouts of laughter from children in a cancer ward.

Sassy (and honorary Beagle Sprite) got into therapy work on the recommendation of their trainer, an evaluator for Therapy Dogs Incorporated. Owner Sydney thought it was a great idea since she knew that if she were in a nursing facility, she would enjoy a visit from a dog. Sassy and Sprite passed the evaluation test and, along with Sydney, began visiting a local facility every other week. They love the attention they receive, and residents look forward to seeing them. Only once has Sassy's nose gotten the better of her, Sydney reports. They went in to visit a patient and Sydney noticed that he had an open package of peanut butter crackers on his nightstand. Sassy saw them too, so Sydney watched her closely. They finished their visit and were leaving the room when Sydney heard the sound of crunching. She looked down and saw that Sassy had a cracker in her mouth, with the other half on the floor. She still hasn't figured out how Sassy sneaked it out from under her gaze.

Your therapy Beagle needs to be clean and free of fleas, and have pretty company manners. No food stealing (well, not too much) or potty accidents! He must pass a temperament test to ensure that he's suited to this type of work. A sweet, tolerant, fearless disposition is ideal since therapy work involves encounters with new or unusual places, people, and equipment. Both of you will attend training classes before visits begin. Be sure to take normal precautions for your dog against falls from shaky aged hands or run-ins with wheelchairs or walkers. A short leash attached to a harness will help you keep control. (For more information on therapy dog certifying organizations, see the appendix.)

Playing Nicely with Children

When they're introduced properly and carefully supervised, Beagles and children are the perfect playmates. While Beagles are tolerant and fun-loving, however, they aren't stuffed animals, and they need to be protected from ear-grabbing and tail-pulling. Any interaction between children and Beagles needs to be grounded in close parental guidance. It's simply not smart to bring home a dog without being willing to supervise, set rules, and teach your child how to behave with the dog.

Even if you don't have children in your home, your Beagle may still encounter them in other places. Be aware of approaching children; toddlers, especially, tend to be unafraid of animals and will run right up to your dog and try to pet him. Intercept the approach so you can control any interaction. Teach a

Fun Things Kids Can Do with a Beagle

Teaching Tricks

Beagles are very smart and can learn how to do all sorts of tricks. Amaze your friends by teaching your dog to sit, beg, dance on his hind legs, speak on command, and play dead (roll over). A good book to learn how to do this is <u>The Trick Is in the Training: 25 Fun Tricks to Teach Your Dog</u>, by Stephanie J. Taunton and Cheryl S. Smith.

Bobbing for Biscuits

You can play this game any time of year, not just at Halloween. It's great fun at birthday parties—yours or the dog's! You'll need a small bowl, four biscuits per Beagle, and a watch with a second hand.

To get started, put some water in the bowl (not too much or the dogs will try to drink their way to the biscuits) and drop in four dog biscuits. One at a time, let the dogs try to get the biscuits. The object is for the dog to eat as many biscuits as he can within the time limit—30 seconds to one minute. No help from the audience, please, but cheering and clapping are okay. The dog who eats the most biscuits in the least amount of time is the winner.

Junior Showmanship

If you want to see what dog shows are all about, junior showmanship is the place to be. It's a great way to learn about dogs and develop good sportsmanship and dog handling skills. It doesn't matter whether your Beagle is show quality. You'll be judged on your ability to present and handle your dog, not on his looks. There are also junior handler programs for agility and obedience. For more information on junior showmanship, contact the AKC (see the appendix).

4-H

These nationwide clubs offer a chance to learn about all kinds of activities, including dog care. The 4-H dog program teaches grooming, training, and other aspects of dog ownership. At the beginner level, 4-H members learn how to choose a dog, feed him, keep him healthy, teach him nice manners, and show him. Intermediate and advanced members learn how to train a dog for obedience or other activities.

young child not to run up to dogs, and hold the child's hand while she strokes him.

Holiday Hazards:
Keeping Your Beagle Safe and Healthy

Naturally, you'll want to include your Beagle in your holiday celebrations. She's a special family member, after all. But the holidays hold a few hazards that you'll want to be aware of so you can make them fun and safe.

New Year's is a loud and raucous time of parties, fireworks, and noisemakers, all of which can be stressful to your Beagle if she's not used to it. Make some time to spend with her before you have a party or go out. If you're having people over, confine her to a quiet room where she won't be disturbed. On the other hand, if your Beagle is a party animal, let her join the fun. Just make sure she's kept well away from chocolate, champagne, paté, and other rich goodies. You don't want her to start the new year with an upset tummy or a hangover.

For most of us, Valentine's Day and Easter mean chocolate—and lots of it. But as you know, chocolate can be hazardous to your Beagle's health, even in small amounts. Keep it up high to prevent nibbling.

Marching bands, cookouts, and fireworks mark Independence Day. If your Beagle goes to the parade with you, keep her on leash and under control. At the picnic, she'll no doubt want a taste of all the goodies, from deviled eggs to hot dogs. Ignore her pleading eyes and ply her with healthy treats, such as carrots or bits of dog biscuit. At night, sparks fly, and the sky is filled with the colorful flashes and whizzing sounds of fireworks. The combination can frighten even the most self-possessed dogs, so be sure your Beagle is indoors or securely restrained during the show. This is the holiday when dogs are most likely to run away, fearful of the strange noises.

Wee ghosties and goblins roam the streets in search of sweet treats at Halloween. The costumed visitors may cause your Beagle to bark or howl when they come to the door. If the stress of these unearthly visitors is too much, confine your Beagle to a room where she can rest in peace without going to pieces. Some Beagles enjoy the fun, though, and will even get in the spirit of things by allowing themselves to be dressed in costume. As with Valentine's Day, keep the candy well out of reach.

The feast of Thanksgiving with its smells of turkey and dressing wafting from the kitchen will start your Beagle begging, but such rich foods aren't good for her digestive system and can lead to vomiting or diarrhea. If you can't resist giving a bite, limit it to no more than a tablespoon of breast meat (dark meat is higher in fat) and forego the gravy and dressing. Neither you nor your Beagle will be very thankful if she has to go to the emergency room with a case of pancreatitis.

Trees, ornaments, and decorative plants are all part of the Christmas celebration, but they can be dangerous to your dog. For instance, the chemicals you put in the water to keep the tree fresh aren't good for your dog to drink, so make sure she doesn't have access to the tree stand. Consider putting the tree in a room that can be closed off when you aren't around to supervise, or putting up

Did You Know?

Millie, President Bush's English springer spaniel, earned over four times as much as her owner in 1991.

Trees, ornaments, and decorative plants are all part of the Christmas celebration, but they can be dangerous to your dog.

a decorative but effective barrier around the tree. Tinsel is hazardous if swallowed, and electrical cords are attractive to dogs who like to chew. Wrap them up and put them out of the way to avoid a shocking experience. Mistletoe, holly, Jerusalem cherry, amaryllis, and other flowering bulbs can be toxic to dogs, so place them out of reach. A chewed poinsettia can irritate the lining of the mouth and intestines.

By taking precautions, you can ensure that your Beagle enjoys an entire year of happiness and safety.

Making Your Beagle a Good Neighbor

To keep your Beagle from getting a reputation as a neighborhood nuisance, you need to ensure that barking and howling don't rise to an annoying level and that you always pick up after him when you go on walks. When he interacts with neighbors, make sure he sits nicely instead of jumping up on them or tangling his leash around their legs. If you do all this, your Beagle may well be the most popular neighbor on the block!

Vacations: Traveling with and Boarding Your Beagle

Beagles are loving and convenient travel companions. They never complain about the length of the trip, and the amount of luggage they require is small. Wherever you're going, you couldn't ask for a better comrade.

Making the Decision

Most Beagles love going on outings, short or long, especially if they've been conditioned to it from puppyhood. When deciding whether to take your Beagle along, consider his previous experiences, his personality, and the purpose of your trip.

An outgoing Beagle who's used to running every errand with you will adore the experience of a long car trip or a stay in a hotel. This dog is open to adventures of all kinds, as long as you're together. One who is more of a stay-at-home dog can find the same experience unnerving, however. The other consideration is what you'll be doing on the trip. If it's for business, your Beagle won't have much fun staying alone in the hotel room in his crate all day. A better option is a relaxing vacation during which you'll have plenty of time to devote to your dog.

Traveling with a Beagle is much easier than with a larger dog. Many hotels welcome small, well-behaved pets. On the other hand, unless you're traveling in France or another dog-loving European country, dogs are generally not welcome in shops, restaurants, museums, or on public transportation. If you travel with your Beagle, make sure that your destination has plenty of places where he can accompany you, such as parks and restaurants with outdoor seating.

Leaving your Beagle in a boarding kennel or at home with a pet sitter is something to consider if you're going on a trip where you won't be able to spend a lot of time with him or to a place where a dog would be unsafe or must stay in quarantine for a long period, such as England or Hawaii. Many boarding kennels provide daily playtime and petting sessions, or even offer dog camp activities such as agility or other games. A live-in pet sitter allows your Beagle to stay in familiar territory, and avoid the stress of encountering strange dogs and people.

Traveling with Your Dog

If you decide your Beagle will enjoy the trip you're taking, all you need to do is make the arrangements. He'll need his own plane reservation if you're flying, and you'll need to pack a bag that includes an appropriate food and treat supply, bottled water to prevent tummy upset, grooming supplies, medications such as heartworm preventive, and a favorite toy. Your veterinarian can provide you with a health certificate, which you may be required to present at the airport or at any state or international border crossings.

Before You Leave If you are moving or traveling with your Beagle, obtain a temporary write-on tag with your new phone number or the phone number of a friend. Temporary tags are available at pet stores or from veterinarians or animal shelters. In the case of a move, you should provide your dog with an engraved ID tag that lists not only your new address and phone number but also a contact name and number in your previous neighborhood. If your dog gets lost along the way, rescuers may not be able to reach you immediately at your new address.

Traveling by Air If your Beagle is small enough to ride in a carrier that fits under your seat in the plane, he can travel in comfort and style in a soft-sided carrier. Choose one that permits your dog to stand up and turn around inside it. Not just any old tote bag will do; the bag must be approved by airlines for carry-on use. These bags are available at pet supply stores or through catalogs. Look for such features as mesh panels with roll-up flaps (flaps can be rolled up or down to give your Beagle a view or privacy), top and front zippers for easy placement and removal of the dog, a zippered end pocket (good for storing documentation), an adjustable shoulder strap that doubles as a leash, and a coordinating accessory bag to carry such items as medication or plastic bags for scooping poop. The bag should wipe clean in case your Beagle has an accident inside it. Some carriers also have wheels for easier transport. Most airlines permit these soft-sided carriers, but it's a good idea to stop by the airport with the carrier before your trip to make sure the airline will permit it on board.

> Sedation alters an animal's natural ability to balance and maintain equilibrium, and increased altitude can create respiratory and cardiovascular problems for sedated animals.

Limit food and water intake for several hours before the flight, to lessen the chance of airsickness. Let your Beagle lick an ice cube or two in flight to assuage his thirst, and give him a few bites of kibble if he seems to be calm and enjoying the trip. If at all possible, avoid shipping your Beagle in the cargo bay. This is a stressful experience for any dog, given the loudness, turbulence, and possibility of other luggage falling on the crate. If for some reason your dog must fly baggage instead of "first-class," you'll need a high-quality plastic crate that is airline-approved.

The American Humane Association recommends against tranquilizing pets for flights. Sedation alters an animal's natural ability to balance and maintain equilibrium, and increased altitude can create respiratory and cardiovascular problems for sedated animals. If your Beagle is so sensitive that you believe sedation is necessary, it may be best for him not to fly at all.

Traveling by Car The image of a Beagle with his head sticking out the car window, ears flapping in the wind, and tongue hanging out is irresistible, but a moving car is not a safe place for a free-roaming dog. Your Beagle should ride in a crate, which will keep him in snug comfort and prevent him from getting underfoot, jumping in the driver's lap, or being tossed out of the car in the event of a wreck. If you plan to show your Beagle or take him on trips with you, the crate must be portable, sturdy, and easy to set up and clean.

Beagles traveling by car, van, or motorhome can ride in style in wire or plastic crates. Some wire crates are specially designed for frequent car or van travel. These come with doors on the side rather than the front, allowing owners to pack around them yet still remove the dog easily. Some of these crates have both side and end door openings. A crate that's frequently used for travel must be well built, made with strongly welded heavy-gauge wire. This is especially important in foldable crates, which tend to be more lightweight.

Plastic crates are lightweight, long lasting, and easy to clean. They're perfect for car travel—simply run the seatbelt through the handle and fasten it to keep the crate from sliding around. One see-through plastic model has a raised seat that gives dogs a ride with a view.

A wire crate allows your Beagle to see out and to enjoy the breeze if the windows are down. When the sun is shining bright, you can cover a wire crate so your dog won't get overheated. Whether you're buying a plastic or wire crate, look for one with strong latches and smooth edges.

If you choose to let your Beagle ride in the car restrained by a canine seatbelt but wish to have access to a crate, a soft-sided carrier or a crate that folds flat may be your best choice, especially if space is at a premium. Look for one with an easy-carry handle.

Hotels and Campgrounds The number-one piece of advice you need to know about staying at a hotel or campground is to call ahead first. Make sure that dogs are permitted before you arrive. If the answer is no, offer to pay a deposit—the usual amount is $25 or $50—or to provide proof of your Beagle's good behavior, such as his CGC or CD certificates.

If the answer is yes, be sure you and your dog are on your best behavior. Don't permit barking, put a cover on the bed-spread to protect it from dog hair, and pick up after him wherever he eliminates.

Most hotels prefer that you not leave your dog alone in the room. If you must, however, confine him to a crate so he won't have an accident or escape when the cleaning people come in. A crate also prevents your Beagle from doing any damage to the room. Stella, who was normally well-behaved for a Beagle, was left uncrated while her owners went to dinner. They returned to find that she had scratched quite a bit of wallpaper off the bathroom wall.

At campgrounds, the same rules of good behavior apply. Keep your Beagle quiet, don't let him foul the grounds or eliminate near streams or other bodies of water, and keep him on leash to protect him from wildlife (and vice versa).

Boarding Your Dog

You should choose a boarding kennel just as carefully as you do a veterinarian. Ask for referrals from friends or your vet. If the breeder from whom you bought your dog lives nearby, ask if she offers boarding services. Many breeders do, and it's ideal if you can leave your Beagle with people and dogs that are familiar to him.

Before You Board If leaving your dog with his breeder isn't fea-
sible, start checking out the places other people have suggested.
Inspect them in person to satisfy yourself as to cleanliness and
the nature of the staff. You don't want to leave your dog in any
but the most loving and trustworthy of hands.

> You should choose a boarding kennel just as carefully as you do a veterinarian. Ask for referrals from friends or your vet.

Look for easy-clean concrete
floors, large runs, and clean
grounds. It's natural for there to
be some odor, given the presence of many dogs, but feces
should be picked up unless
they've only been recently "deliv-
ered." If you do see stools, check to see if they're well-formed; it's
an indication that the dogs staying there are eating a high-quality
food and aren't unduly stressed.

Key Questions to Ask See if the kennel has a grassy play area
where dogs can exercise. Ask how many dogs are let out at a time
and whether an effort is made to segregate them by size. Many
kennels offer camp-style games or will provide your dog with a
set amount of one-on-one attention and petting each day. These
services may or may not be included in the daily boarding cost.
Be sure you understand what's covered and what's not.

Find out what diet the kennel operators feed. You may prefer
to bring your own food supply so as not to disrupt your dog's eating habits. You'll also need to bring any medications he needs;
there may be an extra charge for administering it.

Expect to be asked to provide up-to-date vaccination records.
Most kennels require proof that a dog has been inoculated for rabies, distemper, and parvo within the past year, and they may require a *Bordetella* vaccination within the past six months. If you

have your dog on a triennial vaccination schedule, this may pose a problem, but your veterinarian may be able to provide you with a health certificate that the kennel will accept. The kennel operator will also check to see if your dog is flea-free and may require him to have a bath—at extra expense—if he's not.

Make sure the kennel is staffed 24 hours a day, seven days a week. This is a must for your dog's safety. In case of fire or other emergency, someone needs to be there to handle the situation. Nevertheless, don't expect to be able to drop your dog off or pick him up at any time of the day or night. Just like any other business, kennels have specific hours during which they do business.

Expect the kennel manager to answer your questions openly and readily. A surly attitude or an unwillingness to answer questions is a red flag. Turn right around and leave. There are bound to be better options for your Beagle.

Hiring a Pet Sitter

The advantages of a live-in pet sitter are many. Your dog gets to stay in her own familiar home, with all its comforting scents and toys, plus she'll have someone to keep her company while you're gone. A pet sitter eliminates the stress of staying in a strange place and limits your Beagle's exposure to parasites or disease carried by other dogs.

As with any service, word of mouth is a good way to start the search for a pet sitter. Ask friends if they can recommend someone. Your veterinarian may have some veterinary technicians on staff who moonlight as pet sitters. Once you have some names, schedule personal interviews in your

Leaving a List for the Dog Sitter or Boarding Kennel

Even though you are satisfied with the boarding kennel situation or the pet sitter's credentials and have explained everything thoroughly, leaving behind written instructions helps set your mind at ease. You can detail feeding and medication instructions, exercise and elimination requirements, and favorite pastimes. Consider including some or all of the following information:

○ Feeding/medication times

○ Amount of medication

○ Favorite toys/games

○ Commands dog knows

○ "Secret" passwords to get the dog to eat or potty

○ Favorite hiding places

○ Name and phone number of where you'll be

○ Airline, flight numbers, and departure/arrival times

○ Who to contact in case of emergency

○ Veterinarian's name, address, and phone number

○ Directions to nearest animal emergency hospital

○ Permission for the pet sitter to authorize treatment and guarantee of payment

○ Name and contact number for your pet's guardians in case something happens to you

home so you can see how well they get along with your dog and what she thinks of them.

Ask the following questions when you're interviewing the pet sitter:

○ Are you bonded? Do you carry commercial liability insurance? A positive answer to these questions indicates that the pet sitter takes the job seriously. Expect the pet sitter to show you proof of bonding and insurance.

○ Are you a member of a professional organization, such as the National Association of Professional Pet Sitters? Like bonding and insurance, professional membership indicates that a pet sitter isn't just an animal lover hoping to make a little extra money; he or she has met exacting professional standards.

○ What is your background in pet care? Some pet sitters are veterinary technicians, while others are experienced pet owners. If your Beagle has a medical problem, you may prefer someone who's trained to spot health problems or who is experienced at giving medication or insulin injections.

○ Can you provide references? A good pet sitter should be more than willing to give you the names of other satisfied clients. Don't be afraid to call them and ask about their experience with the pet sitter.

○ What are your prices? The pet sitter should give you a brochure or other written material that details prices and services. He or she may ask you to sign a contract that spells out exactly what will be done. This protects both of you from misunderstanding.

○ Who will take care of my pet if something happens to you? The pet sitter should have a partner or some sort of contingency plan in the event of a personal emergency.

If you're satisfied with the pet sitter's replies, set up an appointment for a few days before your trip so you can explain your dog's routine and show where food, toys, and other necessities are kept.

9

A Lifetime of Love
and Good Health

In This Chapter
- ○ Your Aging Beagle—What to Expect
- ○ How to Keep Your Older Dog Comfortable
- ○ Saying Goodbye

You are fortunate in the breed you've chosen because Beagles generally enjoy a long life span. Barring disease or trauma, a Beagle will be with you for at least 10 years. With good genes and excellent care, he might live 15 years or more. Older dogs have different veterinary and nutritional needs and can benefit from specialized care, health testing, and dietary planning. The following tips will help you keep your senior Beagle in good shape over the years.

Your Aging Beagle—What to Expect

Small dogs such as Beagles often don't show signs of aging until about age 10, but aging can begin as early as seven years of age. Just as each dog is an individual, so is his aging process. Some older Beagles act like pups, while others of the same age slow down tremendously. In general, though, you can expect to see the following signs.

As your Beagle enters his golden years, his muzzle will silver and he'll start to slow down some. His joints may be a bit creakier, and he probably won't race to the food bowl at his old rate of speed, moving instead at a more dignified pace. Dental problems may surface or become worse. His teeth may become weak. Other signs of aging include a thinning coat, brittle toenails, and cataracts, indicated by eyes that appear whitish or blue. Geriatric Beagles may sleep more, pay less attention to what's going on around them, and have less tolerance for hot or cold weather. Some older dogs develop behavioral or mental changes, such as becoming fearful of storms or strangers. They may exhibit this lack of self-confidence by staying closer to you than usual.

Diseases associated with aging are more easily identified if you report small changes in appearance and behavior to your veterinarian or if you bring your dog in for checkups more than once a year. Begin geriatric screenings of your dog when he is seven years old to establish a baseline for his health. Remember that dogs age five to seven years for every chronological year, so problems can develop more quickly. Don't assume that your veterinarian can't do anything for the problems of old age. Veterinary medicine is advancing rapidly, and there are many treatments and medications that can ease your Beagle's passage into this new life stage.

Is Your Beagle Getting Old?

The following questions will help you recognize the signs of aging and take appropriate steps.

Has your Beagle gained or lost weight recently? The gain or loss of a pound or two may not seem like much to you but, for a Beagle, that can be up to 10 percent of his body weight. Weight control is extremely important in dogs, especially as they age. A fat Beagle is more prone to disease, especially diabetes, arthritis, or congestive heart failure. To keep your Beagle's weight at a normal range, limit the number of calories he consumes by switching him to a lower-calorie senior food, feed him several small meals each day instead of one big meal, and increase the amount of exercise he gets. If your Beagle is eating well, even ravenously, but is losing weight, he may have developed diabetes. Weight loss can also be an early, subtle warning sign of cancer.

Is your Beagle drinking more water than usual? Excessive thirst can be a sign of diabetes or kidney disease, which is especially common in older animals.

Has your Beagle's appetite changed? Is he picky or does he act hungry all the time? For most Beagle owners, these are signs of serious problems. If your Beagle is picking at his food, his teeth may hurt. You may need to moisten his dry food or switch to a canned food. Lack of appetite or an excessive (even for a Beagle) appetite can also be a sign of disease.

Does your Beagle have bleeding gums, loose or broken teeth, or bad breath? Older dogs are prone to periodontal

Did You Know?

The old rule of multiplying a dog's age by seven to find the equivalent human age is inaccurate. A better measure is to count the first year as 15, the second year as 10, and each year after that as 5.

disease, which can affect their ability to eat as well. The bacteria in the mouth can also spread through the bloodstream to the heart or other organs, causing serious infections.

Examine your Beagle's stool. Is it dry, soft, or bloody? Is the color different? Does your Beagle strain to defecate? Straining to defecate or producing a hard, dry stool may mean your Beagle is constipated. The opposite condition—a loose or liquid stool—can be a sign of intestinal disease.

Is your Beagle's skin dry, dull, or flaky? Has it developed bald patches? Poor skin condition can indicate nutritional deficiencies, hormonal diseases, allergies, or parasites.

Is there a change in your Beagle's energy level? Lack of energy can signify problems such as anemia or cancer.

Is your Beagle urinating more frequently, or urinating inside the house? Frequent urination often goes along with excessive thirst. It can indicate a bladder or kidney infection or diabetes.

These signs all indicate a need for a veterinary exam so that problems can be stopped before they become serious. If you answer yes to one or more of the above questions, schedule a geriatric exam for your Beagle. A geriatric exam conducted before you see any of these problems can establish a basis for comparison if your Beagle later becomes ill. In addition to a physical exam to check for stiffness, heart murmurs, bad breath, skin lesions, and other typical signs of common aging diseases, a geriatric exam usually includes blood work or other diagnostic tests to determine the status of your dog's organ function and body chemistry. Regular blood testing can help identify diseases in their earliest and most treatable stages. Your veterinarian might also ask if you've seen signs of disorientation or other behavioral changes, and may recommend lifestyle changes such as a different diet, an increase in exercise, or minimizing stress by creating a more stable routine.

How to Keep Your Older Dog Comfortable

No doubt your Beagle has been living in comfort all his life, but there are still things you can do to make life easier as he gets older.

Make sure bedding is extra comfy. Those old bones need plenty of warmth and cushioning. If your Beagle doesn't already have a heated bed, consider purchasing one to keep the shivers away. Heated beds are sometimes available at pet stores but are most often found in pet supply catalogs or through Internet pet suppliers (do a search for dog beds). Choose a bed that comes with safety features to prevent overheating (most do).

Make it easier for him to get around. Provide a stepstool or ramp up to the sofa or bed so he doesn't have to leap quite so high. Giving him a step up also lessens the likelihood of a broken bone from a fall. Be aware of slippery floors, and provide a non-slip covering if possible. Your Beagle may also have trouble negotiating stairs or steps. He's small enough for you to carry if need be, or you can provide a ramp.

Give him plenty of opportunities to go outside to eliminate. The aging bladder doesn't have the holding capacity of its younger years, so spare your Beagle the embarrassment of having an accident in the house. Take him out several times a day or put papers down in the house.

Provide mental and physical stimulation. Just because your Beagle is old doesn't mean he won't still enjoy a fun game or a short walk. Exercise maintains muscle tone, enhances circulation, promotes digestion, and helps maintain proper weight. Reduce your pace a little so your dog doesn't have to strain to keep up. Consult your veterinarian if your dog tires easily or has any trouble breathing.

If your Beagle is too creaky or tired to go for much of a walk, follow the kind example of one family that took their dog for "walks" by pulling him in a child's wagon. Their young daughter rode in the wagon with the dog, and it was her job to describe things to the dog as they rode along. The girl explained this by saying, "My doggie is real old and can't see or walk real well anymore."

Keep brushing those teeth, and don't neglect veterinary cleanings. Dental disease is the scourge of the old Beagle. You don't want your dog to have to gum his food.

Maintain a weekly grooming schedule. Use this time to check for lumps, bumps, or sores that your veterinarian may need to examine.

Age-Related Disorders

With lots of love and good care, your Beagle can live into her teens, but the aches and pains of age are unavoidable. As dogs get older, they are more prone to disease, but if problems are caught early, they can often be successfully treated, ensuring your dog a long and comfortable life. For Beagles, age-related diseases usually begin to appear when they're 10 to 13 years old.

> With lots of love and good care, your Beagle can live into her teens, but the aches and pains of age are unavoidable.

Arthritis is a painful degenerative joint disease that commonly affects dogs seven years or older. You may see subtle signs, such as decreased activity or lagging behind on walks, progressing to a reluctance to run, jump, or climb stairs; stiffness when getting up or lying down; soreness when touched; swollen joints that seem hot or painful; and even behavioral changes such as aggression or withdrawal.

Although there's no cure for arthritis, you can help your Beagle feel more comfortable. Weight loss helps relieve stress on joints, and new anti-inflammatory medications are available to relieve pain and inflammation. These medications are generally safe for long-term use, but be aware of possible side effects involving the digestive system, kidneys, or liver. And remember that, while aspirin and other analgesics work wonders for arthritis pain in people, they should never be given to dogs without a veterinarian's okay. A single tablet of ibuprofen, for instance, can kill a dog, says veterinarian James Roush of Kansas State University.

Cancer is one of the most common problems of older animals. The risk of cancer increases with age, and dogs get cancer at about the same rate as humans. A diagnosis of cancer used to be considered a death warrant, but today it can often be successfully treated if caught in time.

Cancer occurs when cells grow uncontrollably on or inside the body. These uncontrolled growths may remain in a single area or spread to other parts of the body. Most forms of cancer are diagnosed through a biopsy, the removal and examination of a section of tissue. Blood tests, x rays, and physical signs can also indicate cancer. Among the types of cancer commonly seen in dogs are skin tumors, breast cancer, testicular cancer, cancers of the mouth or nose, and lymphoma.

Half of all mammary tumors in dogs are malignant, but spaying your Beagle before her first heat greatly reduces her risk of this type of cancer. Breast tumors are usually removed surgically. Testicular tumors are common in dogs, and Beagles with retained testicles may be especially prone to them.

Testicular tumors are removed surgically and can be prevented altogether by neutering.

Lots of older dogs develop lumps and bumps on or beneath their skin. Fortunately, these growths are usually harmless, but you should always have your veterinarian check them out. If the tumor increases in size or changes in color or texture, this is cause for special concern.

Signs of mouth cancer are a mass on the gums, bleeding gums, bad breath, or difficulty eating. Bleeding from the nose, difficulty breathing, or facial swelling may indicate nasal cancer. Early, aggressive treatment is important for these types of cancer, so don't delay a veterinary visit if your Beagle exhibits these signs.

Half of all mammary tumors in dogs are malignant, but spaying your Beagle before her first heat greatly reduces her risk of this type of cancer.

Lymphoma is characterized by enlargement of one or more lymph nodes. This type of cancer is usually treated with chemotherapy, which has a good rate of success. Fortunately for dogs, they don't suffer the same side effects from chemotherapy as people do; there's no nausea or hair loss, although the dog may be tired for a few days afterward.

Cognitive Dysfunction Syndrome

A newly recognized disorder in dogs is called cognitive dysfunction syndrome (CDS). It's any age-related mental decline that can't be attributed to a condition such as a tumor, organ failure, or hearing or vision loss. Signs of CDS are: disorientation or confusion, such as aimless wandering, staring into space, or seeming lost in the house; fewer or less enthusiastic interactions with family members; changes in sleep and activity patterns, such as sleep-

Signs of Cancer

The signs listed here don't always mean cancer. Some of them are just part of getting old, but have your veterinarian check them out any time you notice them. Whatever your Beagle's health problem, early detection promises a much better chance of treatment and recovery. Don't ignore abnormal swellings that persist or continue to grow, sores that don't heal, unusual or excessive weight loss, extended lack of appetite, bleeding or discharge from any body opening, offensive odor, difficulty eating or swallowing, hesitation to exercise or loss of stamina, persistent lameness or stiffness, or difficulty breathing, urinating, or defecating.

ing more during the day or pacing the house and howling in the middle of the night; and breaking house-training. If your Beagle shows signs of CDS, talk to your veterinarian. She can prescribe medication that can help. Possible side effects to watch for are vomiting, diarrhea, hyperactivity, or restlessness.

Congestive Heart Failure

Another disease of old dogs is congestive heart failure. If your Beagle is coughing, has respiratory distress, is restless at night, or tires easily even after mild exercise, your veterinarian needs to examine her for this disease. Like so many diseases of old age, congestive heart failure has no cure, but it can be managed for a time with diet, medication, and rest. An appropriate diet for Beagles with this condition is low in sodium but has increased amounts of potassium and magnesium. Congestive heart failure is worsened by obesity, so a diet/weight loss plan can help there, too.

Leaving Your Pet in Your Will

Who will care for your pet if you die before he does? Many people neglect to think this could happen, with the result of their beloved pet being placed in an animal shelter after their death. Talk with family and friends and find someone who is truly willing and able to take care of your dog if you should pass. Then speak with your lawyer and include your pet in your will. You may also want to specify a certain amount of money to go to the person caring for your Beagle to offset the costs of food, veterinary care, and other pet-related expenses.

Hearing Loss

Beagles are often accused of having selective hearing, but as they get older their ability to hear really does decrease. They aren't always ignoring you when you call them to come in and they don't respond. To determine if your Beagle's sense of hearing has gotten worse, sneak up behind her and clap your hands. If she doesn't respond, she may have suffered some hearing loss.

Deafness can result from a history of ear infections or simply from degeneration of the sound receptors in the ear. Your veterinarian should examine the dog to make sure her problem isn't related to an ear infection or neurologic disease.

Deaf dogs usually adjust to their condition by making better use of their other senses. You can communicate with a deaf dog by using hand signals instead of verbal commands. When you approach her, be sure she sees you or feels the vibrations from your footsteps so she doesn't become startled and accidentally bite you.

Dental Disease

Dental disease is a serious problem in most older dogs. Signs of dental disease are bad breath, a buildup of brown plaque on the teeth, and inflammation of the gums. Left untreated, the mouth becomes a breeding ground for bacteria, which enter the bloodstream where they can travel to and potentially infect organs such as the heart or kidneys. Keep your Beagle's mouth healthy by brushing her teeth regularly, providing chew toys and hard biscuits to help remove plaque, and taking her in for an annual veterinary cleaning. After a cleaning, your veterinarian may prescribe a course of antibiotics to help prevent bacterial infections.

Kidney Problems

The kidneys are vital organs because they help the body remove waste products and maintain a sufficient level of water, minerals, and B vitamins. With age, kidney function can gradually deteriorate, but if the problem is identified in the early stages, it can be managed through diet and sometimes medication to give your Beagle good quality of life. It's a good idea to make routine screening tests for kidney function part of your older dog's annual exam, particularly if her water consumption appears to have increased. If your Beagle develops kidney disease, your veterinarian will probably prescribe a low-protein diet that won't overwork the kidneys. That doesn't mean, however, that you should automatically feed your old Beagle a low-protein diet. If a normal, healthy dog still has good kidney function, reducing the protein level in her food won't prevent the development of kidney disease.

Kidney failure is the loss of 65 percent or more of functional tissue in both kidneys. The early signs of kidney failure are subtle to nonexistent, so regular testing to detect the buildup of nitrogen wastes in the blood can help you and the veterinarian keep tabs on your dog's condition and institute treatment before the problem gets serious. In the later stages of the disease, your Beagle may exhibit greater than normal intake of water and output of urine. She may begin to have accidents in the house or be unable to hold her urine through the night.

If kidney failure goes undetected and continues to progress, the dog will become depressed, lose her appetite, and develop a dry coat and an ammonia-like odor to her breath. Like kidney disease, chronic kidney failure can be managed with a protein-restricted diet. A change in diet can slow the progression of the disease.

Vision Problems

One of the most visible signs of aging in dogs is called nuclear sclerosis, a condition in which the nucleus, or center, of the eye lens becomes a hazy gray color. Nuclear sclerosis eventually occurs in all old dogs, but it doesn't affect their vision significantly.

Another eye condition associated with old age is cataracts, an opacity of the lens. Cataracts are common in dogs, and cause gradual loss of vision. Every case is different but, in many, a veterinary ophthalmologist can surgically remove the cataracts. If that's not possible for financial or other reasons, be aware that most dogs learn to adapt to sightlessness without much difficulty, especially if they're in a familiar environment. Rearranging the furniture might cause a slight problem, but Beagles are masters at using their sense of smell to navigate, and you can help your dog learn the new arrangement by guiding her around the room. Another tip is to scent the furniture with perfume at the dog's nose level so she can use the smell as a "map." Visually impaired dogs are sometimes fearful of going down stairs. It may be necessary to keep them on the ground floor only or to carry them downstairs. What a way to build your biceps!

Prostate disease

Prostate disease isn't limited to men; it also occurs in male dogs, especially unneutered (or intact) ones. The prostate gland, which plays a role in semen production, surrounds the neck of the bladder. With age, it can gradually become enlarged and more susceptible to infection or structural abnormalities. Signs of prostate disease are a bloody discharge from the tip of the penis, difficulty passing feces, and feces that are smaller than normal in diameter. Your veterinarian may prescribe antibiotics and in some cases will recommend neutering after the infection is eliminated.

Saying Goodbye

There are few things in this life more difficult than losing a beloved pet. It's grievous when human friends or relatives die, but rarely are we the ones who make the decision that it's time for them to go. As caring pet owners, though, that's what we must do for our animals. As much as we'll miss them, it's not fair to extend their lives when they are in pain or no longer find pleasure in their

Did You Know?

The oldest dog ever documented was an Australian cattle dog named Bluey, who was put to sleep at the age of 29 years and five months.

Veterinary Teaching Hospital Grief Hotlines

- University of California, Davis, California, (916) 752-4200, 6:30–9:30 P.M. PST, Monday through Friday

- Colorado State University, Fort Collins, Colorado, (970) 491-1242

- University of Florida, Gainesville, Florida, (352) 392-4700 (ext. 4080); takes messages 24 hours a day; someone will call back between 7:00 and 9:00 P.M. EST

- Michigan State University, East Lansing, Michigan, (517) 432-2696, 6:30–9:30 P.M. EST, Tuesday, Wednesday and Thursday

- Ohio State University, Columbus, Ohio, (614) 292-1823; takes messages 6:30–9:30 P.M. EST, Monday, Wednesday and Friday

- University of Pennsylvania, Philadelphia, Pennsylvania, (215) 898-4529

- Tufts University, North Grafton, Massachusetts, (508) 839-7966, 6:00–9:00 P.M. EST, Monday through Friday

- Virginia-Maryland Regional College of Veterinary Medicine, Blacksburg, Virginia, (540) 231-8038, 6:00–9:00 P.M. EST, Tuesday and Thursday

- Washington State University, Pullman, Washington, (509) 335-4569

daily activities. A painless exit out of their misery is the greatest gift we can offer.

It's hard to know when it's the right time to say goodbye to such a beloved member of the family. It's different for each dog. We all wish that our Beagles could go quietly in their sleep, dreaming of bunnies, but rarely is this the case. When your Beagle is no longer interested in food, finds movement painful, loses bladder and bowel control, and is even indifferent to you, it's time to make that tough decision. "One of the themes that predominates in a Beagle's life is food, and that was a good indicator for us of when it was time to say goodbye to Daisy," says Janiece Harrison. "During the last few days of her life, she stopped eating, and it was clear to us that she was suffering." An understanding veterinarian will give you all the time you need to make your farewells and won't deny you the opportunity to stay with your dog until the very end.

There's nothing wrong with crying when your Beagle dies. He was a special part of your life, one that you'll never forget. And when you're ready, one of the best ways you can honor his memory is to welcome another Beagle into your home and heart.

Dealing with Grief

Euthanasia is one of the most difficult decisions you will ever make, and it's often accompanied by overwhelming grief and guilt. People who don't understand the loving relationship between people and their dogs may try to make you feel better by saying "Beagles are a dime a dozen; you can get another one just like him." Ignore any such insensitive statement, and don't feel any embarrassment in grieving for your dog. Your love for your Beagle is worthy of recognition, and you deserve the emotional support of your friends and family or of a bereavement counselor.

> Your love for your Beagle is worthy of recognition, and you deserve the emotional support of your friends and family or of a bereavement counselor.

When your dog dies, expect to experience all the stages of grief: denial, anger, bargaining, depression, and acceptance. Going through these stages is an important part of the healing process. The length of each stage depends entirely on the length and depth of your relationship with the dog and on the amount

Seeking Pet Loss Counseling

The need for pet loss counseling can begin even before your Beagle's death. Talking to an experienced third party can help you see things more clearly and ask the right questions of yourself and your veterinarian. A good counselor can help you consider a diagnosis and decide whether treatment or euthanasia is the best decision. Questions you and the counselor should consider are whether the condition can be treated or managed, whether your dog can be made comfortable, and whether there is hope for good quality of life. Other important factors are your dog's personality, your ability to provide care, and, much as we might like to think it doesn't matter, the cost involved.

Some clinics offer group counseling sessions for owners of pets with terminal illnesses. Attending these group meetings can help you come to terms with your dog's illness, and recognize and prepare for the day when he must be euthanized.

Your veterinary hospital may have someone on staff who serves as a counselor, or you can call one of the many pet bereavement hotlines provided by veterinary organizations and veterinary colleges.

and quality of emotional support you receive. Don't let anyone tell you that your period of mourning is too long; there is no "normal" length of time that grief should last.

Ways you can deal with grief include allowing yourself to cry and memorializing your dog in a special way. Consider inviting your Beagle-loving friends over for a wake. It can be comforting to swap stories about your dog's antics and to have people who knew him share their favorite memories. Some people place a photo of their dog in a prominent spot and light a candle to his memory each night for a week. You may want to light a candle annually on the anniversary of his death. Donating a sum of money in your dog's name to Beagle rescue or some other pet-related organization is also a fulfilling memorial.

"One of the things that helped me most in dealing with losing a dog is the idea that its life can be honored with a celebration of remembrance," Janiece Harrison says. "We have many mementos of Daisy and Sadie that we keep in a wooden 'treasure' box next to our bed. Their graves are a flowerbed that we try to plant each spring and fall with annuals."

Whatever memorial you choose, always remember that even though your Beagle no longer has a physical presence, he will live forever in your heart and memories.

Appendix: Resources

Boarding, Pet Sitting, Traveling

Books

Dog Lover's Companion series
Guides on traveling with dogs
    for several states and cities
Foghorn Press
P.O. Box 2036
Santa Rosa, CA 95405-0036
(800) FOGHORN

*Take Your Pet Too!: Fun
    Things to Do!,* Heather
    MacLean Walters
M.C.E. Publishing
P.O. Box 84
Chester, NJ 07930-0084

Take Your Pet USA, Arthur
    Frank
Artco Publishing
12 Channel St.
Boston, MA 02210

*Traveling with Your Pet 1999:
    The AAA Petbook,* Greg
    Weeks, Editor
Guide to pet-friendly lodging
    in the U.S. and Canada

Vacationing With Your Pet!,
    Eileen Barish
Pet-Friendly Publications
P.O. Box 8459
Scottsdale, AZ 85252
(800) 496-2665

Other resources

The American Boarding Ken-
    nels Association
4575 Galley Road, Suite 400-A
Colorado Springs, CO 80915
(719) 591-1113
www.abka.com

Independent Pet and Animal Transportation Association
5521 Greenville Ave., Ste 104-310
Dallas, TX 75206
(903) 769-2267
www.ipata.com

National Association of Professional Pet Sitters
1200 G St. N.W., Suite 760
Washington, DC 20005
(800) 296-PETS
www.petsitters.org

Pet Sitters International
418 East King Street
King, NC 27021-9163
(336)-983-9222
www.petsit.com

Traveling Pet Owners of America (TPOA)
P.O. Box 6042
Omaha, NE 68106-0042

Breed Information, Clubs, Registries

American Kennel Club
5580 Centerview Drive
Raleigh, NC 27606-3390
(919) 233-9767
www.akc.org/

Beagles on the Web
www.beagles-on-the-web.com

Canadian Kennel Club
Commerce Park
89 Skyway Ave., Suite 100
Etobicoke, Ontario, Canada M9W 6R4
(416) 675-5511
www.ckc.ca

InfoPet
P.O. Box 716
Agoura Hills, CA 91376
(800) 858-0248

The Kennel Club
(British equivalent to the American Kennel Club)
1-5 Clarges Street
Piccadilly
London W1Y 8AB
ENGLAND
www.the-kennel-club.org.uk/

National Dog Registry
Box 116
Woodstock, NY 12498
(800) 637-3647
www.natldogregistry.com/

Tatoo-A-Pet
6571 S.W. 20th Court
Ft. Lauderdale, FL 33317
(800) 828-8667
www.tattoo-a-pet.com

United Kennel Club
100 East Kilgore Rd.
Kalamazoo, MI 49001-5598
(616) 343-9020
www.ukcdogs.com

Dog Publications

AKC Gazette and AKC Events
    Calendar
51 Madison Avenue
New York, NY 10010
Subscriptions: (919) 233-9767
www.akc.org/gazet.htm
www.akc.org/event.htm

Coping with the Loss of a Pet, Moira
    Anderson Allen
Peregrine Press, 1988

Direct Book Service
(800) 776-2665
www.dogandcatbooks.com/direct-
    book

Dog Fancy
P.O. Box 6050
Mission Viejo, CA 92690
(949) 855-8822
www.dogfancy.com

Dog Lovers Bookshop
P.O. Box 117, Gracie Station
New York, NY 10028
(212) 369-7554
info@dogbooks.com
www.dogbooks.com

Dog World
500 N. Dearborn, Suite 1100
Chicago, IL 60610
(312) 396-0600
www.dogworldmag.com/

How to Survive the Loss of a Love,
    Melba Cosgrove, et al.
Bantam Books, 1976

The Loss of a Pet, Wallace Sife, Ph.D.
Howell Book House, 1985

Mind's Eye Productions
(800) 570-DOGS
www.petvideo.com

*Pet Loss: A Thoughtful Guide for
    Adults and Children*,
Herbert A. Neiburg and Arlene
    Fischer
Harperperennial Library

Popular Dogs—Beagles
Lisa Hanks, Editor
P.O. Box 6050
Mission Viejo, CA 92690

*When Your Pet Dies: How to Cope
    with Your Feelings,*
Jamie Quackenbush and Denise
    Graveline
Simon & Schuster, 1985

Fun, Grooming, Obedience, Training

American Dog Trainers Network
161 W. 4th Street
New York, NY 10014
(212) 727-7257
www.inch.com/~dogs/index.html

American Grooming Shop Associa-
    tion
(719) 570-7788

American Kennel Club (tracking,
    agility, obedience, herding)
Performance Events Dept.
5580 Centerview Drive
Raleigh, NC 27606
(919) 854-0199
www.akc.org/

American Pet Dog Trainers
P.O. Box 385
Davis, CA 95617
(800) PET-DOGS

Animal Behavior Society
Susan Foster
Department of Biology
Clark University
950 Main Street
Worcester, MA 01610-1477

Association of Pet Dog Trainers
P.O. Box 385
Davis, CA 95617
(800) PET-DOGS
www.apdt.com/

The Dog Agility Page
www.dogpatch.org/agility/

Grooming supplies
Pet Warehouse
P.O. Box 752138
Dayton, OH 45475-2138
(800) 443-1160

Intergroom
76 Carol Drive
Dedham, MA 02026
www.intergroom.com

Naming Your Beagle
www.FindaPet.com/petnames.htm
www.petrix.com/dognames

National Association of Dog Obedience Instructors
PMB #369
729 Grapevine Highway
Hurst, TX 76054-2085
www.nadoi.org/

National Dog Groomers Association
of America
P.O. Box 101
Clark, PA 16113
(724) 962-2711

North American Dog Agility
Council
HCR 2 Box 277
St. Maries, ID 83861
www.nadac.com

North American Flyball Association
1400 W. Devon Ave, #512
Chicago, IL 60660
(309) 688-9840
www.muskie.fishnet.com/~flyball/
flyball.html

Pup-Peroni Canine Freestylers
P.O. Box 350122
Brooklyn, NY 11235
(718) 332-8336
Fax: (718) 646-2686
pupfreesty@aol.com

United States Dog Agility Association, Inc.
P.O. Box 850955
Richardson, Texas 75085-0955
(972) 231-9700
www.usdaa.com/

United States Canine Combined
Training Association
2755 Old Thompson Mill Road
Buford, GA 30519
(770) 932-8604
www.siriusweb.com/USCCTA/

Grief Hotlines

Chicago Veterinary Medical
Association
(630) 603-3994

Cornell University
(607) 253-3932

Michigan State University
College of Veterinary Medicine
(517) 432-2696

Ohio State University Pet Loss Support Line
(614) 292-1823

Tufts University (Massachusetts)
School of Veterinary Medicine
(508) 839-7966

University of California, Davis
(530) 752-4200

University of Florida at Gainesville
College of Veterinary Medicine
(352) 392- 4700

Virginia-Maryland Regional College
of Veterinary Medicine
(540) 231-8038

Washington State University
College of Veterinary Medicine
(509) 335-5704

Humane Organizations and Rescue Groups

American Humane Association
63 Inverness Drive E
Englewood, CO   80112-5117
(800) 227-4645
www.americanhumane.org

American Society for the Prevention
of Cruelty to Animals (ASPCA)
424 East 92nd Street
New York, NY 10128-6804
(212) 876-7700
www.aspca.org

Animal Protection Institute of
America
P.O. Box 22505
Sacramento, CA 95822
(916) 731-5521

Beagle Rescue, Education and Welfare (BREW) of Northern Virginia
www.beagles-on-the-web.com/brew

Humane Society of the United States
2100 L St. NW
Washington, DC 20037
(301) 258-3072, (202) 452-1100
www.hsus.org/

Massachusetts Society for the Prevention of Cruelty to Animals
350 South Huntington Avenue
Boston, MA 02130
(617) 522-7400
www.mspca.org/

Morris Animal Foundation
45 Inverness Drive East
Englewood, CO 80112
(800) 243-2345 or (303) 790-2345

Pet Loss Foundation
(513) 932-2270

SOS (Save Our Snoopies) Beagle
    Rescue
(609) 267-5157
sosbeagles@juno.com
www.beagles-on-the-web.com/sos

SPAY/USA
14 Vanderventer Avenue
Port Washington, NY 11050
(516) 944-5025, (203) 377-1116 in
    Connecticut
(800) 248-SPAY
www.spayusa.org/

Medical and Emergency Information

American Animal Hospital Associa-
    tion
P.O. Box 150899
Denver, CO 80215-0899
(800) 252-2242
www.healthypet.com

American Holistic Veterinary Medi-
    cine Association
2214 Old Emmorton Road
Bel Air, MD 21015
(410) 569-2346
www.altvetmed.com

American Kennel Club Canine
    Health Foundation
251 West Garfield Road, Suite 160
Aurora, OH 44202
(888) 682-9696

American Veterinary Medical
    Association
1931 North Meacham Road,
    Suite 100
Schaumburg, IL 60173-4360
(847) 925-8070
www.avma.org/

Canine Eye Registration Inc.
    (CERF)
Veterinary Medical Data Program
South Campus Courts, Building C
Purdue University
West Lafayette, IN 47907
(765) 494-8179
www.vet.purdue.edu/~yshen/cerf.html

Centers for Disease Control and
    Prevention
1600 Clifton Road NE
Atlanta, GA 30333
(404) 639-3311 (CDC Operator)
(800) 311-3435 (CDC Public
    Inquiries)
www.cdc.gov

Infectious Diseases of the Dog and Cat, Craig E. Greene, Editor
W B Saunders Company

National Animal Poison Control Center
1717 S. Philo, Suite 36
Urbana, IL 61802
(888) 426-4435, $45 per case, with as many follow-up calls as necessary included. Have name, address, phone number, dog's breed, age, sex, and type of poison ingested, if known, available
www.napcc.aspca.org

Orthopedic Foundation for Animals (OFA)
2300 E. Nifong Blvd.
Columbia, MO 65201-3856
(573) 442-0418
www.offa.org/

Pet First Aid: Cats and Dogs, by Bobbi Mammato, DVM
Mosby Year Book

Skin Diseases of Dogs and Cats: A Guide for Pet Owners and Professionals,
Dr. Steven A. Melman
Dermapet, Inc.
P.O. Box 59713
Potomac, MD 20859

U.S. Pharmacopeia
vaccine reactions: (800) 487-7776
customer service: (800) 227-8772
www.usp.org

Veterinary Medical Database/Canine Eye Registration Foundation
Department of Veterinary Clinical Science
School of Veterinary Medicine
Purdue University
West Lafayette, IN 47907
(765) 494-8179
www.vet.purdue.edu/~yshen/

Veterinary Pet Insurance (VPI)
4175 E. La Palma Ave., #100
Anaheim, CA 92807-1846
(714) 996-2311
(800) USA PETS, (877) PET HEALTH in Texas
www.petplan.net/home.htm

Nutrition and Natural Foods

California Natural, Natural Pet Products
P.O. Box 271
Santa Clara, CA 95052
(800) 532-7261
www.naturapet.com

Home Prepared Dog and Cat Diets,
   Donald R. Strombeck
Iowa State University Press
(515) 292-0140

PHD Products Inc.
PO Box 8313
White Plains, NY 10602
(800) 863-3403
www.phdproducts.net/

Raw Diet Online Resources
www.onelist.com

Sensible Choice, Pet Products Plus
5600 Mexico Road
St. Peters, MO 63376
(800) 592-6687
www.sensiblechoice.com/

Service and Working Dogs

Canine Companions for Independence
P.O. Box 446
Santa Rosa, CA 95402-0446
(800) 572-2275
www.caninecompanions.org/

Delta Society National Service Dog
   Center
289 Perimeter Road East
Renton, WA 98055-1329
(800) 869-6898
www.petsforum.com/deltasociety/dsb
   000.htm

The Seeing Eye
P.O. Box 375
Morristown, NJ 07963-0375
(973) 539-4425
www.seeingeye.org/

Therapy Dogs Incorporated
2416 E. Fox Farm Road
Cheyenne, WY 82007
(877) 843-7364
www.therapydogs.com

Therapy Dogs International
6 Hilltop Road
Mendham, NJ 07945
(973) 252-9800
www.tdi-dog.org/

United Schutzhund Clubs of
   America
3704 Lemay Ferry Road
St. Louis, MO 63125

Index

W, X

Meet Your Beagle Care Experts

Author   Kim Campbell Thornton is an award-winning writer and editor. During her tenure as editor of *Dog Fancy*, the magazine won three Dog Writers Association of America Maxwell Awards for best all-breed magazine. She has written more than a dozen books and is a contributor to the *American Kennel Club Gazette, Dog Fancy, Dogs USA,* and *Pet Product News,* among others. Kim has been active in promoting the adoption of retired racing Greyhounds, a cause near and dear to her heart. She is a member of the Dog Writers Association of America, serving on its Board of Governors, and also belongs to the Cat Writers' Association and the Authors Guild. Kim shares her home with her cats—Shelby, Peter, and Pandora—two birds, and Bella, a Cavalier King Charles Spaniel.

Trainer   Liz Palika has been teaching classes for dogs and their owners for over twenty years. Her goal is to help people understand why their dogs do what they do so that dogs and owners can live together successfully. Liz says, "If, in each training class, I can increase understanding and ease frustration so that the dog doesn't end up in the local shelter because the owner has given up, then I have accomplished my goal!" She is the author of 23 books and has won awards from both the Dog Writers Association of America and the ASPCA. Liz and her husband, Paul, share their home with three Australian Shepherds: Dax, Kes, and Riker.

Series Editor   Joanne Howl, D.V.M., is a graduate of the University of Tennessee College of Veterinary Medicine and has practiced animal medicine for over 10 years. She currently serves as president of the Maryland Veterinary Medical Association and secretary/treasurer of the American Academy on Veterinary Disaster Medicine, and her columns and articles have appeared in a variety of animal-related publications. Dr. Howl presently divides her time between family, small animal medicine, writing, and the company of her two dogs and six cats.